THE UNMEDIATED VISION

An Interpretation of Wordsworth, Hopkins, Rilke, and Valéry

The Unmediated Vision

AN INTERPRETATION OF WORDSWORTH,

HOPKINS, RILKE, AND VALÉRY

BY GEOFFREY H. HARTMAN

New Haven: YALE UNIVERSITY PRESS, 1954

London: Geoffrey Cumberlege, Oxford University Press

TO MY MOTHER

CONTENTS

INTRODUCTION: *A Short Discourse on Method*

W HAT IS HIS APPROACH? Whenever a critic of literature is discussed, this question tends to preface all the rest. More than any other it rings in the student's ears the first weeks at graduate school. I could not understand it then, and still cannot. Approach? Either one has the truth about a poem or one does not. Approach? Just as a thousand misunderstandings will not alter in the least the possibility of a correct understanding, so a thousand varied approaches cannot negate uniqueness of meaning.

Then I began to eat of the tree of knowledge, so that my eyes were multiplied, and where I had seen but a single *text* I now perceived the formidable legion of variant, if not discordant, *interpretations*. The philologist and the philosopher, the sociologist, the humanist, the various historians—of ideas, of literature, of politics, and of economics—the psychoanalyst and the empirical psychologist, the theologian and the lay Jewish and Christian critics, the more orthodox and the less orthodox—all had their "approach," believed themselves in possession of the truth, demanded a hearing, quarreled suavely or with verbal spittle, and insisted that even when the text did not quite fit, their analysis clarified a truth dimly perceived in the original. Still more evidence came from the history of interpretation itself: inexplicable changes of taste, wilful decontextualizations, sublime absurdities, and finally that cheerful bird of prey the skeptic, with corpses enough, yet attacking both the living and the dead.

Having tasted these multiple modes of interpretation, I fell in love with the art of interpreting and could not return to my original state. I realized that the study of literature, like that of history and physical phenomena, had advanced beyond intellectual naivete, that just as we had laid hands on nature, unwillingly, and pried into history, unwillingly, so we were now, unwillingly, forced to consider literature as more than an organic creation, a social pastime, a religious trope, an emotional outlet, a flower of civilization, more even than an exemplary stage for ideal probabilities. Literature was being recognized as a moral force in its own right, an institution with its own laws, and, incipiently, a distinctive form of knowledge. The recognition meant labor, hard labor. The criticism of Voltaire and the classical writers, relying on an instinctive sense of decorum, as on the free and common consent of a class of gentleman readers, seemed to have perished like Atlantis. In its stead appeared the work of the owl-eyed philologist or historiographer with broad sympathies, the professional scholar with his "field," and the unpredictable responses of a profane crowd of enthusiasts, journalists and college students. Reflecting on these things —the passing of instinctively accepted (though fully educated) criteria of judgment and the extreme increase in modes of interpretation—I wondered if "criticism with approach" was an inevitable thing, or if there might be found once more a method universal in its appeal, a method of interpretation which could reaffirm the radical unity of human knowledge.

The essays of this book are in pursuit of such a method. They attempt to present a way of analysis sensitive to each author as individual and to each work of art as such, and a principle of synthesis applicable to all authors and to every literary work of art. They would respect both the persistent ideal unity of the work of art and the total human situation from which it springs. In short, the essays would be an example of "criticism without approach." Though nothing is more presumptuous than to believe one's thought free of assumptions, this book is offered as an exercise in that kind of presumptuousness which does not trust any but *complete interpretation,* so as to realize in criticism the "art of ideas and of the orders of ideas" preconized by Valéry.

In order to gain a method of complete interpretation, the book evolves as a threefold study. The first part comprises four essays on poets of varying character and from three different countries, each essay centering on a single poem but through that poem touching the rest of the author's work. After each poet has been considered individually, two final essays are added, one to attempt an explanation of the ideal tendency of all symbolic process, especially that by means of language, the second to describe the dilemma of what is here called simply modern poetry, which results from an almost total break from Judeo-Christian traditions. In this way each poet is studied as individual, as poet (*sub specie poetae*), and finally as poet of a particular historical moment.

The title of the book, *The Unmediated Vision,* refers to a theme present throughout but hidden (even to the writer) up to the final chapter. I would not be a revealer of secrets. It is easy to let great truths spring from the tongue as if they were natural to the human mind and understood as quickly as spoken. That they are neither natural nor immediate can be seen by this fact, that ideas can be lost, utterly lost; and even if found once more, are then impure. Many a time the poem is but the fragment of an original intuition, and many a time the critical essay contains the original idea, but it is lost among arbitrary associations. If these essays leave certain things *in potentia,* it is because they would not be a revealer of secrets.

Yet I have often wished that someone with authority would issue a writ of *habeas corpus* to the professional students. We have barely started to attempt to understand literature as a distinctive mode of knowledge in which the processes, or, better, the desires of the human mind find their clearest expression. Art, furthermore, has this advantage over the other modes of knowledge: it, alone, is in the service of no one, not even of truth. For truth, even when sought for its own sake, will surely destroy in the searcher his consciousness of human responsibilities. Abstraction is never less than total. Great poetry, however, is written by men who have chosen to stay bound by experience, who would not—or could not—free themselves by an act of knowledge from the immediacy of good and evil.

Some procedural detail should finally be noted. These essays claim unity of theme and method but not of form. Each essay will start from a single text and proceed by successive interpretations, sometimes of the same poem, sometimes of the author's work as a whole; but in the number and sequence of successive analyses it is guided by the text itself as well as by the central interests of each author. While the final aims of the essays are to demonstrate the common tendency of all symbolic process and the specific tendency of modern poets, the immediate aim of each is to show that a unified multiple interpretation of poetry is textually justified, even required; that, since the poem brings the complete man into activity, its symbols are open to various explanations equally valid as long as the unity or identity to which all tend is found.

Furthermore, no attempt has been made to give exhaustive analyses or develop all meanings (moral, economic, historical, anagogical, epistemological, and so forth), but rather to present complete interpretations that could stand without further development. For if poetry is to be the object of specialized study, it should go the whole way and never stop short of completeness by contenting itself, for instance, with a few remarks on syntax, sound, meter, genre, *topoi,* and unity. There is no order of discrete things: the poem should be taken as a whole, and the poet's work as a whole, or not at all.

With such as its aim, then, this book is proposed as a small contribution to that empirical discourse on method still lacking for the fine arts.

In its original form, the study was presented as a doctoral thesis at Yale University, and I am grateful to that company of students and scholars who afforded me the necessary years of hard study and creative leisure for its production. I am indebted with more than the ordinary debt that a student bears his teachers to the trust, the open-mindedness, and the alternation of discipline and encouragement shown by René Wellek, Sterling Professor of Comparative Literature, who supervised the thesis, spent much time reading and correcting both manuscript and proofs, and without impairing either freedom of thought or standards of scholarship bridled and directed my lust for interpretation. Henri Peyre gave me comfort and counsel, encouraging half-expressed thoughts, yet guarding me against too barbaric a contact with philosophical terms. Herman Weigand spent many hours training me to regard the detail without losing Nietzschean fire. Kenneth Douglas and David Horne read the manuscript and trimmed the style. I also give my thanks to many others who were always willing to hold conversations long and short. I would finally express my appreciation to Yale University Press, which accepted a book without cost to its author in an age when scholars have to buy the right to publish. Its editorial department firmly guided an impatient novice through the technical process of publication.

The Lord talked with you face to face in the mount out of the midst of the fire. I stood between the Lord and you at that time, to shew you the word of the Lord: for ye were afraid by reason of the fire, and went not up into the mount.

DEUTERONOMY 5:4–5

WORDSWORTH

Five years have past; five summers, with the length
Of five long winters! and again I hear
These waters, rolling from their mountain-springs
With a soft inland murmur.—Once again
Do I behold these steep and lofty cliffs,
That on a wild secluded scene impress
Thoughts of more deep seclusion; and connect
The landscape with the quiet of the sky.
The day is come when I again repose
Here, under this dark sycamore, and view
These plots of cottage-ground, these orchard-tufts,
Which at this season, with their unripe fruits,
Are clad in one green hue, and lose themselves
'Mid groves and copses. Once again I see
These hedge-rows, hardly hedge-rows, little lines
Of sportive wood run wild: these pastoral farms,
Green to the very door; and wreaths of smoke
Sent up, in silence, from among the trees!
With some uncertain notice, as might seem
Of vagrant dwellers in the houseless woods,
Or of some Hermit's cave, where by his fire
The Hermit sits alone.

From *"Lines* composed a few miles above Tintern Abbey, on revisiting the banks of the Wye during a tour." July 13, 1798. *The Poetical Works of William Wordsworth,* ed. E. de Sélincourt and H. Darbishire.

THE SUBJECT MATTER of "Tintern Abbey" is not sublime in the Miltonic sense, at least not at first glance. There are no pagan or poetical gods, no divine machinery; it is a personal experience, date and place noted, which leads to various meditations. The theme of these is thankfulness to Nature which never has betrayed, never betrays, nor ever will betray the heart that loves her. But although the subject matter is not lofty, the argument is. The former starts from impressions received on beholding a sweet valley encompassed by steep and lofty cliffs, but the latter recounts the lasting influence of the humble, secluded scene.

The poet's delight at hearing once more the rolling waters of the Wye is almost taken for granted; as if something long foreseen and bound to continue were now given a certain physical reality: "and again I hear," "Once again/Do I behold," "when I again repose," "Once again I see." There is certainly some disproportion felt between the intense emotion that has preceded, is present, will probably ensue, and the actual scene causing this emotion. We find no climax, although the placing of the second exclamation mark is curious. Why is there such surprise at smoke rising from the trees? The sentence, in any case, even as after the first exclamation, does not stop, but goes on to a leisurely close. Climactic effect is avoided both by the Wordsworthian period organized loosely, comparable to the progress of a stately stream, and by the meter's internal surge and fall:

> five summers, with the length
> Of five long winters! and again I hear
> These waters, rolling from their mountain-springs
> With a soft inland murmur.

The feeling of disproportion mentioned has nothing in common with an idealist's disappointment in the presence of a thing long hoped for. It is the feeling that these sights and sounds, waters,

cliffs, trees, hedgerows, pastoral farms, and wreaths of smoke, raise
an emotion that no amount of thought can explain, and no feature
of these objects considered in themselves can justify. The emphasis
is on *these* waters, *these* steep and lofty cliffs, *this* sycamore, *these*
plots of cottage-ground, *these* orchard tufts, *these* hedgerows, *these*
pastoral farms, as if the poet were thinking: what I now see are
not waters in general, cliffs in general or even smoke in general;
I have an inexplicable affection for these particular hedgerows
(hardly hedgerows, little lines of wood run wild)—which seem to
reciprocate by offering me, a mute demonstration of love. Surely
they have a special bearing on my destiny; yet neither can they tell
me nor can I discover more than this present image and emotion.

Wordsworth, in other words, can no longer see external nature
with neoclassic eyes as an assemblage of fair and universal forms
duly marked by ticketings of "the," or as a garden demonstrating
divine love; but at the same time neither does he wish to number
the streaks of the tulip or to supply the absence of divine intent
from the strength of the subjective spirit. Wordsworth knows one
thing only: the affection he bears to nature for its own sake, the
"quietness and beauty" which the presences of nature give to his
mind; and this dialectic of love makes up his entire understanding.
The poet thus bears an affection to external nature which cannot
be more than stated, nor can the objects of it be more than described.[1]

The description of objects and the statement of emotion that
these objects bring are expressed by separate operations. There is
no attempt to relate anything specific in the description to any
specific feeling in the statement, no simple or complex attempt to
reconstitute some nexus of cause and effect. The waters remain
these waters, and should we try to find out exactly the content of
the emotion caused by them, we are bound to fail; they are "feelings," "sensations sweet." Wordsworth is best recognized in such
conceptions as "the sounding cataract haunted me like a passion,"
where the object and the emotion are considered independent
powers inevitably associated.

The period of the sounding cataract is, of course, Wordsworth's
"second" stage; but though there have been critics who have found

as many as five stages of intellectual development, it is difficult, at least from "Tintern Abbey," to discover more than two (the "glad animal movements" excepted, which are mentioned only in passing, and in brackets): (1) the time when perception and joy are simultaneous, an appetite, and (2) the time when perception and joy are no longer simultaneous, and meditation must supplement what is no longer an intrinsic interest. However, the link between the emotion and its object, whether immediate or through the space of memory, cannot in either case be found. Even in the perfect and, as it were, mystical act of cognition described later in "Tintern Abbey"—where the object and mind both remain whole and a state of suspension is created in which physical and intellectual activity cease—understanding does not bring concrete knowledge of relationships, but simply "the power of harmony," "the deep power of joy," the essentially unspecific seeing "into the life of things."

What marks the thought of Wordsworth is this profound respect for both partners of the act of understanding. He refuses to employ the language of analysis either on himself or on external nature. He is not like previous poets of a religious bent beset by an imperative to comprehend immediately the purpose of Creation (*res creatae*). The impulse of Henry Vaughan, for instance, to whom the Lake Poet is often compared, is to search out the appearances of God, and his complaint is the futility of attempting this by an act of will. Search as he might, "It whispered: Where I please." [2] But Wordsworth seems to have renounced beforehand that knowledge which would explain to him the necessity of things, or of their relation, or even the necessity of his own existence. *Wordsworth's understanding is characterized by the general absence of the will to attain relational knowledge,* that is, knowledge which may be obtained in direct answer to the Why, the What, the Wherefore, and the How.

The beginning of "Tintern Abbey" develops as a sequence of four sentences each keynoted by a "Once again." Its mood is not surprise or exaltation, but an intense matter-of-factness. What does the poet tell us about the reason why this valley in particular, these waters, and these hedgerows have exerted such an influence on him?

Is it a childhood scene? Was his first love experienced there? Does it remind him of medieval Christianity or of England's glory? He has been inexplicably influenced; his only duty is acknowledgment; and his method is thus one of simple statement: Time has passed slowly! and again I hear, repose, view, see. Strictly speaking, the poet does not even tell us that time has passed slowly; there is no suggestion of "subjective" time: these first two lines defy logical analysis, for in spite of the feeling of compressed longing which they evoke, they state, quite simply and by a peculiar redundance, that five years have passed, five summers with five winters which have the length of long winters. No word of blame passes the lips of the poet on the subject of mutability. Time is a justness of nature, a matter of fact; and the heart of the poem is surely an acceptance of a natural order which he does not try to explain, and which includes even time—that time is past . . . not for this faint I, nor mourn, nor murmur.

Indeed, we occasionally feel that such formulas as "That time is past," "There was a time," "The day is come" are too frequent and give the impression that Wordsworth is continually writing his own epitaph. His fondness for the epitaph as genre is well known; he wrote on it at length and declared once "the occasion of writing an epitaph is matter-of-fact in its intensity." [3] (One marvels how poetry can be written that is matter-of-fact in its intensity, and in which the will toward relational knowledge is absent.)

Yet Wordsworth is the first English poet to consider and use personal experience as his "sublime argument." Before him, autobiography did not enter into serious poetry without being legitimized by a score of mythological references, or being set into the explicit frame of the Christian religion. In George Herbert's *The Temple* almost every poem is referable to a sacred object or ceremony. Milton will not express his grief at a friend's death except in a pastoral monody that invokes a goodly member of ancient gods. The plan of a nature poem of the eighteenth century, such as Pope's *Windsor Forest,* is determined not so much by an intrinsic love of the scene or by personal reminiscence as by its convenience for and suggestiveness of political glory. [4] But in "Tintern Abbey" even

the smoke that ascends from among the trees awakens poetic delight, and for no apparent reason. Literary history provides us with
perhaps only one other famous example of poetical smoke, when
Du Bellay, stranded at Rome, dreams of his sweet Angevine:

> Quand reverrai-je, hélas, de mon petit village
> Fumer la cheminée?

Yet even this is not entirely out of the simplicity of the poetic spirit,
but is based on the authority of Homer's *Odyssey,* and the love for it.

However, the very reason why Wordsworth feels free to use his
own individual experience in a mode of expression which restricts
itself to general nature is that this same experience is considered
by him as a matter of fact. The theory of impersonality is not a
modern invention: it becomes necessary as soon as a poet wishes
to speak in his own person. But only the very greatest poets
have achieved this matter-of-factness, the correlative of true mysticism.

Wordsworth, at the beginning of "Tintern Abbey," is striving
toward the expression of a mystic feeling. We saw he was trying to
convey a disproportion between his high feelings and the visible
character of the scene, one that is pointed up by the frequency of
the demonstrative (these waters, these cliffs). There is that "intensity of the matter-of-fact" which made us speculate that the only
condition allowing the poet to introduce personal experience in
a direct way was to treat his personality itself as a matter of fact.
We may therefore offer the following explanation of the poet's
mood as he looks on the Wye valley. Whenever Wordsworth considers external nature of that familiar kind which alone enters into
his experience, he is beset by an urge to consider it with the same
enthusiasm that affects Milton contemplating a nature neither
external nor familiar, that is, the very spirit of God seen through
the mind's eye; but this valley, these waters and cliffs, these pastoral
farms never, even at the most intense, convey more than the suggestion of a *possible sublimity.*[5] This is the basic experience. The
objects do arouse a sense of beauty, but the emotion of the mind in
beholding them is far too strong to make this evident beauty its
explanation, and far too sincere to make this independent beauty

its function. We glimpse a universal paradox inherent in the human and poetic imagination: it cannot be, at the same time, true to nature and true to itself. If it is true to the external world, it must suspend all will toward relational knowledge; if it is true to itself, it must alter the external world by an action of the creative or moral will. The first leads to imbecility or mysticism, the second to artifice or sophistry; both spell the end of art.

The conflict of intense matter-of-factness and passionate fiction, of the human and the enthusiastic imaginations, of the passive and the creative mind, of the remission of the relational will and its assertion, of familiar and sublime argument—this conflict is vital to the peculiar strength of "Tintern Abbey," as, perhaps, to all of Wordsworth's poetry. We have remarked a few of its consequences: (1) the disproportion between the sublime intimations in the poet's mind and the merely possible sublimity of the scene before him; (2) the direct use of personal experience, but only with an intense matter-of-factness; (3) the strict separation of the statement of emotion from the description of objects, so that no facile nexus of cause and effect may be found between them, and so that, if associated, they are so without explanation, inevitably; and (4) the general absence (in this poem) of the will toward relational knowledge, at least of that will which would demand expression in the language of analysis, to which might be added (5) the very choice of blank verse,[6] which suggests that Wordsworth challenges both Milton and the tradition by using a meter consecrated to sublime subjects for the conveying of familiar experience (although the way had been prepared by Thomson and Cowper). But how wrong it would be to conclude that "Tintern Abbey" is primarily concerned with the workings of the Imagination. To a degree it is, but the struggles of the human imagination are for the poet subsumed under a more important and more immediate experience, the dialectic of love between man and nature. To understand the dialectic in all its parts is our immediate task.

2

We have mentioned that the two "moments" of the poetic imagination either were an intense matter of fact or were passionate fiction.

In the first the creative will is absent, and a "wise passiveness" has taken its place, in the second the human mind freely imposes its spiritualizing powers on the scene before it.[7] But both tend toward a third moment, as toward an ideal, when the creative will of man is either spontaneous or suspended. And the common denominator of all these moments of apperception will be a *principle of generosity* whether it issue from man, from external nature, or from their contact.

Let us go once more to "Tintern Abbey." It begins in a mood intensely matter-of-fact. The poet, though tempted by the scene, refuses to free his creative power. To Nature alone is given the attribute of will and generosity: the waters roll with a soft inland murmur, the lofty cliffs connect the landscape with the quiet of the sky, the orchard-tufts "lose themselves" amid groves and copses, the pastoral farms are "green to the very door." His restraint is admirable. He might have chosen to burst into a panegyric of Nature, to release the energy of his excited mind in celebration of this humble landscape and pipe, as Spenser did, to shepherd swains within this grove of chivalry; or he might have settled on some British tale unsung by Milton, which Nature could accompany with gleams "like the flashing of a shield." [8] He respects, however, the intrinsic and unfictional loveliness of the Wye valley and the superior energy of his mind, contenting himself with the simple statement "Once again do I behold."

But there comes the moment when his creative fancy is almost too strong, when he cannot refrain from a transcendent image, a supernatural suggestion, and this, curiously enough, comes in the description of the smoke:

> and wreaths of smoke
> Sent up, in silence, from among the trees!
> With some uncertain notice, as might seem
> Of vagrant dwellers in the houseless woods,
> Or of some Hermit's cave, where by his fire
> The Hermit sits alone.

Wandering gypsies and a hermit appear, part of the traditional romantic landscape, though much will eventually have to be said on Wordsworth's use of the hermit figure. The smoke, however, claims our first attention.

Smoke and mistiness are often imaged by Wordsworth. A memorable example is the invocation to his sister at the end of "Tintern Abbey":

> Therefore let the moon
> Shine on thee in thy solitary walk;
> And let the misty mountain-winds be free
> To blow against thee:

The image here is suggestive of freedom, expressing that double generosity of Nature toward man and man toward Nature, always present in the impassioned Wordsworth. The misty winds, like the smoke, suggest a liberty of movement, the possibility of passionate fiction that makes the mind wish to "wanton with graceful joy in the exercise of its own powers . . . loving its own creation." [9]

But more: the mists are sudden and go as quickly as they come. Dorothy's *Journal* is full of darkenings and lightenings, and one of the finest passages Wordsworth has written is about Michael:

> he had been alone
> Amid the heart of many thousand mists,
> That came to him, and left him, on the heights.

Like the smoke that rises from the woods, these mists seem to be produced by invisible generation. They suggest not only a liberty of movement, but one emanating from an invisible source.

Yet a third characteristic may be added. Only an infinitesimal space of time exists between the rise of the sun and the conversion of dew into mist, between sunrise and the smokiness of human activity. This is the time of absolute peace, the mystic moment proper, the first and original splendor of creation, the prospect from Westminster Bridge

> All bright and glittering in the smokeless air.

> .   .   .   .

> Ne'er saw I, never felt, a calm so deep!
> The river glideth at his own sweet will:

> Dear God! the very houses seem asleep;
> And all that mighty heart is lying still!

The smoke rising from the woods of the Wye valley gives only a faint intimation of this central peace, of the river moving at his own sweet will, of a spontaneous generosity of movement. The smoke and the mist already impede themselves by their very visibility; there is a fine passage in the journals of Dorothy Wordsworth (often used as a source book by Wordsworth) which indicates this:

> The shapes of the mist, slowly moving along, exquisitely beautiful; passing over the sheep they almost seemed to have more of life than those quiet creatures. The unseen birds singing in the mist.[10]

It will be noted that the mist hides, not simply because it impairs visibility but because, like a Nessus' garment, it robs the sheep of the very life that it might bestow on them. The feeling is far too deep ever to become a conscious theme in Wordsworth. But the underlying metaphor of the garment reappears at several critical junctures in his description of his own development. Thus, when the energy of new manliness is dissipated in revelry, he writes

> It seemed the very garments that I wore
> Preyed on my strength, and stopped the quiet stream
> Of self-forgetfulness.[11]

More curious even is the episode of the drowned man. The very first week that the boy Wordsworth is entrusted to his sweet valley he perceives on the opposite shore of the lake a heap of garments:

> Long I watched,
> But no one owned them; meanwhile the calm lake
> Grew dark with all the shadows on its breast,
> And, now and then, a fish up-leaping snapped
> The breathless stillness.[12]

Someone is merged with the quiet stream of self-forgetfulness; he has put off the garments. The next day he is brought up, a specter shape of terror but, adds the poet, no soul-debasing fear

> for my inner eye had seen
> Such sights before, among the shining streams
> Of faëry land, the forest of romance.[13]

It seems therefore as if Wordsworth were working toward an image evocative of a power that, like the Nessus' garment, is a condition, the source even, of life, but which inevitably impedes itself because of its own strength.

   This is confirmed in a passage from the very beginning of *The Prelude*. The poet states that though Nature first woke the mind to a sense of its own power, the mind has now become a power in its own right, and so strong that it can find satisfaction neither in Nature nor in itself:

> For I, methought, while the sweet breath of heaven
> Was blowing on my body, felt within
> A correspondent breeze, that gently moved
> With quickening virtue, but is now become
> A tempest, a redundant energy,
> Vexing its own creation.[14]

"Vexing its own creation" must be construed in two ways. The redundant energy not only vexes what it creates, the things on which it wishes to impose its imaginative power, but also vexes itself *into* creation, wishing to generate itself by its proper force, disowning Nature. Is this not the general dilemma of the imagination?

> Imagination—here the Power so called
> Through sad incompetence of human speech,
> That awful Power rose from the mind's abyss
> Like an unfathered vapour that enwraps,
> At once, some lonely traveller. I was lost;
> Halted without an effort to break through;
> But to my conscious soul I now can say—
> "I recognise thy glory": in such strength
> Of usurpation, when the light of sense
> Goes out, but with a flash that has revealed

> The invisible world, doth greatness make abode,
> There harbours; [15]

The simile of "unfathered vapour" springs to mind because mist has become an indispensable symbol for a liberty of motion or creation that, insofar as it becomes visible or causes creation, impedes itself and the things it creates by a strength too generous for the objects for which it is employed. But the dilemma is here overcome by the nature of the situation. This is not only a power given by an invisible source, it is "unfathered," for Wordsworth, who has just learnt that he has crossed the Alps, is caught off guard, before his mind can prepare for and transmute the event. The imagination usurps him, he is lost, and makes no effort to break through. The episode takes us back to what has been called the inherent paradox of the imagination, whether in Wordsworth or in any other poet: the imagination, because it depends on a human will "vexing its own creation," hiding itself or its generating source like mist, cannot be true either to itself or to Nature, unless usurped by a third power (here the immortal soul) at the moment when the creative will is at rest, as after an intense expectation or when the possibility of willed recognition has been removed.

It is noteworthy that Wordsworth seems to have discovered for himself, and in himself, one of the most persistent religious problems often handed on by scriptural interpretation rather than by a conviction having its origin in personal experience. This paradox of the imagination is not an intellectual construct, but inevitable as soon as we ascribe to man any kind of creative power. Wordsworth intends to describe a principle of generosity which, while it is shared by Nature and the mind, transcends both. How this principle of generosity comes to reveal itself to the poet, and how it informs his poetry, is our next concern.

3

The fifth book of *The Prelude* gives us the episode of the Boy of Winander. He stands by the lakeside at evening, when the earliest stars were moving along the edges of the hills, "rising or setting," and he hoots to the silent owls, who reply across the lake with "long halloos and screams, and echoes loud" until

> a lengthened pause
> Of silence came and baffled his best skill,
> Then sometimes, in that silence while he hung
> Listening, a gentle shock of mild surprise
> Has carried far into his heart the voice
> Of mountain torrents; or the visible scene
> Would enter unawares into his mind,
> With all its solemn imagery, its rocks,
> Its woods, and that uncertain heaven, received
> Into the bosom of the steady lake.[16]

This boy may be compared to the later poet. The poet also calls on a responsive Nature in whom the principle of generosity is everywhere apparent—one cannot say why the stars move along the edges of the hills, rising or setting, yet one feels that they do it for the sheer joy and splendor of motion—but the poet is not given moral or creative strength according to the exertion of voice and will. He is formed, and his imagination rises, precisely at that moment when he, like the Boy of Winander, has ceased exertion and hung listening.[17] "Hung" is frequent in Wordsworth as a verb indicating a suspension both physical and mental, when a force other than that of personal effort seems to sustain mind and body:

> Oh! when I have hung
> Above the raven's nest, by knots of grass
> And half-inch fissures in the slippery rock
> But ill sustained, and almost (so it seemed)
> Suspended by the blast that blew amain,
> Shouldering the naked crag, oh, at that time
> While on the perilous ridge I hung alone.
> With what strange utterance did the loud dry wind
> Blow through my ear, the sky seemed not a sky
> Of earth—and with what motion moved the clouds! [18]

In "with what motion moved the clouds!" we find a typical case of what might be called the absentee referent, where the poet sim-

ply states that something is a very special kind of motion and emotion, but refuses to qualify by an exertion of the creative will.

It is a principal theme of *The Prelude* that neither the creative
will, by which is meant the will to call up experience in all its affec-
tive qualities, nor the moral will, that is, the will to understand
and interpret experience, have very much in common with the
true imagination. This is not to say that the poet leaves off moraliz-
ing or that he is never aware of his creative struggles, for Wordsworth is evidently one of our last poetic moralists, and his *Prelude*
seeks to be the biography of the growth of a poet. It means that
the moral message, whenever explicit, is kept causally separate
from the narrated experience, that, similarly, the description of
experience is kept pure of the arbitrary or associational connec-
tions which are the necessary product of a searching mind, like that
of Coleridge "Debarred from Nature's living images,/Compelled
to be a life unto herself." There are, in the best poems of Wordsworth, in "Tintern Abbey" and *The Prelude,* neither moral nor
objective correlatives, although there is morality and epistemology
in abundance. Though he moralizes through a whole paragraph
before the Boy of Winander episode, this latter remains unencum-
bered. Though all kinds of conclusions, mystic and moral, are ap-
pended to the story of the Plundering Boy ("Thanks to the means
which Nature deigned to employ"), no extraneous considerations
mar the story itself.

The cardinal point, then, concerning both the poetic and the
human imagination (Wordsworth refused to distinguish between
them) is that their power stems neither from the creative will nor
from the moral will but from an inherent generosity found now in
Nature, now in man, which belongs ultimately neither to Nature as
external nature nor to man. It is an "interchangeable supremacy,"
and often has no access to man except by way of usurpation.

This of course sounds as if it were a disguised metaphysical position, yet it is not, at least not when active through his poetry. Wordsworth has no qualms about professing his belief in God, the be-
neficence of Nature, or the existence of an immortal soul; but he
knows that this profession is an incidental and almost arbitrary
way of naming what is a psychological fact, and may only be repre-

sented as such. His aim in *The Prelude* is therefore not to justify the ways of Nature to man, nor to sketch the growth of an idea, but to present the growth of the whole mind, never disguising the fact that the bases of belief lie too deeply submerged in childhood to be more than glimpsed by the reasoning reason.[19]

The principle of generosity is not only an aesthetic principle, but one that influences the totality of human effort. There is in Wordsworth none of that "chessboard psychology" with which Herder reproached the philosophy of Kant. If the imagination fails, it is because the poet has failed with respect to his soul. The first important event of *The Prelude* tells us of such a failure:

> It was a splendid evening, and my soul
> Once more made trial of her strength, nor lacked
> Aeolian visitations; but the harp
> Was soon defrauded, and the banded host
> Of harmony dispersed in struggling sounds,
> And lastly utter silence! "Be it so;
> Why think of any thing but present good?" [20]

The episode sets the cheerful note of the entire epic. The "Once more" almost like the "Once again" of "Tintern Abbey" suggests that this incident is only one of very many opportunities the poet has to commune with Nature. The failure is not radical. Furthermore, no problem of subject and object exists. The evening *is* splendid, the soul *does* exist. Wordsworth is a poet as affirmative in his way as Milton. "Splendid" is ordinarily a rather common adjective of appreciation, used here to show not a special gift of joy, but a common joy immediately replied to, a joy open daily to the eager in heart, not granted the poet by divine dispensation. A serious note, however, subsists. Why is the poet defrauded of his poetry, why must he resign himself with the calm thought, "Be it so"? True to his custom, Wordsworth does not presume to tell us; he states (1) the experience, (2) his acceptance, and no attempt is made to justify one in terms of the other.

Certain other episodes in a more mystical vein, such as "Crossing the Alps," already cited, help to answer this question. They are always concerned with the testing of the soul. Wordsworth insists

that the soul is *creative*. It will eventually be seen that this term
is used in a literal sense. But though the soul is creative, it cannot
will itself to power, it cannot test its own strength. Wordsworth
does not seem to be at all consistent in his use of terms; at times
the soul is described as the active "under-power," but then it is the
heart that cannot help itself:

> Gently did my soul
> Put off her veil, and, self-transmuted, stood
> Naked, as in the presence of her God.
> While on I walked, a comfort seemed to touch
> A heart that had not been disconsolate:
> Strength came where weakness was not known to be,
> At least not felt; and restoration came
> Like an intruder knocking at the door
> Of unacknowledged weariness.[21]

But whatever the term used, it is certain that the soul's strength
cannot be tested by man himself. In the above episode it was the
cold, raw, untuned air that helped to reveal the secret fullness of
the heart, and if the poet lost his poetry, it may have been because
he sought to test his creative strength instead of waiting for the
"usurpation." [22]

If it cannot be willed into action, how does the principle of generosity reveal itself, how is the soul made apparent? One of the famous passages in *The Prelude* is that dealing with skating at night.
Clear and loud the village clock tolled six, the boy

> wheeled about,
> Proud and exulting like an untired horse

he and his companions hiss along the ice, a pack after the hunted
hare

> So through the darkness and the cold we flew,
> And not a voice was idle; with the din
> Smitten, the precipices rang aloud;
> The leafless trees and every icy crag
> Tinkled like iron

> .   .   .   .

> and oftentimes
> When we had given our bodies to the wind,
> And all the shadowy banks on either side
> Came sweeping through the darkness, spinning still
> The rapid line of motion, then at once
> Have I, reclining back upon my heels,
> Stopped short; yet still the solitary cliffs
> Wheeled by me—even as if the earth had rolled
> With visible motion her diurnal round!
> Behind me did they stretch in solemn train
> Feebler and feebler, and I stood and watch'd
> Till all was tranquil as a dreamless sleep.[23]

"When we had given our bodies to the wind" is not only descriptively fine, but suggests the very joy of giving, a joy of free movement sparked by the spirits of Nature, very similar to that constant delicacy of intent, though virile, stronger, so reminiscent of Sidney's *Arcadia*, which we find everywhere in Dorothy's *Journals:* "The wind blew so keen in our faces that we felt ourselves inclined to seek the covert of the wood," or, "the little birds had given over singing." [24] But the main point of the scene is that the motion of Nature—and "motion" whenever used ("a spirit and a motion," "with what motion moved the clouds!") has for Wordsworth the connotation of Nature revealing herself as an active or sustaining force—is here made manifest, so that even the cliffs, which most easily give the impression of stock-still solitude, are now seen to participate in the general movement that informs the earth, one that is, moreover, a perpetual and daily thing, not a miraculous and sudden infusion. Though it seemed as if ("Proud and exulting like an untired horse") the source of this energy were simply in the animal spirits of the young boy, the scene being dark and cold and bare with ice, Nature soon responds to the activity of the skaters, just as when the owls replied to the Boy of Winander. The precipices ring, the trees though leafless make a sound, the reflection of the still stars flies along the ice—and then, when the moment of relaxation comes and they give their bodies to the wind, she reveals her secret motion in its entirety. Many are the moments in Words-

worth's verse or his sister's *Journal*, when the spirit of Nature is
caught as a visible thing. One could compare the view of the trees
outside the poet's window that seem to "rock the moon," [25] or this:

> As we were going along we were stopped at once, at the dis-
> tance perhaps of 50 yards from our favourite birch tree. It was
> yielding to the gusty wind with all its tender twigs, the sun
> shone upon it, and it glanced in the wind like a flying sun-
> shiny shower. It was a tree in shape, with stem and branches,
> but it was like a Spirit of water.[26]

The tree "yields" to the wind, the boys "give" their bodies: the tree
is transformed into a shiny spirit, and for them the motion of the
earth is made visible.

But the finest touch, perhaps, is that whereas the boy had
"wheeled about" at the beginning of the episode, at the end it is
the earth that "wheeled by" him. He has given Nature life, but
only a life that was there originally, and of which he is, finally, only
a part. *His spontaneous action has uncovered a far deeper generosity.* And though Nature replied immediately to the animal energy
of the skaters, she did not open herself entirely until the boy ceased
to skate, when he reclined on his heels, stopped short. Then both
the motion and the central peace are made apparent. Once again
the mystical suspense is gained after exertion, when the will is at
rest, and Nature is empowered to take over.

One could mention, finally, that the difference between Coleridge and Wordsworth is nowhere so obvious or essential as in their
respective views on the relation of will and soul or will and imagination. Both depreciate the fancy and a poetry of the will, and, at
the outset, their theoretical position is practically coincident. Yet,
perhaps through his contact with Schelling's philosophy of transcendental synthesis (which grants the possibility of perceiving the
essential harmony of man and nature through an intuitive and
voluntaristic act), Coleridge comes to satisfy his theological bent
and stresses man's power to humanize nature.[27] He seems therefore
to abandon his friend's basic separation of the imaginative and the
wilful, though the difference remains one of degree and depends
mainly, perhaps, on his greater emphasis on the "shaping spirit of

the imagination." The ode *Dejection* indicates the germinal difference very clearly. Such statements as

> I may not hope from outward forms to win
> The passion and the life whose fountains are within

or

> O Lady! we receive but what we give,
> And in our life alone does Nature live

could not really come from someone who, like Wordsworth, believed in the reciprocal generosity of man and Nature. The boy
Wordsworth receives much more than he gives; the man Wordsworth thinks that to receive depends not on what we give, but on
how spontaneously it is given. Poetically, at least, Coleridge does
not often stand comparison with Wordsworth; his fine conceit from
the same ode

> And those thin clouds above, in flakes and bars
> That give away their Motion to the Stars

is still merely a fine conceit, reminiscent of the subject of his poem,
the will to give away; while Wordsworth's description of his grove
at the onset of inspiration, if not immediately lengthened by the
tame tail of moral comment, would have been more than a conceit,
and have outpoesied his friend's achievement both in theme and
in effect:

> my favourite grove
> Tossing in sunshine its dark boughs aloft,
> As if to make the strong wind visible.[28]

4

How do the principle of generosity, and the dialectic of love of
which it is the source, affect the poem as poem? For it is difficult to
see how a poem, which always remains an artifact, can do justice
to an experience that has its roots in childhood and mystical visita-
tions.

In a poetical preface to *The Excursion* of 1814, Wordsworth
claims his work to be "the spousal verse" of a "great consumma-

tion" which, it seems, has taken place for him, but not as yet for man in general. His voice proclaims

> How exquisitely the individual Mind
> (And the progressive powers perhaps no less
> Of the whole species) to the external World
> Is fitted:—and how exquisitely, too—
> Theme this but little heard of among men—
> The external World is fitted to the Mind;
> And the creation (by no lower name
> Can it be called) which they with blended might
> Accomplish:—this is our high argument.[29]

It is the last of the three subjects that holds our attention. The first two are not without importance; but this "fitting and fittedness," as Blake called it in contempt,[30] is hard to understand, unless it should refer to a common theory of cognition going back at least to Plotinus, active in scholastic philosophy and revised by Kant. But the last statement seems of different caliber. It claims that Mind and World blend their might to produce a creation, and the poet puts emphasis on "creation." It is not, however, to be thought that this simply designates the modifying powers of the imagination. The prose preface of 1815 specifically states that the imagination not only modifies but also *creates*.[31] The idea of a modifying imagination is, in any case, nothing very extraordinary, but was toward the end of the eighteenth century a commonplace of epistomology, being found, among most other topoi, in *L'Imagination* of the Abbé Delille.[32] Wordsworth says "creation," and he wants to be taken literally. The poet has felt, and has been given the power to reproduce, a cognition not only organic, but also immediate and transcendent, one to which both mind and external world are necessary. Can we show by what process Wordsworth's poetry suggests this great consummation at once mystical and commonplace?

When the poet writes

> Once again
> Do I behold these steep and lofty cliffs,
> That on a wild secluded scene impress
> Thoughts of more deep seclusion

the reader who believes in a literal reading may at first be puzzled. How can one inanimate thing impress on another inanimate thing thoughts, the property of animate beings? The difficulty would resolve itself if one were to take this passage as a concentrated piece of writing that has omitted an obvious intermediary of perception. But he who knows Wordsworth and his claim to verbal accuracy will doubt that concentration is a sufficient, let alone valid, cause. The poet starts by saying "I behold," a favorite and scriptural verb referring more to the visionary than the visual sense, and negating the question whether what is seen is willed or received by the mind. The rest of the sentence, by omitting an obvious intermediary of perception, gives the effect that the impress of external nature on the mind is, by the mind, immediately reconstituted as the quality of the scene before it, and as an inexplicably profounder quality. We thus find preserved the organicity, immediacy and mystery of cognition in an ordinary, unpretentious circumstance.

Yet, curiously, we receive an impression that the thought itself has deepened. The phrase "of more deep seclusion" has a referent of which we are hardly conscious because a transcendent one immediately suggests itself. It is the cliffs that cause the scene to appear more secluded, it is the thoughts that are by nature more secluded even than the scene, but the suggestion persists that the cliffs and the scene have, by the very fact of entering the mind, caused a deepening there.

The figure that makes possible this last interpretation is not readily explained, but since, in one form or another, it occurs rather often in Wordsworth's poetry, we shall give it a name. We may call it "incremental redundance": the quality of a thing redounds on the thing it qualifies and is perceived as its very cause; the part of the whole appears greater than the whole of which it is the part. "Thoughts of more deep seclusion" means thoughts that are more deeply secluded, or thoughts that concern, or belong to, a more deep seclusion.

The process is supported by the repetition of the adjective "secluded" as well as the noun "seclusion": the scene is secluded, thought is even more secluded, but on coming together through perception there is apprehended a kind of seclusion deeper than

either, something "far more deeply interfused." It would seem as
if cognition and perception are imperceptibly one and the same
act, because of a subsistent ground of vision.

A single instance could not bear such weight, but the principle
is often and unobtrusively used in Wordsworth's poetry. There is
one case especially, again in "Tintern Abbey," reflection on which
would have saved some misunderstanding. When the poet says that
the dwelling of something far more deeply interfused is "the light
of setting suns," the emphasis is really on the first member of the
partitive construction: the light seems to belong to the suns, but
is actually something that transcends them, the *light* of setting suns.
So the erudite Coleridge is said to lack the *light* of knowledge.[33]
If the phrase is read in this manner no suggestion of pantheism
may be derived. The figure is more than a common ambiguity or
a simple synecdoche. There is involved a most subtle type of per-
sonification, of a "power" or "presence" rather than of a substance
or quality.

The emphasis of Wordsworth is never on knowledge as a completed state; the simple words "I hear," "I see" have magic for him.
His concern is with a subsistent, that is continuing, spirit: "Thou
soul that art the eternity of thought." He is correctly said to be ob-
sessed with the brooding, immediate presences of things, for he
believed in a kind of imperceptible cognition, in an effortless blending of the might of mind and nature to produce the recognition
of a transcendent principle of love.[34] The eighteenth century had
an understanding for powers and presences,[35] but in order to allow for deep, imageless feeling it had to fall back on a theory of
sublimity—"that comprehension and expanse of thought which
at once fills the whole mind, and of which the first effect is sudden
astonishment, the second rational admiration." [36] The poetry of
the century is full of verbs and nouns that have become adjectives
(J. Thomson's "the astonish'd eye," "disaster'd") as if no strong
feeling or thought could be unviolent, continuous, or operative
beyond prehension and will. But in Wordsworth understanding,
though mystical, is never "divine rape" or "annihilation of the
mind" but the revelation of the sustaining spirit, an innate power
that works on us, and in our most common perceptions. In these

famous lines from "Tintern Abbey" the emphasis is on the power
and the life, on what the poet has just termed the *"living* soul":

> While with an eye made quiet by the power
> Of harmony, and the deep power of joy
> We see into the life of things.

The idea that cognition is not a special state but an imperceptible and continuing process (though Wordsworth realizes that, as
man gets older, his recognitions of transcendent power are not
habitual and take the form of usurpations) is also conveyed by a
technique of verbal redundance. Perhaps the adjective is repeated
as noun ("secluded," "seclusion") or the noun repeated in its verb
("with what motion moved the clouds!") or something attributed
to one member of the action returned as a function of the other
(the "wheeled" of the skating scene in Book I). It is always the same
force that becomes variously manifest in the subject and its predi-
cates.

Even the rhythm, which in Wordsworth has become a major effect of style, helps to realize the continuous ebb and flow of the
sustaining power. Unaccented syllables are picked up and gradually brought forward to the reader's attention until accentuated,
as if a wave (of sound or sea) were bringing closer a far-away sound
and redispersing it in its echo. In the account of the skating, for
example, echo (which has metaphysical significance) is rendered by
"with the din/Smitten, the precipices rang aloud," where the sharp
high *i* of "din" is progressively accentuated, while the vowel plus
n or *ng* is first (in "smitten") deaccentuated, but picked up again
in "rang." The nature of overflow lines (that break in the first or
second or even third foot of the following verse) could also be noted
as contributing toward the ebb and flow effect; ". . . /Smitten"
is one example.

However, the use of ebb and flow is hardly anywhere so apparent
as in the beginning of "Tintern Abbey," where the vowel plus *r*
or *rs* and the vowel plus *n* or *ng* are alternately accentuated and
deaccentuated: years-summers-winters-hear-waters-murmur; win-
ters-again-rolling-mountain-springs- [referring back to other *ng*

combinations] inland. Even, of course, when the subject does not warrant it onomatopoetically, the technique persists; at the end of our passage "With some uncertain notice" the *ice* of "notice" is picked up by "Hermit's" and finally accentuated by "sits," while "dwellers" and "houseless" provide side echoes. The permanence of ebb-and-flow rhythm suggests those swellings of the spirit that pervade the "undecaying mind."

Indeed, Wordsworth's poetry is pervaded by images of waters, rivers, lakes and seas. The river Derwent had flowed through his dreams. Perhaps the sea that increases and diminishes, yet whose force remains constant, suggests to him a fundamental analogy to the life of the emotions and of faith. Even to the loose stones on the highway he gives a life:

> the great mass
> Lay bedded in a quickening soul [37]

and with this metaphor comes explicit suggestion that the soul's life and power is like that of the sea, and this sea is not an external sea, we are imbedded in it; it is an "inland ocean."

The paradox of the quickening soul is essential with him. How may the soul become the "living Soul" of "Tintern Abbey," how may that which is a power independent of human life, on coming into life (quickening), not only not lose its power but increase it (quicken) during life, like a river that gains speed in its course?

> and again I hear
> These waters, rolling from their mountain-springs
> With a soft inland murmur.

All these rivers that come rolling from the mountains, gaining speed in their course, will never reach the sea, at least not an external sea. They are part of that inland ocean with which man also is in daily and continuous contact.

Through syntax, sound, and imagery, then, we arrive at the same conclusion. A technical summary would run as follows: for Wordsworth, cognition is the confluence, the almost imperceptible confluence, of mind and external world which springs from and reveals the transcendent principle blending both. The transcendent is, for

Wordsworth, that principle of generosity or love we have already described. Therefore the ultimate referent of Wordsworth's poetry may be seen as a mystical principle, as the origin of the cognition, as well as the result of it. That Wordsworth's poetry does suggest a mystical substratum to experience is hardly to be doubted, although the means by which the poet achieves this are difficult to trace, but should be traced in order to understand him fully. They depend on the general device of incremental redundancy which, as has been said, effects subtle personifications of powers and presences, making what appears to be only part of a whole suddenly appear greater than the whole of which it is a part. They depend, further, on effects of rhythm and imagery which convey the impression of a subsistent and sustaining ground of vision. How subtle the process is whereby perception imperceptibly becomes cognition, whereby the might of the mind receives fulfillment through blending with the might of Nature, may be shown in this example from "Tintern Abbey," where the poet addresses the river Wye as if it were a salvational force to relieve him from the fever of the world

> when the fretful stir
> Unprofitable, and the fever of the world,
> Have hung upon the beatings of my heart—
> How oft, in spirit, have I turned to thee,
> O sylvan Wye! thou wanderer thro' the woods,
> How often has my spirit turned to thee!

"How oft, in spirit, have I turned to thee" indicates the desire of the poet to commune with Nature; "How often has my spirit turned to thee" may indicate the very same thing, but may also, and almost imperceptibly, suggest that an active and generative principle has fulfilled in fact what was only a potentiality in human desire.

5

Concepts of the imagination as creative and of the poem as creation reveal a consummation at once mystical and commonplace: the imperceptible blending of man and the external world, of the mind's might and Nature's, of ordinary perception and the subsistent, transcendent power uniting heaven and earth. We shall now see whether this terrestrial paradise, of which *The Prelude* and *The Excursion* are a "spousal verse," has, like Milton's heavenly paradise, a real topography, whether, in other words, there can be found in Wordsworth a sustained allegory.

An allegorical element is essential to every poem that wishes to present a world picture. For Dante the allegorical meaning gave a synthetic view of human history in the light of divine history— Fall, Redemption, Last Judgment. In order to conceive an allegory, the writer must believe that he can see human events prophetically subsumed under a divine or transcendent scheme of reference. Allegory, therefore, is also a statement on the nature of revelation.

Though Wordsworth talks directly about his own life, such a scheme of reference is present, as well as a statement on the nature of revelation. But contrary to Milton, he considers that his revelation can be expressed in the forms and symbols of daily life. The human soul, furthermore, is often thought to need the external world in order to know and express its divine origin.

The poet's prospect is almost always, as in "Tintern Abbey," from a height looking into a valley. The latter is the "chosen Vale," as he calls it in Book I of *The Prelude* while he journeys toward his "hermitage." It is also a "deep Vale," heaven's earthly counterpart.[38] He has, in any case, escaped the "vast city" and aware of his new liberty echoes, in "The earth is all before me," Milton's comment on Adam and Eve expelled from Paradise.[39] There is another important place where he echoes Milton, this time in *The Excursion,* describing again a valley suddenly revealed (like that of the Wye) among a waste of huge hill tops:

> when, all at once, behold!
> Beneath our feet, a little lowly vale,
> A lowly vale, and yet uplifted high
> Among the mountains; even as if the spot
> Had been from eldest time by wish of theirs
> So placed, to be shut out from all the world!
> Urn-like it was in shape, deep as an urn;
> With rocks encompassed, save that to the south

Was one small opening, where a heath-clad ridge
Supplied a boundary less abrupt and close;
A quiet treeless nook, with two green fields,
A liquid pool that glittered in the sun,
And one bare dwelling; one abode, no more!

.   .   .

Ah! what a sweet Recess, thought I, is here! [40]

It is Adam who, on being informed that he has to leave Paradise, sadly calls it "our sweet Recess." [41] But Wordsworth, who is trying in his epic to lead up to the crowning idea of the "Recluse," sees Paradise possible in any sweet though bare nook of the earth, and whereas for Milton a total retreat from human life in order to gain contemplative contact with God had for its prerequisite the unfallen state of man and the separate region of Paradise, for Wordsworth Paradise lies *before* man, not *behind* him, and the Recluse would have been he who perceived God in the simplest sign of Nature, by living with her in the valley of love and utter solitude:

Paradise, and groves
Elysian, Fortunate Fields—like those of old
Sought in the Atlantic Main—why should they be
A history only of departed things,
Or a mere fiction of what never was?
For the discerning intellect of Man,
When wedded to this goodly universe
In love and holy passion, shall find these
A simple produce of the common day. [42]

Wordsworth formulates his concepts of retirement and spiritual liberty in conscious criticism of Milton. Both poets had, of course, turned to a life "Private, unactive, calm, contemplative" after political disillusion. For both, liberty had first seemed a political fact, and is then perceived as a spiritual fact. But while Milton seeks revelation only in the scriptures, and firmly expresses his belief in an ethic of stand, wait, and, if necessary, condemn, Wordsworth seeks revelation in all the forms of rural nature, and voices an ethic of immediate sympathy with repose in abstract moral judgments.

Indeed, Wordsworth comes to express through his poetry a feeling for *continuous revelation*. The mystical moments are referred to as "spots of time" or as flashes of light, "gleams like the flashing of a shield"—derived, it should not be forgotten, from the "common face of nature." When the poet wishes to evoke an image of tranquillity he chooses the glitter made by light on wet things, on the grass "By mist and silent rain-drops silvered o'er." We remember Dorothy's favorite birch which appears in the sun a "Spirit of Water." Another passage from Dorothy's *Journals* is even more remarkable.

> Sat a considerable time upon the heath. Its surface restless and glittering with the motion of the scattered piles of withered grass, and the waving of the spiders' threads. On our return the mist still hanging over the sea, but the opposite coast clear, and the rocky cliffs distinguishable. In the deep Coombe, as we stood upon the sunless hill, we saw miles of grass, light and glittering, and the insects passing.[43]

Let us note only the dry grass of the deep Coombe, light, restless and glittering. Is not the idea implicit that here is, as it were, an ocean of glittering grass? In *The Prelude* the "presences" of Nature are said to make

> The surface of the universal earth
> With triumph and delight, with hope and fear,
> Work like a sea . . .[44]

One might think that the earth is a sea of liquid light which gives forth waves of light and sound. "The trees almost *roared*," writes Dorothy of a storm, italicizing her brother's favorite verb for the noise of mighty waters.[45] The Wordsworthian valley is, moreover, filled with murmur of "inland streams"; in one fragment found among the jottings of Dorothy's *Journal*, "a mighty vale" takes the very semblance of the sea, its fields green "as is the greenest billow of the sea," its hills rising like islands, "and the dome of Heaven/And waters in the midst, a second Heaven." [46] The Heaven, therefore, is also of the waters, or is it that the sky merely serves to divide one heavenly ocean from the other?

> And God said: "Let there be a firmament in the midst of the
> waters, and let it divide the waters from the waters." And God
> made the firmament and divided the waters which were under
> the firmament from the waters which were above the firma-
> ment; and it was so. And God called the firmament Heaven.

There is always in the corner of the poet's mind this vision of
a flooded world, in which the spirit of God hovered over the face
of the waters. Paradise is not separate from the earth, and neither
is Heaven. The firmament is a simple division of two presences of
the spirit of God, two waters.

Revelation, then, is continuous, though fainter than at the origin;
God did not withdraw from the earth with the creation of an uncertain heaven.[47] This constitutes a second criticism of Milton, and
a second feature of a new allegory. Book XI of *Paradise Lost*
(Wordsworth and his sister wept on reading it) reveals to Adam
the future destruction of man through the Flood. The lesson of
the Flood is stated to be

> To teach thee that God attributes to place
> No sanctity, if none be thither brought
> By Men who there frequent, or therein dwell. (XI, 836 ff.)

Nothing could be more in harmony with the moral teaching of
Wordsworth than that man should bring sanctity to his home,
should wed this goodly universe in holy passion. But the optimistic
Wordsworth does not like to envisage the Flood as a consequence of
man's Fall. His divine cosmology is still based primarily on the
first chapter of Genesis. Dorothy's "Spirit of Water," and all the
other watery presences that hover over the face of "universal earth,"
do not presage the waters of sin, but those of God's primary and
continuous revelation.

A few more instances should be given to show the pervasiveness
of the concept and imagery of continuous revelation in Wordsworth. The very prospect that made him a dedicated spirit suggests itself as a prototype of his total vision. It is a picture of a sweet
and common dawn, with the sea "laughing at a distance," and
the solid rocks that shine (like clouds!) "drenched in empyrean

light." [48] There is no doubt that the mountains are more solid and nearer to us than the sea; yet both mountains and sea are images of liquid light. This blending of the mountains and the sea is complemented by the marriage of heaven and earth,[49] also a watery vision, as in the description of young Hartley Coleridge's fairy boat of life

> Suspended in a stream as clear as sky,
> Where earth and heaven do make one imagery.

The humble yet glorious valleys of Wordsworth are full of these "perpetual streams," [50] prompting thoughts "Of Life continuous, Being unimpaired," [51] sending up their inland murmur. The air itself is caught as if inhabited by the spirits of water. "There was no *one* waterfall above another—" writes Dorothy, "it was the sound of waters in the air—the voice of the air," and this voice in winter reaches even the top of the mountains.[52]

Thus, the general body of Wordsworth's imagery may be related to the idea of an inland ocean partially ebbed from the face of the earth, but visible in the distance, and audible everywhere—even to the top of the mountains. The finest passage expressing this is found in *The Excursion:*

> I have seen
> A curious child, who dwelt upon a tract
> Of inland ground, applying to his ear
> The convolutions of a smooth-lipped shell;
> To which, in silence hushed, his very soul
> Listened intensely; and his countenance soon
> Brightened with joy; for from within were heard
> Murmurings, whereby the monitor expressed
> Mysterious union with its native sea.
> Even such a shell the universe itself
> Is to the ear of Faith; and there are times,
> I doubt not, when to you it doth impart
> Authentic tidings of invisible things;
> Of ebb and flow, and ever-during power;
> And central peace, subsisting at the heart
> Of endless agitation.[53]

The incident serves to express most fully Wordsworth's vision of the earth as an ocean at ebb tide. This shell is found away from the sea-shore—it is the earth itself—and the poet is like an inquisitive child for whom every original contact with the unknown ocean is a joy-ful mystery. The sea has retreated, but the earth, when *listened* to, expresses "Mysterious union with its native sea." Faith is an act of listening, and in "tidings" we find a very rare Wordsworthian pun: they are, of course, gospel tidings, as well as tides of the sea.

One may also recall the poet's dream in the fifth book of *The Prelude*. This time the vision is of a desert and an Arab fleeing through the desert to save the two precious products of the human mind, the shell and the stone, poetry and geometry, from the pur-suing flood:

> mine eyes
> Saw, over half the wilderness diffused,
> A bed of glittering light: I asked the cause:
> 'It is,' said he, 'the waters of the deep
> Gathering upon us;' [54]

If we remember Dorothy's description of the deep Coombe as withered grass, restless and glittering, if we remember the pervasive image of the earth as an ebbed inland ocean, then we may read this dream without difficulty. The great flood that has ebbed is returning to claim its own; the mysterious union with the sea is to be re-effected; the sea, though an image of terror, is not a sign of vengeance but of spiritual fulfillment as prophesied by the "pro-phetic blast of harmony" put out by the sea-shell poetry. If it is an image of terror, it is so because the deluge will destroy even the frail shrines that men have built for what, to their mortal eyes, seemed a deathless spirit. [55]

We reach the last station of Wordsworth's divine cosmology. In-stead of Heaven's Paradise, terrestrial Paradise; instead of the Flood of sin, the Flood of life and continuous revelation; instead of the Passion and the Redemption, this Apocalypse of the returning tide of mighty spiritual waters.

For it is the Apocalypse which is here suggested, and the Arab is the type of a recurrent apocalyptic figure, also represented by the wanderer and the Hermit. But into the Arab of Book V there has entered a quixotic element; we feel that it is no Quixote, symbol of the poetic spirit running actively after its visions (as Wordsworth had done at the time of the French Revolution) who will survive the Flood and save the intellectual effort of mankind. The true ideal is entirely contemplative, and the hermit its true representative. In *The Excursion,* the Wanderer muses what impulses drew

> Through a long course of later ages, drove,
> The hermit to his cell in forest wide;
> Or what detained him, till his closing eyes
> Took their last farewell of the sun and stars,
> Fast anchored in the desert? [56]

"Fast anchored in the desert": the vision of Book V works on as a sunken image; the Hermit alone will survive the Deluge that is to return and submerge the ebbed ocean bed of earth.

But why, finally, is it the Hermit who will survive? He is, first of all, Wordsworth's prophetic figure *par excellence.* In "Resolution and Independence" we find the following curious stanza to which the poet attached some importance since he cites it as an example of "Imagination." [57] It describes the aspect of the oldest man "that ever wore grey hairs":

> As a huge stone is sometimes seen to lie
> Couched on the bald top of an eminence;
> Wonder to all who do the same espy,
> By what means it could thither come, and whence;
> So that it seems a thing endued with sense:
> Like a sea-beast crawled forth, that on a shelf
> Of rock or sand reposeth, there to sun itself;
> Such seemed this Man   (stanzas 9 and 10)

That Wordsworth should have chosen such a grotesque image in order to illustrate the workings of the imagination is more than curious—but the old man is evidently a relict of the spiritual flood. He is a "sea-beast" stranded by the ebbed tide, and in search of the waters of pools "dwindled long by slow decay." The entire atmosphere of the poem is pervaded by the sound of waters: in the night

the wind roars, the rain falls in floods; in the morning, the air is
filled with pleasant noise of waters; traveling on the moor the poet
"heard the woods and distant waters roar"—and he adds, "Or heard
them not, as happy as a boy," for hearing them he is at moments
returned to the unconscious life of boyhood. The very voice of the
Leech Gatherer has the sound of waters, scarce heard because it is
the voice of the first boyhood flood that is past, and the second flood
that is to come, which will gather up man into the stream of life:

> The old man still stood talking by my side;
> But now his voice to me was like a stream
> Scarce heard.

There is at least one other place where this original image of a voice
that has the sound of waters is found, namely in the Apocalypse of
St. John:

> And his head and his hairs were white, as white wool and as
> snow. And his eyes were as a flame of fire: And his feet like unto
> fine brass, as in a burning furnace. And his voice as the sound
> of many waters. (1:14–15)

The Leech Gatherer and the Hermit figure in general refer us
to this vision and voice of St. John.[58] The figure prophesies the
flood of a new revelation, is itself a flood of revelation. If the apparition sometimes takes the peculiar form of a Hermit, it is because
he exemplifies contemplation, having retired to the desert or the
woods in order to "subdue" his eyes, and await the flood "fast anchored." The Hermit of "Tintern Abbey" is an image of transcendence: he sits fixed by his fire, the symbol, probably, for the pure or
imageless vision—the ultimate end of the greater and partially un-
avowed journey Wordsworth makes into the chosen vale and to
his "hermitage." [59]

Dante and Milton at particular moments of their work feel compelled to apologize for having represented spiritual essence as if it
were a thing outward and visible. Wordsworth does not make the
apology. Although it can be argued that his final tendency is toward
an imageless vision, he claims the necessity of the external world
for this end. "Tintern Abbey" is subsumed under an allegorical

scheme, even if this be kept as an under-sense and never given either dogmatic or conceptual foundation. The poet starts by a vision into the mystic vale. The river of life sends up its inland murmur, reminding him of its far-away source, but also of its continued presence, perhaps also of the future consummation. But though the cliffs connect a secluded landscape with the quiet of the sky, erasing the dividing line of heaven and earth, the forms of external nature do not shed their concreteness, at least, not until the poet shows toward them a generous yielding of his moral and creative will equal to their own apparent generosity: the pastoral farms are green to the very door. There begins the dialectic of love, when the poet succeeds in suspending his will toward relational knowledge and, by an act of faith, comes to hear and feel, within him and abroad, the ebb and flow of the immortal sea. An inherent principle of love is discovered, smoke rises from the dark woods as if it were a visible sign from an invisible source, of the freed will; and the Hermit appears, fixed near his fire, freed in his perception from the forms of the external world, a relic of eternity and prophet of the immortal sea's return.

6

This is the first of the essays on different poets in which we shall suggest a method of complete interpretation. It is not to be supposed, of course, that a single effort can exhaust the meanings of a particular poet.[60] But an attempt will be made to justify a unified multiplicity of interpretation, though justifying it as more than subjective—as, in fact, textually required.

We first examined the most literal level of meaning, that concerning the poet's immediate experience of the world, the dialectic of love between man and Nature. Seeking then to find the faculties of the mind put into play by this dialectic, we arrived at Wordsworth's concept of imagination, its link with a transcendent principle of generosity. This in turn led to an anagogical concern, "the testing of the soul." How the poem as artifact could suggest the principle of generosity, and how this principle depends on a theory of cognition was our next subject, and we showed the nature of the great consummation which is supposed to be realized by the poem, as by the creative imagination. We went on, finally, to indicate an allegorical meaning, the setting of Wordsworth's poetry into the frame and image of the great consummation, pointing out that, insofar as a poem has allegorical meaning, it is also a statement on revelation.

Nothing, except the poem itself, stands in the way of adding to these meanings. It is possible to derive a moral or sociological interpretation, as we have slightly indicated in mentioning Wordsworth's attitude toward liberty. And it must be mentioned—though this may throw doubt on the credibility of our interpretation and on the validity of the method—that a psycho-sexual analysis of the first part of "Tintern Abbey" is not impossible. The danger has to be run. There is no safeguard except common sense, a knowledge of the entirety of the poet's work, and an understanding of the nature of symbols that allow neither exclusive nor divergent interpretations.

We would now concern ourselves more closely with the nature of these symbols. Our problem throughout has been how poetry may deal with mystical experience. We do not insist on "mystical." "Metaphysical" would do just as well, except that it has been specialized to signify a purely intellectual relation. Mystical experience is metaphysical experience seizing the whole of man. Taking up the romantic definition of poet and genius which Coleridge expresses in *Biographia Literaria,* we would ask how the poet brings the whole soul of man into activity, or, in our more technical terms, how poetic symbols lend themselves to that unified multiplicity of interpretation exhibited in the previous sections.

One could first take the case where the poet tries to convey a metaphysical idea and fails, not because the idea is poor or false, but because it does not accord with the language of poetry. The following passage is typical of *The Excursion,* and, in its original version dating back to 1798, supported Coleridge's shift from Hartley and Godwin: [61]

> For, the Man—
> Who, in this spirit, communes with the Forms
> Of nature, who with understanding heart

> Both knows and loves such objects as excite
> No morbid passions, no disquietude,
> No vengeance, and no hatred—needs must feel
> The joy of that pure principle of love
> So deeply, that, unsatisfied with aught
> Less pure and exquisite, he cannot choose
> But seek for objects of a kindred love
> In fellow-natures and a kindred joy.
> Accordingly he by degrees perceives
> His feelings of aversion softened down;
> A holy tenderness pervade his frame.
> His sanity of reason not impaired,
> Say rather, all his thoughts now flowing clear,
> From a clear fountain flowing, he looks round
> And seeks for good; and finds the good he seeks: [62]

It is, on the whole, a skilful passage, pleasant to read, and the moral purpose is patent. Wordsworth, like Schiller,[63] advocates here an ethic based on the "constraint of love": *one cannot choose but love,* and seek the world in love, if one has communed with Nature.

Coleridge, no doubt, liked the passage because it substitutes a necessitarianism of the heart for one of the intellect. But the language does not entirely lend itself to the argument. It is said that a communion with Nature will gradually bring about a compulsive love. Yet the very word "communes" in the second line indicates a spirit of action already present which need only be set in motion; the phrase "with understanding heart" likewise. We thought at first that Nature would effect the change by her own agency, force the hard heart to love and spread love; we now perceive that the heart must already be understanding before love can come to it. At one point the poet represents man as passive, "he by degrees perceives/His feelings of aversion softened down;" at another point as active, already possessing what he is to possess, "who with understanding heart/Both knows and loves." The very end is the only successful part. It betrays the real argument, which is that man acts, looks round, seeks, finds, not simply through the exercise of his will,

but through a transcendent, pure principle of love that makes his
heart understand before it has tried to understand.

Poetry then seems to proceed by absolutes; Wordsworth's "understanding heart" forestalls and invalidates the entire logical sequence. "Understanding" is used in an absolute sense. We do not
wish to ask what the heart understands, or how, etc. In one word,
we would forgo relational knowledge. But the poet has put it into
an argumentative context, so that we are forced to ask questions
about "relations," the what, how, and why, and where, and so, finally, to disparage. Successful metaphysical statement, if it is to
occur, must occur without prompting the mind to seek knowledge
of relations.

Let us examine a metaphysical statement where the will toward
relational knowledge is not excited. Consider

> Fair seed-time had my Soul, and I grew up
> Fostered alike by beauty and by fear (*Prelude* I)

and compare it to the Psalmist's "It is a good thing to give thanks
unto the Lord." The passages are well-known; they need not be
quoted in full. The first makes an oblique assertion of beneficent
Nature, the second makes an assertion very directly. Both remain
poetry: the degree of directness has evidently no necessary pejora-
tive effect. If both succeed as poetry, it is because neither asks to
be developed in a relational way. Do we want to ask, What is this
Soul? Who is this Lord? How may seeds be planted in an immaterial thing? Why should it be good to give thanks? Neither the creative will, in the light of which all objects answer to the demand
made of them by the searching mind, nor the moral will, in the
light of which they are subsumed under a prior law of duty, is here
put into effect. Both poets assume something beyond wilful assump-
tion; their statement is of the kind: "it is so," and not "it ought
to be so" or "if you consider 1, 2 and 3, then 4." The will toward
relational knowledge plays no part because whatever relation is,
is. It may be accepted, and thanksgiving result, it may be rejected
and complaint result, but the relation holds.

But what is this relation so immediately perceived, and so immediately stated, that our moral and creative will forgoes its cus-

tomary harassment? In good poetry we do not seek for proofs, practical values, personal applications. There is what has been variously described as suspense of judgment, poetic faith, the objectification of the will. We call it the statement of a relation in such immediate terms that no incitement to relational thinking remains. The poet, insofar as he writes poetry, feels himself, and is able to express himself, as fundamentally in relation, not with any particular, in any particular way, for any particular reason (though with some thing, in some way, for some reason), but *in relation;* so that poetry is more immediate, that is, less dependent on a relational use of symbols, than ordinary discourse.

Let us first take a naive piece of writing, but one we instinctively recognize as good. An extract from Dorothy Wordsworth's *Journals* will do as well as any other.

> *April 22nd, Thursday.* A fine mild morning—we walked into Easedale. The sun shone. Coleridge talked of his plan of sowing the laburnum in the woods. The waters were high, for there had been a great quantity of rain in the night. I was tired and sate under the shade of a holly tree that grows upon a rock, I sate there and looked down the stream.[64]

All the sentences are simple, unsubordinated phrases, and not merely because these are the jottings of a journal, for even when a rare causal clause appears, as to explain why the waters were high, it is of such naive character that it too has to be taken as more than explanatory, as existing in its own right. Dorothy says "I was tired," giving no reason. "It is so." The statement is the same matter-of-fact but intrinsically significant kind as the causal "for there had been . . ." She sits in the shade of a holly tree "that grows upon a rock," descriptive phrase but one which must have some reason beyond simple description. And why does the writer repeat "I sate [there]" twice? Though there is hardly a relational thought, linking one event with another, explaining one event in terms of another, the effect as a whole is most strongly that the writer feels herself so immediately "in relation" that she can forgo comment. The sun is hers, and if she is tired, this is also worth noting because in some way it is as much "intended" for her as the sun, the high waters, and the fact that they are high because it rained in the night. Even the act and direction of her glance become naturally significant. Why else should we be told that she looked down the stream?

However, the importance or value of a poem does not reside in the simple feeling of relatedness or intentionality, which, after all, is a constant of perception. It lies in the immediacy with which a fundamental relation is perceived and expressed. Like Emerson, the poet will never speculate on why the Rhodora or anything is where or how it is, unless his mind raises the same question about itself, and simultaneously. The poet does not engage in relational thinking because he knows certainly that there is relation.

Can the individual character of this relation be determined through a study of Wordsworth's poetry? We propose to do so by a trilogy of proof that shows the radical unity of Wordsworth's greater works, of the Great Ode, "Tintern Abbey," and *The Prelude*.

First the Great Ode. In the midst of springtime sound and festivity, writes the poet,

> To me alone there came a thought of grief:
> A timely utterance gave that thought relief,
>   And I again am strong:
> The cataracts blow their trumpets from the steep;
> No more shall grief of mine the season wrong;
> I hear the Echoes through the mountains throng,
> The Winds come to me from the fields of sleep,
>   And all the earth is gay;

This is a puzzling passage; we are not told the nature of the thought of grief,[65] but if we knew what the timely utterance was we might come to understand. It is evidently a momentary thing, an event, but the syntactical disjunction makes it possible that the sounding cataracts were part of this event, perhaps the utterance itself, or at least, together with the echoes and the winds, of the same nature as the event, and its continuing presences. The phrase "No more shall grief of mine the season wrong" may be a thought of the poet in his own person, but could equally well refer to the announcement of the cataracts, as interpreted by the poet. In any case the timely utterance, the strength-restoring event, occurs amid continuing presences that the new feeling of strength makes more apparent.

The light of rainbow, rose and moon, though these also are presences, did not prompt the utterance relieving the thought of grief. The poet describes and feels their joy, yet it is not light but sound which seems to restore him. In stanza 4 there is at last the exclamation "I hear, I hear, with joy I hear!" followed by the complaint that tree and field—objects discernible mainly by sight—no longer yield the visionary gleam. While *sound* still brings on the intimations of immortality, *light* seems to have lost its power to do so.[66]

The timely utterance, then, may perhaps be the sound of the cataracts, or of the same origin as this sound. In a later ode Wordsworth is to write "A Voice to Light gave being," [67] and this is more than a conceptual reference to the Logos. It does not, of course, mean that in his youth light and sound were as one, but that sight acted on him as if it were sound, having in sound its origin. Thus the Great Ode starts by expressing the dilemma that light no longer acts on him like sound, but is mere silent light; the intimation is received only through presences like that of the perhaps invisible cataract.

This intimation, however, is of a specific nature. The cataracts blow their trumpets from the steep. Is there not an indication here of the Last Judgment and its trumpeting angels? We recall the line of *The Prelude*, "The stationary blasts of waterfalls," where "stationary" [68] may be more than a brilliant visual observation. The passage as a whole is loud with voices and deals with the "Characters of the great Apocalypse." The timely utterance and the trumpeting waters are very probably the same thing, both referring to an intimation of the Apocalypse, the Last Judgment, which is always represented in Wordsworth as the prophecy of a great flood: "And his voice as the sound of many waters." [69]

We must, finally, step beyond the bounds of the poem in order to discover that fundamental relation at the base of perhaps all of Wordsworth's major poems. For why should this hint of the Last Judgment dispel the thought of grief and restore his strength? In

The Prelude, Book XIV, as a climax to the entire poem, occurs the
famous account of the moon's apparition on the top of Mount
Snowdon. The travelers mount, they are soon girt round with mist,
and with no time "to ask or learn the cause," the moon's light falls
like a flash at the poet's feet, while the moon "hung naked" in the
firmament above a silent sea of mist that "usurped" upon the main
Atlantic—save that through a rift in that ocean, the roar of waters
is heard mounting "innumerable, roaring with one voice," heard
over sea and earth, and even felt by the heavens.

The mist we have met before. The imagination rises after exertion, and before time is given "to ask or learn the cause." The moon
hangs in the heavens, parallel to the suspended or self-sustained will.
The solid vapors cover even the Atlantic, suggesting thus an inland
but now silent ocean, so that the poet refers to his place in the
mountain as "the *shore* whereon we stood" (my italics). Through
the vapors there mounts the roar of waters, prophetic of those that
have covered and will again cover the world. The moon over the
roaring waters becomes

> the emblem of a mind
> That feeds upon infinity, that broods
> Over the dark abyss, intent to hear
> Its voices issuing forth to silent light
> In one continuous stream; a mind sustained
> By recognitions of transcendent power.[70]

Wordsworth, like this moon, like the Child of the Great Ode,
broods over the abyss to catch these voices issuing to silent light.
The voices come in a continuous stream, a continuous revelation.
Through them rise recognitions of immortality and, simultaneously, a repose in the moral and creative will, since they suggest
both the final peace and the final judgment which is God's alone.
The only time in *The Prelude* that the poet quotes from the Scriptures is at the end of this passage, to describe the peace of a mind
caught by the "inevitable mastery" of heaven's harmonic sounds

> that peace
> Which passeth understanding, that repose

> In moral judgements which from this pure source
> Must come, or will by man be sought in vain.

We now perceive the experience acting as common denominator to the Great Ode, *The Prelude* and "Tintern Abbey." The poet meditates on the mature man's loss of and compensations for a feeling and a love that, in youth, had no need of a remoter charm "By thought supplied, nor any interest/Unborrowed from the eye." The world of eye and ear which in its essential purity proved his sole pleasure and guide cannot with the gradual advance of age retain its autonomous hold either on his senses or on his spiritual being. The light of sense no longer speaks directly to his eyes. Similarly for the poet of the Great Ode. The light is silent and no longer brings intimations or spiritual repose. A thought of grief, perhaps a movement of moral or creative wilfulness, assails him, but at that moment, perhaps borne to him from the cataract, a sound arises, one of those that halt angels on the wing, and dispels the thought of grief, suspending the moral will and its judgments: "The Winds come to me from the fields of Sleep." The trumpets of the cataracts, which haunted the poet in his youth, are those of the Last Judgment and the Apocalyptic Waters. The fundamental relation may be described as one between light and sound, light and revelation. *In the imagination of Wordsworth everything tends to the image and sound of universal waters.*[71]

Let us return once more to Dorothy Wordsworth's account:

> The waters were high, for there had been a great quantity of rain in the night. I was tired and sate under the shade of a holly tree that grows upon a rock, I sate there and looked down the stream. I then went to the single holly behind that single rock in the field, and sate upon the grass till they came from the waterfall. I saw them there, and heard Wm. flinging stones into the river, whose roaring was loud even where I was. When they returned, William was reading the poem: "I have thoughts that are fed by the sun." It had been called to his mind by the dying away of the stunning of the waterfall when he came behind a stone. When we had got into the vale heavy rain came on.[72]

His sister's entry, which we now quote more at length, confirms that surprising and, as it were, instinctive apprehension of thing and event in relation to the sound and image of great waters. One wonders whether the rock has not suggested to her, as single rocks stranded in the landscape invariably do to Wordsworth, the evidence of an ancient flood. Could not the rock and the holly in whose shade she is sitting have intimated that she too has her growth in hard soil, from which the waters have ebbed? Why does she look down the stream? The water theme continues as we are told that her brother's poem was started by his perception that the "stunning" of the waterfall died away behind a rock. The "roaring" of the river, she also tells us, was loud even where she sat.

This interpretation, though apparently extravagant, is made possible by this fact of the poetic mind: its cognition and statement are not relational, but immediate and in relation. If we think that Wordsworth's sister figured out the analogy between herself and the rock and the holly, the interpretation is made ridiculous. If we realize that the analogy is perceived and stated not as a relation but as an identity in which perceiver and perceived cannot be divorced, then the interpretation may appear credible. Poetry does not deal with relations, but with the totality of a relation, with identities.

The confusion of relation with identity has always been held against poets and poetic philosophies. But it is only a sufficient theory of identity that will ever give a satisfactory theory of figurative or poetic language. The painters of the earlier fifteenth century would place the Cross anywhere in the landscape but knew that, wherever they placed it, the rest of the represented world would have to be seen in its light and figure. In the perfect work of art every sign, without losing its commonplace origin or rich connotation, will refer itself to a fundamental relation. When the poet says he hears "These waters rolling from their mountain-springs" we are to imagine and understand not only the Wye, a river we may never have seen, or any particular river accidentally associated in our mind with that name and created thing, or even an abstract river, its qualities washed away by itself, but, ultimately, one prompting in us the *cogito, This river: I am.*

If poetry, then, is a way of expressing statements of identity, we may not think that the value of simile, metaphor, and poetic symbols in general stands in proportion to "points of likeness." We may consider "the stationary blasts of waterfalls" a brilliant image because the poet has noticed that the most torrential thing in nature is frozen by distance.[73] Or we may think it effective because it suggests that the maximum of movement returns to stillness. Or finally we may point out the hint of the trumpeting angels. But neither effect nor value comes from each relation taken separately; they both exist as a function of their immediately perceived identity, and this identity reposes upon the mind's capacity for nonrelational and simultaneous apprehension.

We would, finally, distinguish and sum up the attributes of this power whereby the human mind may perceive, and the poetic faculty express, mystical ideas. A first attribute concerns the act of interpretation. The text reveals a unified multiplicity of meanings verifiable in it as a more than subjective response. A second attribute concerns the possibility of symbols. This results from the mind's immediate, sustained perception of an identity between itself and the thing perceived. A third attribute concerns the will. Wherever poetry is, the will that has been, and will again be, is suspended. A fourth attribute concerns the depth and breadth of sensation. The moral and creative will suspended, human sympathy finds itself limitless—"He saw one life, and felt that it was joy." A fifth attribute concerns the indestructibility of sensation assured by the memory, and its first essential purity, assured by an inviolate quality of the individual mind. A sixth attribute concerns the nature of understanding. Though understanding reposes on a capacity for simultaneous apprehension, the enabling act which reveals Life continuous, Being unimpaired is as complete a mystery in our day as in Plato's time. How are the sensual aroused from their sleep of death? What is it blending the might of mind and of the external world to produce the great commonplace consummation for which the poet writes a verse at once prophetic and spousal? A seventh and ultimate attribute concerns the object sought by the understanding and revealed to it as a pure principle of love sustaining and moving that by which it is sought.

H O P K I N S

THE WINDHOVER: *To Christ our Lord*

I caught this morning morning's minion, king-
   dom of daylight's dauphin, dapple-dawn-drawn Falcon,
       in his riding
  Of the rolling level underneath him steady air, and striding
High there, how he rung upon the rein of a wimpling wing
In his ecstasy! then off, off forth on swing,
   As a skate's heel sweeps smooth on a bow-bend:
      the hurl and gliding
  Rebuffed the big wind. My heart in hiding
Stirred for a bird,—the achieve of, the mastery of the thing!

Brute beauty and valour and act, oh, air, pride, plume, here
  Buckle! AND *the fire that breaks from thee then, a billion*
Times told lovelier, more dangerous, O my chevalier!

  No wonder of it: shéer plód makes plough down sillion
Shine, and blue-bleak embers, ah my dear,
  Fall, gall themselves, and gash gold-vermilion.

Poems of Gerard Manley Hopkins, 3rd ed., ed. R. Bridges & W. H. Gardner.

THE BIRD called the windhover takes its name from an ability to hover steady over one spot in the face of the wind. The subject of our poem is, in the octave, the poet's admiration for a balance achieved in the face of violent motion by countermotion; in the sestet, the sacrifice of both admiration and admired ideal to the transcendent example of Christ. The poem's argument thus turns on Hopkins' interpretation of Christ and Christian action, and will be discussed in detail later on.

The immediate difficulty of "The Windhover" lies less in the complexity of its ideas than in its aesthetic surface. Hopkins, counter to general belief, tends to use rather simple ideas without theological complication, as if his purpose were confined to the medieval *manifestatio*—an illustration, not argumentation, of sacred doctrine. But his poems do not seem to progress by thought to which word and image are subordinate, rather by word and image distilling thought. Where another poet might use statement, elaboration, suggestion, or grammatical emphasis, Hopkins will use word on word, image on image, as if possessed with a poetic kind of *horror vacui*. Consciousness of the word is so strong in "The Windhover" that the poem's very continuity seems to derive from an on-the-wing multiplication of the sound of one word in the next, like a series of accelerating explosions: "morning" to "morning's" to "minion"; "king" takes the *in*, "daylight" picks up the *d* of *dom* and "dauphin" the *in,* as well as an echo of the *au* from "caught"; a sort of climax is reached in the triple adjective before the main noun with its repeated *d* and *aw*. In the next lines the *r* is multigraphed and combined with the dominant nasal glides of "striding," "rung," "rein," falling away into the *in* and *im* before the movement is broken to a new direction with the wheeling of the bird in the fifth line, where a fresh beat of the wing is felt ("then off, off forth on swing"). Moreover, the clash of words is hardened, not softened, by every kind of alliterative and assonantal

device, and the poem from the first line on is marked by an excited-
ness of individual perception ("caught" is an intensive verb, hint-
ing the swift, empathic, mastering glance of the observer) that omits
the smoothing article and relative pronoun.

Every means is used to gain an asyndetic style with a minimum
of grammatical subordination. Hopkins is a master of extreme
suspension (hyperbaton) but not for the sake of subordinating one
word or thought to another. The two main objects of the first three
verses, falcon and air, are strongly suspended by apposition and
adjective- noun- verb- qualifiers, but only to crowd each line with
an asyndetic rush-of-breath movement, maximizing the density of
the verse. Just as windhover, air and dawn are seen not as three
separate elements, but as one whirl of action, so noun, verb and
modifier are similarly viewed as one massed element with mini-
mized grammatical distinctions. Hopkins favors the verbal noun,
(of which he constructs new examples: "the hurl," "the achieve")
because it brings out the freshness of a verbal root at the expense
of a purely linguistic form having no direct source in sense perception. What, we can imagine Hopkins asking, corresponds in
my sense-seizure of this bird to noun, verb, adjective and the rest?
Grammatical distinctions have no intrinsic value, and become subordinate to word-painting. Thus such images as bow-bend (line 6)
make evident the indifference of linguistic form. "Bow" is an Anglo-
Saxon equivalent of "bend," and adds no element of meaning to
"bend" that might not have been rendered by "bend" alone; both
words refer equally well to a curve or to the flexing of the knee
necessary in skating or taking a curve. Yet these meanings, common
to either word, might not have been conveyed by either in isolation with the exact physical stress. Hopkins, aware of the atrophied
or simplified sense-root of words, combines them to suggest their
original identity in a physical percept.[1]

The physical nature of sight, sound, and movement are vividly
rendered in "The Windhover." Hopkins is much aware of spatial
position and angles of sight ("I caught . . ."). Rarely do we find
such awareness of air as a medium, actively affecting vision, dis-
tributing light, lighted in return, inseparable from the object it
surrounds. The notebooks are full of fine observations wherein

sight is conceived as a physically near, self-conscious gathering in and going out: "Cups of the eyes, Gathering back the lightly hinged eyelids. Bows of the eyelids." [2] Hopkins has written a poem to compare the Blessed Virgin to the air we breathe ("Wild air, world-mothering air . . ."). But air is also a field of sound. The "whorled ear" corresponds to the "cup" of the eye. Sound and sight are combined in "The Windhover" by such words as "rolling," "rung," "the hurl," where an act and its echo appear as simultaneous. Air is a true theater of action, dense with event. The density of space and the physical nature of sound and sight are found in all of Hopkins' poetry. We may add this passage from the poem "Spring" where the thrush (itself a sight-sound image) "through the echoing timber does so rinse and wring/the ear, it strikes like lightnings to hear him sing. . . ."

The rhythm of the poem moves against a like density. In the first eight lines of "The Windhover" only two connectives are found, both more ecstatic than conjunctive. The poet employs a system of hard fillings which, on the level of meter, forces weak words into a position of emphasis and, on the level of syntax, jams a group of grammatically assorted words before the suspended noun ("Of the rolling level underneath him steady air"). A counterpoint rhythm evolves that respects the abrupt and singular nature of each word, while emphasizing the one-breath swing of every line, hovering at the repeated end-rhyme, moving forward in a series of glissando movements, but never receding from the forward surge.

While rhythm is not necessarily imitative of a physical movement, with Hopkins it is. The hurl and gliding of his verse render the "hurl and gliding" of "The Windhover." We do find a similar rhythm in some other poems (e.g., "Look at the stars! look, look up at the skies! . . . Down in dim woods the diamond delves! the elves'-eyes!") [3] and this makes us suspect that the thrust and glide of his verse is descriptive of more than the particular motion of the windhover, that the windhover's motion is only a type of a more fundamental rhythm. But the rhythm, in any case, has a physical basis, and many comments could be added to show that Hopkins conceived his words and technique in terms of physical imitation. Of his use of the rather ugly "back" in "The Leaden and the Golden Echo" he writes, *"Back* is not pretty, but it gives that feeling of physical constraint which I want." [4]

There is, even in the best of Hopkins, an unwillingness to release his mind from the physical contact of words, which are conceived not only as the means but also and very strongly as the materials of expression, and used with the undiluted stroke of some modern painters who wish to let color or *touche* speak for itself. Rhythm, sound, and sight involve for Hopkins a sense of the body, the total and individual body, and his poems and notes are full of pride and despair at the inseparably sensuous character of his vision ("my taste was me;/Bones built in me, flesh filled, blood brimmed the curse").[5] The drama of Hopkins is played out between his senses and the thing observed, and perception becomes act in the full sense of the word. But though perception is sensuous and distinctively individual (not therefore personal or characteristic), neither the act of sight nor the true medium are found to change the nature of the thing perceived. In the poem comparing the Blessed Virgin to the air we breathe, Hopkins addresses the reader. How the air is azured, he cries; lift your hand skyward and the rich blue sky will lap round and between the fingers:

> Yet such a sapphire-shot,
> Charged, steepèd sky will not
> Stain light. Yea, mark you this:
> It does no prejudice.
> The glass-blue days are those
> When every colour glows,
> Each shape and shadow shows.[6]

So in his poem on spring the blue is described as all in a rush with richness; air diversifies, reveals, intensifies the intrinsic character of leaf, blossom and timber. There is no blending or blurring between object and object, object and air, object and observer, such as is often found in impressionist painters who are just as sensitive to the "act" of sight as Hopkins; nor is echo (as for example in Shelley) the disembodiment of sound, its spiritual form, but each reverberation in Hopkins is a singular, incisive beat which "strikes like lightnings."

Hopkins' poetry is first an expression of sense experience and wants at first to be taken as such. *The act of sight has become a moral responsibility*, and whereas Milton or Wordsworth might talk about a chastity of the mind, Hopkins would talk about a chastity of the sense. A poet who can write "The Windhover" or "Harry Ploughman" does not share the great religious subject of the century of Marvel and Milton: the dialogue between the re-solved soul and created pleasure. But a poet who works in the belief that "Man's spirit will be flesh-bound when found at best" [7] may yet claim for his theme the dialogue between the created senses and created beauty. We will not understand "The Windhover" unless we first understand this dialogue neither of soul and body nor of mind and nature but of eye and physical event. Hopkins once avowed that "God's Grandeur" was written to accommodate its fine first images, which would not mean that the poet does not think, or thinks by spurts, but that he renders his thoughts in terms of natural perception. Moral and religious meaning do not belatedly disclose themselves to reason, judgment or rationaliza-tion, they are given in the very act of perception, and when Hop-kins catches sight of the windhover, he sees it first in its individual and brute beauty.

2

"The Windhover" bears a religious dedication: *To Christ our Lord,* and yet contains no explicit element of traditional religious sym-bolism except the archetypal falcon. Its imagery is one of natural perception and its one simile, comparing the motion of the bird to a skate heel's turn on a bow-bend, expresses only ease and balance, physical grace. Hopkins, at times, even tries what has rarely been done before him in a sonnet: to introduce technical terms and ob-servations. Thus "rung" may be a word adopted from falconry to suggest the spiral ascent of the windhover.[8] But more significant is the mention of "blue-bleak embers," for Hopkins has noticed the bluish tinge of coals when in full heat but not yet burst or died; and instead of using "blue" absolutely in order to indicate Mary's color and the color of the sky, like the more conventional religious poet, he will use it only in context of a technical observation on the physical world, and so sees the presence, or here the absence, of Mary in a piece of coal.[9] The religious dedication is quite genuine, even required. As in other poems that start with some kind of invocation ("Glory be to God for dappled things"), end with a benediction ("Praise Him"), but in between offer a series of fiercely sensuous and quite untraditional symbols, it indicates that dedication to God is also possible by means of natural perceptions which are, as it were, the first fruits of the senses.

Although religious and natural perception fall together in Hopkins, this is not without its difficulty. The poems after "The Windhover" echo with a plaint on the "skeined stained veined variety" of life.[10] Our present purpose is to find by what means and with what success Hopkins reconciles the sensuous and the religious imperatives, how he passes from a vivid and immediate sensing to religious insight without rejecting or modifying the former. It should first be said, however, that Hopkins is in no way a mystic, except perhaps in one of his late sonnets, "Carrion Comfort," where the combat with God is conceived as a personal one. Even here the concern is merely that of all his poems in its extremity: in my actions, in my perceptions, is it God I feel and credit, or myself? "O which one? is it each one?"

The mystic, seeing the windhover, would be snatched away by it, divinely raped like Ganymede by Zeus the Eagle. Hopkins describes the particular bird, his individual pattern in the air. This, if it cannot suggest the mystic, might make of Hopkins a divine analogist, who sees or seeks in the windhover resemblance to godly action, and such a view is implicit or explicit in most studies so far written on the poet. But Hopkins sets no store by a system of correspondences, perhaps because he acknowledges just one correspondent, Christ—"the Master,/*Ipse,* the only one, Christ, King, Head" [11]—and so the image of the windhover must give way in the poem's second part to the figure of Christ. Yet this Christ, as in the first part, is not symbolized through the traditional symbols or the original story of the New Testament. He is found rather in clay and coal. Thus the real and increased question before us is how Christ can be considered not only the component of natural perception but also the component of a material or physical world.

What catches the eye of the poet is the windhover's mastery of the wind, the control of a proud rider over his tumultuous horse, the strong stress and balance. The simile on the skate heel's smooth turn is also based on a feeling for stress, and whatever image we choose in Hopkins, perhaps "When weeds, in wheels, shoot long and lovely and lush" or "With the gnarls of the nails in thee, niche of the lance," or "For rose-moles all in stipple upon trout that swim," the odds are that there will be found in it a sensitivity if not to actual stress then to touch, muscular action, and pressure. *The sense of pressure or stress is the sixth and radical sense in the experience of Hopkins.* It is evident to the tongue on reading his poetry. Even words like "rung" (upon the rein) and "rolling," which seem to take their effect from a simultaneity of sight and sound, stem from this deeper sense. Also, there is a construction in Hopkins which does not often seem to have been remarked, about which one is not absolutely sure, but which may be exemplified in our poem by "plough down sillion." It gives a figure of thought rather than of speech, and is an attempt to describe muscular action: the strip of land is there to have a plow pushed through, a thing is conceived in terms of the physical action prompted by it.[12] So thing and perceiver, thing and actor, tend in the sight of Hopkins to be joined to each other as if by electrical charge; they are connected like windhover and wind in terms of stress given and received.

Action under stress or by stress is not only a particular condition in Hopkins' universe, but the one condition showing forth the *resilience* of things, their inexhaustible individuality. Whether we consider the relation of eye to object, of creature to creature, or of any of these to the medium—air, water, earth—in which they live, we find that Hopkins has rendered this relation in terms of resilience. There is, for example, the pressure of eye against object and answering pressure of object against eye, each intensifying the "deep-down-thing" freshness of the other. The water in which the trout moves, the movement itself, does not disturb but increases the poet's sensuous apprehension. The blue sapphire-light of the sky which the leaves and blooms of the pear tree are said to brush does not with its strong monotone draw out other shapes and colors but adds to their resistant individuality. The fact is further pointed up in the poem "Spring" by describing the pear tree as "glassy." Even when, as in a snowfall, it seems least possible to remark the individual forms of things, Hopkins still manages to do so:

> It tufted and toed the firs and yews and went to load them till they were taxed beyond their spring. The limes, elms, and Turkey-oaks it crisped beautifully as with young leaf. Looking at the elms from underneath you saw every wave in every twig . . . and to the hangers and flying sprays it restored, to the eye, the inscapes they had lost.[13]

His concern is evidently with the spring of the trees, their resilience; and we meet the word "inscape" which together with "instress" [14] is the poet's technical term describing the individual form of resilience as the quality or effect of a particular thing. The above is also noteworthy in point of style, for by the double indirect object ("to the hangers," "to the eye") Hopkins indicates the compulsion exercised by object on eye.

The act of hard perception, then, where the naked eye becomes an instrument of analysis, does not decrease a thing's individuality, but affirms it.[15] The stronger the pressure of sight or sense, the greater the sensuous yield, but also the resilience, of what is observed. Parallel to God's grandeur, it "gathers to a greatness, like the ooze of oil/Crushed" ("God's Grandeur"). Nowhere is the resilience or "springiness" of the world so directly expressed as in this sonnet, and we realize that there the eternal and unchanged regeneration of the act of sensing and of the world is taken by Hopkins as a mark of the divine. Yet Hopkins' sonnet, however original, is not *sui generis*. It expresses a deep and common religious experience also described in Herbert's "The Flower":

> How fresh, O Lord, how sweet and clean
> Are Thy returns!

But whereas Herbert is witty, homely, almost *ad hominem,* not bothering in the least about oil, foil, and the like to express his delight, citing just a common, unspecified flower, Hopkins cannot speak except with the whole body, with the awareness and justification of all his senses. Hopkins is engaged on a theodicy, and has taken for his province the stubborn senses and the neglected physical world.

But this idea of the world's resilience, however strong in Hopkins and however made clear to the imagination, is an old idea, active in Heraclitus and other pre-Socratic philosophers, incorporate in Aristotle's principle of the eternity of matter, and set forth by the poet himself in the first part of "That Nature is a Heraclitean Fire"—"Squandering ooze to squeezed dough, crust, dust." [16] But to be more in his celebration of oil, clay, and coal than an extreme, modern, industrial pagan, Hopkins must surpass Greek philosophy. And this he does by interpreting the resilience of the world to mind or body, to thought or use, as the source of that individuation of which the culminating point is found in Christ.

For Hopkins leaves aside all speculation on whether the physical universe has or has not a soul and what kind of soul. He is concerned in it with only one thing, its "pitch of self," and he knows that each thing's pitch of self is distinctive and incomparable with any other, and that man's pitch or individuality is the highest. The religious poet before Hopkins often based himself on *Romans* 8:19, (*Etenim res creatae exerto capite observantes expectant revelationem Filiorum Dei*) in order to be permitted to think of the purpose of nature in the divine economy. One of Vaughan's most tragic poems is written under this heading:

> Can they their heads lift, and expect
> and groan too? Why th'elect
> Can do no more.[17]

and Hopkins himself has a poem written on the same theme which, though imperfectly thought out, addresses the Ribbesdale landscape simply as "Earth, sweet Earth. . . . That canst but only be, but dost that long." [18] The landscape, then, like the modern poem, cannot mean, but must be. Hopkins has broken with the age-old belief that nature is the language of God; or, rather, this language is not to be understood in conceptual terms but accepted in its concrete immediacy and resilience to sight. Hopkins does not ask

What is nature for, How can man use nature for his spiritual or material welfare: when he catches sight of the windhover, final and mediate cause are out of mind, he is concerned only with a description of the bird's individual beauty or mode of action, knowing that whether it has a soul or not, a purpose or not, it has resilience and a "pitch of self" which, if felt and acknowledged, will affirm in man his own greater resilience and "pitch of self": "that taste of myself, of *I* and *me* above and in all things, which is more distinctive than the taste of ale or alum, more distinctive than the smell of walnutleaf or camphor." [19]

We see then that man is more highly pitched than anything else. He is as Hopkins elsewhere says, the "clearest-selved spark" of nature.[20] These two metaphors of pitch and flame are fundamental to Hopkins, first because pitch and flame are the two evident types of resilience,[21] and because in them the action of a thing and its nature are identified. This is clear in "As kingfishers catch fire":

> As kingfishers catch fire, dragonflies draw flame;
> As tumbled over rim in roundy wells
> Stones ring; like each tucked string tells,
>   each hung bell's
> Bow swung finds tongue to fling out broad its name;
> Each mortal thing does one thing and the same:
> Deals out that being indoors each one dwells;
> Selves—goes itself; *myself* it speaks and spells;
> Crying *What I do is me: for that I came.*

"Tucked," "hung," "swung" are not simple, sensory adjectives, but (like perhaps "plough down" in "The Windhover") indicate a physical act inseparable from the nature of the thing they qualify: the grammatical sign betrays their status: they are not qualities but proleptic forces: they should be joined to the noun, as they sometimes are, by dashes: the craftsman who constructed this bell though he (no doubt) conceived it instantaneously, created on the first day resilience, on the second day its infinite thingness or self out of resilience, and on the third day its capacity for self-revelation.

But supposing this bell to be of the same make as man, since no distinction exists in this poem between inanimate and animate nature, there being mentioned only "Each mortal thing," then the craftsman must have been faced with this problem: everything has durance, thingness, revelation through resilience; as bird is manifest in flame, so bell in pitch, so earth in being plowed; but what is the manifest of man? The poem continues:

> I say more: the just man justices;
> Keeps grace: that keeps all his goings graces;
> Acts in God's eye what in God's eye he is—
> Christ—for Christ plays in ten thousand places,
> Lovely in limbs, and lovely in eyes not his
> To the Father through the features of men's faces.

Christ, a corporeal Christ, *Ipse,* is for Hopkins the manifest of man, as ringing is of the bell, fire of kingfishers, hurl and gliding of the windhover. We perceive the great identity established in the poems of Hopkins, an identity of all things, all mortal things, in resilience, infinite individuality, God. But this identity, close to the central principle of Aristotelian philosophy, and expressed in the first part of "That Nature is a Heraclitean Fire," is then transcended by a further identity, exclusive to man, in resilience, highest pitch of self,[22] Christ, hence—resurrection! Hopkins would deduce the necessity of resurrection not from a certainty of soul or intellect, but from a physical datum. To "That Nature is a Heraclitean Fire" is added "and of the comfort of the Resurrection":

> Manshape, that shone
> Sheer off, disseveral, a star, death blots black out; nor mark
>   Is any of him at all so stark
> But vastness blurs and time beats level. Enough! the Resurrection,
> A heart's-clarion!

In this way Hopkins goes from the perception that crushed oil gathers again to "a greatness," to the affirmation of Christ. For if all nature have resurgence, should not man? And how can the resurgence of man be conceived except through Christ's example and resurrection? Certain difficulties are to be noted. First, that Hopkins prefers to take his instances of resilience from the world of coal and clay, from the earth as earth, because resurgence is there more evidently inexhaustible than in the animal creation, and when he sees the windhover he catches sight of him not in isolation but in battle with an element, as if the windhover had not like man quite freed himself, selved, from the earth; but this may not satisfy the philosophic mind pointing out that resilience far from being the source of individuation is dependent on the indifferent and undifferentiated character of the earth, and that man's individuality is at the expense of resilience and resurgence; second, that Christ, as he appears in Hopkins, is dangerously near to physical man, while man is still dangerously near to physical beauty, so that Hopkins' work becomes an ode on the eternal nativity of Christ in the physical and sensuous world. In that ode, "The Windhover" is one of the finest stanzas.

3

The poet in the octave marks the "pitch" of the battling windhover, his individual brute beauty, and this is seen deeply in terms of resilience. The poet is in a stage of mere attention, not of analogy; and the hidden heart does not stir for the windhover itself as much as for a bird in general, its balance under extreme stress. Now, a poet is known by his invocations. If Hopkins had felt the windhover to be an immediate symbol for Christ he would have addressed it as spontaneously as he apostrophizes God in "The Wreck of the Deutschland" or "The Loss of the Eurydice"; but when his invocation "O my chevalier" comes in the sestet, the riders have changed, and it is no longer the windhover astride the wind, but Christ's example mastering the poet, which is referred to.

The sestet results from a sudden intrusion of the thought of Christ. For the ideal marked and admired in the windhover by the poet was of elegant balance in the center of stress, and this stress is sought by, not imposed on the falcon who seems to know that a storm center is necessary to display the "achieve" and the "mastery." Yet Christ while also of his own will seeking the center of stress did this not for the sake of elegant balance, but to suffer without mastery the "unshapeable shock night." [23] "Buckle," therefore, addressing the windhover or its accouterments of sensuous magnificence, would be in the nature of an optative and mean more than "buckle on meeting this heart which, thinking of the ascetic Christ, must refuse its admiration"; it suggests, "Let yourself like Christ militant for sacrifice be destroyed in submitting to a storm center greater than the power of beauty, valor, or act, and let this example grapple with, become a buckler for, dent my heart." [24]

Thus the flame breaking from windhover or the Christ-assaulted heart indicates self-destruction in the maximum of stress. But why should the AND be in capitals and the resulting flame be described as a billion times lovelier (aesthetically seductive) and more dangerous (morally seductive) than the windhover's previous proud image? The AND expresses the poet's surprise that the splendor of self-destruction should surpass the splendor of equilibrium: the image of the flaming windhover or of the crucified Christ becomes a greater spiritual temptation than could ever have been exerted by the former image of elegant equilibrium. Then Hopkins, in the final tercet, adds "No wonder of it," for he finds that even the humblest things bear the mark and splendor of Christ's sacrifice imprinted on them like a physical law, even the lowliest thing galls itself and gashes flame, so that the poet feels ("ah, my dear") fear? regret? resignation? perceiving Christ's Passion as a universal and haunting phenomenon. He has not escaped brute beauty: the very means which caused him to reject the windhover have revealed to him a different beauty, less elegant indeed, but just as brutally evident, lovely and dangerous.

The poet, then, sees the sacrifice of Christ imprinted like a physical law in even the lowliest corner of nature. He thought Christ superinduced on the windhover to be unique, but finds the call to sacrificial action also in coal. This physical law, which holds for all inanimate nature, is quite simple and contains three things: maximum stress, the disintegration that follows maximum stress, the flame that follows or is the visible sign of disintegration. In such process Hopkins comes to see an imitation of Christ's Passion, Crucifixion, and Resurrection; and this fact haunts him, that what should be written large as a necessity of matter has not become the fatality of man.

If we regard the images of the sestet we find them all kinaesthetic in nature, determined by the sense of stress or muscle. Even syntax helps toward this: the grammatical status of "Buckle" cannot be fixed with absolute precision, Hopkins often using words to describe more than qualities, things, relations: "Buckle" mimics a muscular movement, a physical act. "Buckle" is not meant to suggest simply the actual object or the act of buckling, but the process whereby when two stresses clash one has to give way, to buckle or be buckled, and this would catch the senses by a displacement of, for example, light flashing from an uneven breastplate—"AND the fire that breaks from thee then." For whereas a lesser poet than Hopkins might have used "fire" in a purely figurative sense, in Hopkins the figurative sense is always derived from physical phenomena. The same thing can be shown of the other images in the poem which are also conceived as emitting light: the coal obviously, but also the "shine" of "plough down sillion": it is neither the shining plow nor the new earth but the kinaesthetic effect of plow-breaking-through-earth. Thus our three images are seen to express contacts and disintegrations that have caused a surprising outward burst of splendor greater than the original splendor of equilibrium.

Stress, disintegration, and flame are caught as one process and almost rendered as such in Hopkins' poetry. But we may go somewhat further to determine how Christ enters this purely physical observation. Here is a skyscape recorded by the poet:

> . . . below the sun it was like clear oil but just as full of colour, shaken over with slanted flashing 'travellers,' all in flight, stepping one behind the other, their edges tossed with bright ravelling, as if white napkins were thrown up in the sun but not quite at the same moment so that they were all in a scale down the air falling one after the other to the ground.[25]

Though in tenor entirely descriptive, the passage reflects a kind of instinctive epistemology on Hopkins' part: the brilliance of the particular depends on individuation, but individuation also, because group intensity is lacking, tends to destroy brilliance; therefore the moment of greatest brilliance in the particular is in its just-emergence from the group, when a measure of off-balance catches the sun—in the moment of disintegration.

Another passage should be given in support, this time in description of a thunderstorm:

> I noticed two kinds of flash but I am not sure that sometimes there were not the two together from different points of the same cloud or starting from the same point different ways— one a straight stroke, broad like a stroke with chalk and liquid, as if the blade of an oar just stripped open a ribbon scar in smooth water and it caught the light; the other narrow and wire-like, like the splitting of a rock and danced down-along in a thousand jags.[26]

The two flashes are compared to the splitting of a rock, and the ribbon scar caused by the stroke of an oar on smooth water. Both images, kinaesthetic, repeat that the greatest brilliance of the particular is in the moment of disintegration or off-balance from the group to which it belongs, and both remind us of the images in "The Windhover." If we now recall that Christ for Hopkins is the highest pitch of self, the summit of human individuation, we also perceive the identity inevitably made between the highest pitch of self, Christ, and the greatest brilliance of the particular, disintegration. Thus the antinomy of self and self-sacrifice would be resolved: the oil has to be crushed before it may gather to greatness. This identity shows the temptation undergone by Hopkins to equate Passion and Salvation. It is not absent from "The Windhover."

In this poem the balance of the bird in the storm wind is rejected for the buckle that flames up when struck or made uneven, the furrowing act of the plow that catches light like the furrow made by the stroke of an oar on smooth water, for the dull embers that suddenly flare forth in falling apart like volcanic rock or jagged lightning or like the grandeur of God which "will flame out, like shining from shook foil" [27] or like the body of the crucified Christ who galled himself and gashed gold-vermilion. The brilliance, brutality, stress and necessity of individuation are connected and apperceptively fused with the sacrifice of Christ and turned by him into a figure for resurrection. The windhover, chevalier in perfect mastery of his winged horse, fitted out with all the accouterments of an elegant-brute-beauty, suddenly falls, buckles, flames, and Christ appears, chevalier of true-brute-beauty, and valor and act.

4

It is possible to apply to Hopkins the same categories of analysis used in our study of Wordsworth. One could examine his psychology, his theory of cognition, the statement on revelation contained in his poetry. It would then be pointed out that (Hopkins places great faith in the hard, direct, vision which tries to seize an object in its immediate and mind-unprejudiced beauty, and makes the act of mere attention a sine qua non for knowledge.) This in turn could be related to the effort of impressionist painting, and perhaps to the phenomenological spirit in general, which tries to obtain the eyes' or the senses' "figura rasa." [28] It could be linked to the historical development that, starting with Occam's and Duns Scotus' criticism of the *species intelligibilis,* leads to Hume's merging of impression, image, and idea and to Wordsworth's trust in what we have called imperceptible cognition. (Hopkins differs, of course, from both Wordsworth and more modern philosophy by putting the unity of cognition not in the nature of event as process (very roughly, Whitehead), nor in the event as occasional awareness of the divine and subsistent ground of vision (Wordsworth), but in the event as Christ. No one has gone further than Hopkins [29] in presenting Christ as the direct and omnipresent object of perception, so deeply ingrained in the eyes, the flesh, and the bone (and the personal sense of having eyes, flesh, and bone), that the sense of self and the sense of being in Christ can no longer be distinguished.) This is surely the *agon* of the late sonnets:

Cheer whom though? the hero whose heaven-handling flung me,
    foot trod
Me? or me that fought him? O which one? is it each one?

It is possible; in Hopkins there is a viewpoint on cognition; but whatever faculty we choose for analysis we come squarely against the poet's conception of Christ, just as wherever we start in Wordsworth we return to the dialectic of love between man and nature. Whatever interpretation is given to Hopkins, in order to hold true it must be based on his understanding of Christ. It is this understanding we have tried to set forth in previous sections. Hopkins is the most Christ-possessed of the modern Christian poets whose religious fervor is beyond doubt but who, like Wordsworth and Eliot, either do not mention Christ at all or introduce him under the strange, litotic and rather inconceivable figure of *Christus absconditus*. Though Hopkins actually names Christ infrequently, and though some critics have refused to consider him as a specifically Christian poet, it is precisely here that his interest lies. He attempts to conceive Christ as hardily and heartily as did the poets up to the time of Crashaw. It is Hopkins as modern poet dealing with Christ, Hopkins as celebrant of "the dense and the driven Passion," who must finally concern us.

In "The Windhover" some ideal of elegance is on the point of fading away, and this is more swiftly evident in the style than in the theme, as if on the creation of a new style everything depended. Hopkins is in revolt not only against a residual diction of generality but also against the diction of sweetness which at the time of his writing was uttering its swan-song in the work of Pater and the Pre-Raphaelites. Like Verlaine, Hopkins would wring the neck of eloquence. In this respect there are certain evident things to say: (1) he is a plosive and guttural more than a liquid and murmuring poet; (2) he prefers words of Anglo-Saxon and dialect coin; (3) he aims at an essentially asyndetic style; (4) he is not afraid of cacophonous repetition, seeks it even, whether in the chime of vowels—the *i*'s and *ī*'s of "does so rinse and wring/The ear, it strikes like lightnings"—or in word repetition—"morning morning's" of "The Windhover"; (5) he cultivates a rhythm in which nothing hypnotic remains and which, as in the octave of "The Windhover," may be used in description of physical movement.

These features militated against the half-way house of nineteenth century eloquence which, while admitting more and more the poetic values of the concrete, stubborn, irreducible material world, favored melic euphemism in religious and what Hopkins derides as "blethery bathos" in sensual poetry.[30] Pater's awareness of physi-

cal beauty, while real, is nevertheless an ideal limited by Greek
example and too soon exhausted by the delicacy of a rose. "Who
would change the color or curve of a rose-leaf for that . . . color-
less, formless, intangible being Plato put so high?" [31] We are leagues
away from the oil and foil of Hopkins' poetry which employs words
with the avowed attempt to transcribe the full physicality of created
things and created senses. Although Hebraic and Asiatic metaphor
is often more audacious than his, no poet before Hopkins has made
such a precise use in religious poetry of what Irving Babbitt, de-
crying post-romantic literature as illegitimately engaged in word-
painting,[32] calls in his *New Laocoon* "local impressions." Babbitt
is scarcely wrong except in judgment; Hopkins does indeed use
eye and sense as plot for, and not merely clothing of, subject or
idea; and he differs from his contemporaries precisely in the entire
and unrestrained acceptance of word-painting. "Word-painting,"
he writes in 1887, "is, in the verbal arts, the great success of our
day." [33]

If Hopkins placed such emphasis on local impressions and word-
painting it was because he wished to restore to God physical compulsion, and this involved the use of words to render the immediacy
of the senses as nerve and muscle and sensation. "The Windhover"
tells not only of the passing of an ideal of eloquence but also of
the passing of a concept of divine Grace. The love that goes from
God to man and from man to God is not, for Hopkins, a human
or yet an intellectual love, and if it be love at all it is hidden and
conceived under the divine attribute of material immensity. "Thou
mastering me/God!" begins his first great poem; two centuries
before, Newton, to have God accord with his cosmology, suggested
that *Dominus* be replaced by *Deus,* and even preferably by *Aeter-
nus,* since the first and even the second implied a personal rela-
tionship as of master to servant inconceivable in a universe regu-
lated by strict eternal law: the polemics against this by Blake and
Wordsworth are well known. But Hopkins, whose persistent cry
is *Dominus,* Master, has instinctively accepted the fact that the
act of God's mastery over man is indistinguishable from the act
of God's mastery over matter. And "The Windhover" shows that
this is not mastery at all—for the control and "achieve" of the bird
over the elements is rejected—but *an inexplicable law of sacrifice*

given by God in Christ, evident even in the inorganic world, yet lacking in man. For Hopkins, as for the modern poet, the compulsion to God is not through an evidence of the intellect or of the sweet-violent soul but through a mark left physically on man and his sensing, whereby he becomes, as Claudel has said of Rimbaud, a mystic in the savage state.

Therefore in Hopkins, against tradition,[34] Christ the human and spiritual intermediary between man and God becomes Christ the supreme physical revelation and physical compulsion. This could be expressed better by saying that Hopkins views the world through the actual body of Christ, instead of through His spiritual body, which is the Church. Hence his relative indifference to theological questions, and his extreme sensitivity to physical media, whether word,[35] air, or his own body, which at the end wrestles with itself as with Christ, not knowing any longer how to distinguish one from the other, or soul from self, Christ being but the supreme *haecceitas*. But Christ is such only by sacrifice, and Hopkins' attention is taken by the sacrificial body,[36] his steady quest being to show man as fated in Christ as He was in man and the body of man:

> . . . How a lush-kept plush-capped sloe
> Will, mouthed to flesh-burst,
> Gush!—flush the man, the being with it, sour or sweet,
> Brim, in a flash, full!—Hither then, last or first,
> To hero of Calvary, Christ,'s feet—
> Never ask if meaning it, wanting it, warned of it—men go.

This passage from the eighth stanza of "The Wreck of the Deutschland" makes clear how Hopkins represents a wished-for fatality of the spirit as a possible compulsion of the body: like the ripe sloe (a kind of communion wafer!) which will burst beneath the stress of the mouth, man, entirely sensed and under divine stress, inevitably imitates the sacrificial action of Christ. We are reminded of "The Windhover" with its embers that fall and gash gold-vermilion: "gash" is a transitive verb made intransitive as if to suggest that the coal's wound like that of Christ is self-inflicted. For "The Windhover" also is haunted by the thought that the material world is nearer to Christ's Passion, Crucifixion and flaming Resurrection than free-willed man.

R I L K E

DIE ERWACHSENE

Das alles stand auf ihr und war die Welt
und stand auf ihr mit allem, Angst und Gnade,
wie Bäume stehen, wachsend und gerade,
ganz Bild und bildlos wie die Bundeslade
und feierlich, wie auf ein Volk gestellt.

Und sie ertrug es; trug bis obenhin
das Fliegende, Entfliehende, Entfernte,
das Ungeheuere, noch Ungelernte
gelassen wie die Wasserträgerin
den vollen Krug. Bis mitten unterm Spiel,
verwandelnd und auf andres vorbereitend,
der erste weisse Schleier, leise gleitend,
über das aufgetane Antlitz fiel

fast undurchsichtig und sich nie mehr hebend
und irgendwie auf alle Fragen ihr
nur eine Antwort vage wiedergebend:
In dir, du Kindgewesene, in dir.

Neue Gedichte

THE GROWN-UP

All this stood on her, was world
and stood on her with all things, fear as well as mercy,
as trees stand, growing and upright,
totally image and imageless like the ark of the covenant,
and solemnly, as if placed upon a nation.

And she endured it; bore up under
the swift-as-flight, the evanescent, the far-away,
the monstrous, and that which was still to be learned—
calm under it and submissive like the water-carrier
under a full pitcher. Till in the midst of play,
transforming and preparing for new things,
the first white veil fell with smooth silent fall

over her open face almost opaque and never to raise itself again,
and somehow returning
one vague answer to all her questions:
within yourself, you one-time-child, within yourself.

THIS POEM deals with a subject rarely treated in literature, but through the iconography of the life of Mary quite familiar to painting: the first moments in which a girl reaches physical maturity, her sudden ripeness. The mysterious and sudden process whereby the child becomes the mature girl is often contemplated in Rilke's poetry. In this poem it is described as follows: open to experience, the child endures the world with its anxiety and grace (stanza 1); she endures, bears up under the evanescent, the nightmarish, the unknown, until surprised in the midst of both suffering and play by a first intuition of completeness which descends on her and encloses her like a veil (stanza 2). It is a veil almost opaque, which never lifts, and which to all her self-questionings intimates only that her childhood is past, and that the source of the future is not in the outside world but in herself (stanza 3).

We would first stress the originality of subject. Although childhood and adolescence become a theme of mystical speculation in the seventeenth century (Jacob Boehme, the Cambridge Platonists), they do not become a major concern of poetry till the romantic movement of the late eighteenth century. Henry Vaughan is an exception, and he was probably influenced by his brother Thomas, an ardent and productive Platonist. But childhood as seen by Vaughan is simply a glorious nearness to God, the age of "white designs." [1] Wordsworth and Blake are perhaps the first to bring out both the glory and the terror of adolescence; the German romantics and later the French are still content to celebrate the naive felicity and divine innocence of the child. An exception again is the painter Phillip Otto Runge, whose child figures have, besides a resemblance to blossoming flowers, a look of terror, sternness, even wickedness. But Rilke's emphasis on the death-experience of the young, present in his earlier poetry,[2] haunting in *Malte Laurids Brigge,* and leading to the fine evocation of death-in-children ("der Kindertod") in the Fourth Duino Elegy, is quite unparalleled in intensity, though the *roman d'adolescence* and Freud come onto the literary scene toward the end of his career, and though surrealism and the modern cinema have exploited it. In the poem before us the death-experience is but hinted at, and as always in Rilke, associated with maturation or the experiencing of an original, creative force.

Rhythm, sound, and mood of narration will be familiar to readers of Rilke. The poem comprises three (perhaps four) periods whose rhythm is perpetually rising or falling, so that we rarely feel a climax, only suspension. We are tempted to use a single breath for each, while the voice prefers instead of accentual emphasis a chant-like uniformity of pitch, slowing down and lengthening the words. The tendency is aided by Rilke's strong, often consecutive assonance: "gel*assen* wie die W*a*ssertr*ä*gerin," "d*er er*ste w*ei*sse Schl*ei*er, l*ei*se gl*ei*tend," "über das aufge*tane A*ntlitz fiel." It would be precarious to ascribe to such effects a more than arbitrary significance if they were not part of a complete series of signs including, for example, the pleonastic phrasing and the repetition of *und* in the first stanza. The impression obtained is that of a rhythm rising and falling by regular and almost imperceptible degrees, one we associate with the opening and closing of flowers or with a circling like that of the stars. Nor is it difficult to locate other passages in Rilke where the same effect is achieved by approximately the same means. We append one example in which the subject is actually the great round of the stars:

> und dass um diese Klage-Welt ganz so
> wie um die andre Erde eine Sonne
> und ein gestirnter stiller Himmel ging,
> ein Klage-Himmel mit entstellten Sternen—: [3]

Yet the movement of the heavens and the opening and closing of flowers are but instances of a process continually evoked in Rilke's poetry. Contemplated in the earlier poems, especially the *Book of Hours,* it causes deep faith and a naive understanding of providence. Later poems express it as quiet amazement at a fatality indifferent to, though shared by, man. So Mary Magdalen reflects on the dead Christ: "Wie gehn wir beide wunderlich zugrund"; *

---

* "How strangely both of us decline!"

and so the angel, as the poet conceives him, is ruled, and thus set free from all limiting duties, by this eternal force: "das ewig Kommende, das kreist." * What is this circling power on which depend flower and star and, in its very ignorance, human life? It is a law of inevitable growth identified by Rilke with Nature.

"Die Erwachsene" is cast as a portrait in which human development is described in terms which might be used to represent one's experience of nature, in particular, of a landscape. The technique, used here only in part, prevails in many of Rilke's poems, sometimes as lightly applied as in his evocation of the Venetian courtesan (whose glance is said to have secret intercourse with the canals because the sea in her eyes ebbs, flows, and is changeful) at other times with more serious intent as when the returning Eurydice is described as being untouchable in her sex, too much like a young flower at nightfall. A great number of Rilke's poems, if not actually landscape portraits, contain instances of the technique which indicates the poet's will to experience the human subject in the same way as the natural subject.

What are the qualities of this experience? A first clue is given by Rilke's early interest in painting. Painting as a genre tends to picture all things suspended in an eternal and fateful present, in what Lessing called "the fruitful moment." The painted figure, moreover, is mute, and forced to speak, if at all, in gestures, in a single gesture by which it stands eternally characterized. In Rilke's *Tagebücher aus der Frühzeit* we find the following fragment of poetry:

> Ich bin ein Bild.
> Verlangt nicht dass ich rede.
> Ich bin ein Bild. Und mir ist eine jede
> Gebärde schwer.
> Mein Leben ist: die Stille der Gestalt.
> Ich bin Anfang und Ende der Gebärde.[4] †

Now these two qualities—*life* conscious only of the present, eternal in the present, fated by the present, and *speech* mute, essentially

* "That which comes eternally, and circles."

† "I am a picture. Do not require me to talk. I am a picture. And every single gesture is a heavy task for me. My life is: the *stillness* of form. I am the beginning and the end of gesture."

natural, speech by means of the body—are identical to those in
Rilke's experience of nature. The special point of view of painting
facilitated their transfer from nature to the human subject. Basi-
cally mute, the subjects and personae of Rilke seem to step for
a moment out of their fixed destinies, to gesticulate, to recite with
the help of the poet a continual inner monologue, and to subside.
"Sieh, wie sich alles auftut: so sind wir" * is the cry of the women
to the poet.[5] This "opening" is related to the "opened face" ("das
aufgetane Antlitz") of the girl in our poem.

"Auftun" is one of Rilke's more general word-concepts to suggest an action as of flowers in the sun, but not of flowers alone; it is
a gesture common to women as much as to the world of flowers.
And their "Sieh" (Behold) is a cry of mute imploring, as of things
that have no adequate voice yet affect powerfully. The "Sieh" which
is most frequent in Rilke imitates a sign whose locus and significance are neither in sight nor in sound taken individually: behold!
is the essential gesture of what Rilke calls "things" ("Dinge"), indicating by this term that he does not distinguish between the human
and the natural subject. For this "behold!" is no more than an
insufficient hieroglyph to suggest the call and summoning ("Lock-
ruf") of all Creation, one which finds its full description in the
Duino Elegies, especially the first:

> Es muteten manche
> Sterne dir zu, dass du sie spürtest. Es hob
> sich eine Woge heran im Vergangenen, oder
> da du vorüberkamst am geöffneten Fenster,
> gab eine Geige sich hin. Das alles war Auftrag.†

Here the present is felt to be so instinct with fate that its essence
is to pass ("a wave rose up imminent in the past"), and we suspect
that the before-mentioned "behold!" is, like the star's emanation,
the violin's self-offering, and the incessant appeal of Creation, some
hieratic gesture expressing a fine tragedy of transience: "How
strangely we two decline."

* "Look, how everything unfolds: *we* are like that."

† "Many a star placed its faith in you that you would sense it. A wave rose
up imminent in the past, or as you came by the open window a violin offered
itself. All this was mission."

That which enables Rilke to look on people and things with the same point of view is a profound feeling for gestures. It assures the continuity and symbols of "Die Erwachsene." We recognize similes such as "wie Bäume stehen" or "wie auf ein Volk gestellt" to represent gestures and to be of a type frequent in his poetry. They are often sentences rather than phrases, and at first glance pleonastic. Many examples could be given, but perhaps the following passage from the *Book of Hours* will suffice:

> Und meine Hände welche blutig sind
> vom Graben, heb ich offen in den Wind,
> so dass sie sich verzweigen wie ein Baum.
> Ich sauge dich mit ihnen aus dem Raum,
> als hättest du dich einmal dort zerschellt
> in einer ungeduldigen Gebärde,
> und fielest jetzt, eine zerstäubte Welt,
> aus fernen Sternen wieder auf die Erde
> sanft, wie ein Frühlingsregen fällt.*

The last simile bears wholly neither on the nature of the objects nor on the nature of the actions compared, and so manages to suggest a broad identity. In the case of "wie Bäume stehen," the objects compared are world and tree, the actions compared are manners of standing, but by repeating the verb *stehen* Rilke suggests that the real comparison is not between one object and another or one action and another but between two gestures. The whole of the first stanza is imagined in terms of this gesture "to stand," the root form (*auf*) *stehen* being repeated four times—*stand, stand, stehen, gestellt*.

Gesture cannot, of course, be translated into human speech. It is a speech essential to the body, and as such has no discernible end or object, only direction. So God is defined not as an object of desire but as its inevitable orientation.[6] "Ich bin Anfang und Ende der Gebärde." Rilke desires to know the common end of

---

* "And my hands, bloody from digging, I raise and open up to the wind, so that, like a tree, they cross their branches. By means of them I suck you out of space, as if you had once shattered yourself there with an impatient gesture, and were now, a world crumbled to dust, falling again to earth from the distant stars, softly falling like spring rain."

all the gestures made by people and things alike, but his poetry swarms with prepositions which have given up their function of pointing to specific place, and are inseparably attached to verbs, as if action had no visible beginning or end but purely direction— "der reine Bezug." [7] One finds *in-, an-, auf-, nieder-, ein-, aus-, zu-, hin-, über-,* and *da-.*

This feeling for directionless or inevitably transcendent direction gives to Rilke's poetry its dominant elegiac note. "Siehe, ich lebe, Woraus?" he cries at the end of the Ninth Elegy. Nor is this cry rhetorical: the metaphor of direction remains one of Rilke's most serious metaphors. He wishes to conceive the source and end of life as subsumed in a purely physical process, as if one could say, I draw my life out of this well, I carry it in this pitcher (my body), and I pour it out into that river. This is, moreover, one reason why the young girl of our poem suddenly appears as *Wasserträgerin:* Rilke seeks a gesture through which the body could express itself as body (as also in Greek art), an act so perfectly suited to it that it is seen to have, necessarily, a purely physical origin.

But this, the quest of sculpture and of some painting, would be an entirely new quest for poetry. It would force poetry to give up its search for subject and symbol in religion, history, society. It would, in short, eliminate everything we call story interest. "Die Erwachsene" is the representation of a fruitful moment, one that belongs not to any particular plot (for example, Medea about to kill her children) but to the general plot of the human body. The poet, like the sculptor, deals more with the speech or gestures of men's bodies than with their actions.

Rilke's feeling for gesture was doubtless confirmed on meeting Rodin, but that he had it before the meeting is sure: the *Book of Hours* is crowded full of types culled from painting and sculpture, men and women whose life is summed up in a single sacramental gesture—*gisants,* those who kneel, those who humble themselves, those who have buried themselves in the earth, the pilgrims, and a weeper "dem sich das Weinen in die Hände schlug." But in Rodin he saw a sculptor for whom the expression of the face, or of character in general, was subordinate to certain primary and primitive acts that seemed to rise from and return to the body alone, as if that were an organism in its own right, having its own history, its own will. The Rodin essay of 1903 gives lyric descriptions of figures and elemental gestures that were to people Rilke's imagination the rest of his life. Here are the "Passant" of the Burghers of Calais, the "Still Voice" of the Hugo Memorial, the Walker St. John who prepares for the Walker Balzac, the Primeval Man who stands as trees stand and who is afraid, like the girl in our poem, because the fruit and plenitude of the summer is already out of the roots, rising slowly, and standing in the trunk around which the winds will blow. We recognize from this how the poet's imagination is guided by what could be called a liturgy of gestures, which has no interpretable history, no social relevance, no theology. *Stehen* is but one act of this liturgy. *Tragen* is another. In the second stanza of our poem, "Und sie ertrug es: trug bis obenhin," the *tragen* that signifies a spiritual quality comes to signify the physical act, and suggests finally the figure and gesture of the water-carrier. Thus qualities that seem to belong to mind or soul may be shown inherent in the body and its fundamental gestures. Rilke is like an orator who in order to illustrate his argument, no matter how transcendent, could find no other example than the body.

We do not wish to discuss the philosophic implications of a notion which makes a tree but the gesture signifying *stehen* by a God whose name is lost, and to this gesture belong the seasons and the winds and death; or a growing girl but another gesture of this same God, signifying perhaps immanent fertility. But it resembles to a surprising degree the basic conception of *phusis* in pre-socratic philosophy, to which German philosophy after Schelling and Nietzsche has been returning.[8] It is doubtful in any case whether Rilke realized this.

However, our present poem "Die Erwachsene" already exhibits an extreme identification of human destiny and physical order. Rilke has tried to envisage maturation as a purely organic process, and has chosen for this purpose a moment in human development where the physical does indeed seem determinate. It is suggested, moreover, that the entire development of this girl depends on a physical will inherent in the body—not in the human body conceived as a creature cut off from the "body" of the earth, but in the human body as joined to it through the gestures of what might be described as an indiscernible centaur. In his interpretation of Rodin, Rilke again and again praises the sculptor (and incidentally Baudelaire) for recognizing that the human body is an organism with its own will and history; and not only with one will, for it seems to be will in every part, so that one may speak of the will and history of the hands! [9] Rilke is quite serious; and his explicit interest in a *physical will* is hardly found in any other literary figure. One could only adduce certain playful and far-reaching premonitions of Diderot in his *Rêve d'Alembert,* where it is pointed out, for example, that bees by simple aggregation come to form one body having both a collective will and a will in every part.[10]

There are fine passages in Rilke's interpretation of Rodin that go even farther in their imaginative strength. Rodin, he writes, "created bodies which touched and cohered in every part like inter-locked struggling beasts that fall like a thing into the depths; human bodies listening like faces and gesticulating like arms; chains of bodies, wreaths and tendrils, and heavy grape-bunches of forms. . . ." [11] Many instances could equally well be found in Rilke's poetry illustrating the working of a physical will, one which seems to create these heavy clusters of forms parallel to Diderot's cluster of bees. One of the finest examples is the "tree of mutually built motion" constructed by the acrobats of the Fifth Duino Elegy.

The body, then, has its own designs, a will quite independent perhaps of the mind's conscious purpose, an ontology that speaks mutely out of its features, and above all a destiny more assured than that which human mind and will arbitrarily infer. For this conception of a physical will, like that of the "thing," stems pri-marily from Rilke's desire to conceive destiny in purely physical terms, such as are expressed in gesture and weight. Thus, strength of expression for Rilke lies more in the torso than in the face, and the loss of the face is an almost obsessive theme in *Malte Laurids Brigge,* not because Rilke does not know the eloquence of expres-sion, but because like Rodin he knew no other way to render it except as landscape or part of the body's language.

Therefore to obtain a correct interpretation of "Die Erwachsene" as of Rilke in general, we must recognize that the body is used as subject and as plot. Rilke's poetry has undeniable social, historical, psychological, even theological relevance, but its starting point is not in any of these. We could say that whatever interpretation is given to the text, this text is the body with its untranslatable gestures. In one respect Rilke stands very close to Wordsworth, Rousseau, Novalis, and the romantic movement. For he feels that language no longer has much in common with the things it would refer to, just as the life of most city-dwellers has lost its kinship with the earth.[12] Yet in another respect Rilke stands very close to the reaction of Baudelaire, Flaubert, and many impressionist painters, for he refuses to ascribe to his experience of Nature an immediate human significance, feeling her sublime indifference rather than her sympathy. This distinction shows at once the unity of romantic and post-romantic in an issue that has become dominant for Rilke: how to discover the meaning of the body and of the physical world, and how to render this meaning in a language which, anthropomorphic, has lost the power of concreteness.

2

Our choice of "Die Erwachsene" was not dictated, as is the case with other poems considered in these essays, by its intrinsic value. It is a typical rather than a major poem. We have chosen it because it presents a fine example of an embryonic symbol which Rilke tries to imbue with life in the majority of his poems. This symbol we would call that of the *pure physical fruit*. I want to conceive God, writes Rilke in the *Stundenbuch*, in the same way that the earth conceives him.

The acrobats, to whom the poet devotes his Fifth Elegy, desire to construct a tree of mutually built motion. Why a *tree*? The figure of the pure physical fruit is evident. The acrobats try in vain to fuse themselves into a human design that would mimic the automatic and immanent fertility of the natural world. In vain, for whatever falls from their tree is unripe, and whatever stays on this tree never achieves ripeness. The boy who tumbles from the top of the pyramid is described as falling off like unripe fruit,[13] and the transcendence which these acrobats achieve in their short moment

of perfect balance is called an "empty too-much," because it lacks
two major qualities of the pure physical fruit, true heaviness and
a perpetual at rest.

Associated with these is a third quality subsuming all others.
This also the acrobats fail to attain. The tree they form completes
its cycle of spring, summer, and autumn in but a few minutes. Now
inasmuch as the pure physical fruit is a more spontaneous product
of Nature (*phusis, natura naturans*) than the rest of nature (*natura
naturata,* "die Kreatur") the acrobats have achieved their end. But
there is one season they cannot imitate, a season almost unknown
to man, namely true winter. "O Bäume Lebens o wann winterlich"
is the opening cry of the Fourth Elegy. What is the significance of
this winter which the acrobats cannot counterfeit?

It signifies the stasis known to all of creation except man, a season
in which life is secretly and radically renewed, the season of death
preceding resurgence. The acrobats traverse an eternal sequence
of spring, summer, autumn, without producing visible fruit. The
fruits they do produce are like those of a milliner who lays claim
to the name Death (Madame Lamort), and who produces a purely
artificial thing, cheap semblances of fruitful destiny, "billige Win-
terhüte des Schicksals." While the fate pursued by the acrobats is
man-willed and artificial, the fate of the rest of creation is a com-
pliance, secret, immanent, inevitable, to Nature's purpose and
fertility. And this constitutes the third subsuming quality of the
pure physical fruit: hidden growth, *Verborgenheit,* that perpetual
and winter-like stasis in which the secret ripeness gathers. "Denn
unter Wintern ist einer so endlos Winter." [14]

How then can Rilke or the poet or even man in general be considered as a pure physical fruit, that is, truly in contact and at one
with Nature, if his life is spent puzzling about the purpose of existence, contriving cheap analogues of destiny, a tightrope between
utter sterility and the premature act?

Instances of Nature's sublime indifference vis-a-vis man abound
in Rilke's experience. Her beauty is, like that of the Angel, only
the initial of her entire terrible name. Whereas Wordsworth felt
Nature's sternness only at rare moments and with the aspect of
traditionally sublime phenomena, Rilke knows it as the constant

of any "thing." To portray Christ he does not choose the moment
of the eclipse, but His lonely ascent of the Mount of Olives: "Da
schlafen Hunde, und da liegen Steine." [15] * The fundamental
arythmos of man and Nature, of human destiny and the natural
world's secret life, lies immanent in his thought. "Herr: es ist Zeit:
der Sommer war sehr gross." [16] † When, if ever, will *he* attain ripeness? Rilke's poetry is a repeated, incipient cry: "Herr: es ist Zeit."

But the concept of the pure physical fruit persists. In a profound
page of *Malte Laurids Brigge* Rilke describes an essential relation-
ship of woman to man. "Resolute and fateless, like one having
eternal life, she stands beside him who lives in perpetual metamorphosis. The woman who loves always transcends her beloved,
for life is a greater thing than destiny." [17] There is a figure in Rilke's
poetry embodying this concept of the ideal woman, of the pure
physical fruit, of immanent fertility and a perpetual repose—
namely Eurydice:

> Sie war in sich. Und ihr Gestorbensein
> erfüllte sie wie Fülle.
> Wie eine Frucht von Süssigkeit und Dunkel,
> so war sie voll von ihrem grossen Tode,
> der also neu war, dass sie nichts begriff. [18] ‡

Eurydice at the mouth of the underworld appears in an inviola-
ble state resembling death. In front of her is the ascending Orpheus.
Her walk is gentle, heavy, uncertain. She is at rest like the things
of Nature, and this rest is the likeness of death because for those
who live in Nature the maximum of life is indistinguishable from
death. Eurydice represents the ideal harmony of the human and
the physical.

Yet there is one quality which the orders of creation exhibit imperfectly, and mainly during the winter-stasis, which, nevertheless,
constitutes the very force of Nature, and by this quality Eurydice
becomes the pure physical fruit surpassing all the orders of crea-

* "Here dogs lie sleeping, and there lie stones."

† "Lord, it is time: the summer was immense."

‡ "She rested in herself. And her being-dead fulfilled her like fulness. Like
a fruit with sweetness and darkness, so was she filled with her great death, which
was so new that she understood nothing."

tion. Not only does she share their *vis inertiae,* but she shares it so absolutely as not to know the moment of blossoming. Now blossoming is the unveiling of Nature's secret power. But Eurydice, to whom (according to the myth) death came all at once, has, according to Rilke, a maturation sudden as her mythical death, one that is called by Rilke a pure descent ("der reine Untergang").[19] In "Die Erwachsene" maturity came suddenly and was pictured in the semblance of a veil, as if this girl were going straight from childhood to the mature woman without a period of awakening. And this precisely is the pure descent: never or hardly ever to know Nature except as an immanent power, to go from childhood directly to maturity without having to pass through a moment of "blossoming." Rilke's physical fruit is matured by Nature alone; it is born and falls asleep; it goes directly from the bud to the ripening fruit; it jumps the knowledge of man:

> Abbruch der Kindheit
> war euch nicht Schaden. Auf einmal
> standet ihr da, wie im Gott
> plötzlich zum Wunder ergänzt.[20] *

The stanza, addressed to the sisters of Eurydice by the poet, bewails his irrecoverable childhood and subsequent fruitlessness. At one point the women are compared to a tree of sleep (*Schlafbaum*). The image at once recalls one of Rilke's finest and latest poems "Das stieg zu ihr aus Erde, stieg und stieg." [21] There is also an Annunciation in which the angel tells Mary, "Ich bin der Tag, ich bin der Tau. . . . Ich bin das Beginnende. . . . Ich bin ein Hauch im Hain"—each followed by the refrain: "du aber bist der Baum." [22] In yet another poem, the meaning of this tree is more explicit

> O, der ich wachsen will,
> Ich seh hinaus, und in mir wächst der Baum.[23] †

But the significance of this tree, independent of human will, that grows and is fertile within Mary, the poet, and Eurydice is most clearly expressed in the Sixth Duino Elegy:

* "The crumbling away of childhood did not harm you. All at once you stood there as if rounded out to a miracle in God."

† "O I who want to grow, I look outward, but the tree grows within."

Fig tree, how long has this had its significance for me, that you almost wholly hasten past the blossom and, uncelebrated, thrust your pure secret into the swift swelling fruit. Like the fountain's conduit your bent branchwork drives the sap down and up: and it leaps out of slumber, almost without wakening, into the bliss of sweetest achievement. Behold: like the God into the swan. . . . But we linger, ah, it is our pride to blossom, and we enter betrayed the retarded interior of our finite fruit.[24]

The *tree of sleep* is another sign to indicate, like Eurydice and the winter of concealment, the possibility of a pure physical fruit, growing by secret growth, independent of human will, suddenly ripe. Is not "Die Erwachsene" an early embodiment of this symbol, and does not it also contain the image of the tree of sleep?

The poem's central image is that of the water-carrier. We have said that Rilke intended by this image to evoke an act so finely suited to the body that it could not be conceived as of other than physical origin. But the water-carrier may also be seen as a variant of the tree of sleep. For she is introduced in part to illustrate a quality of the young girl which Rilke calls "gelassen," a word that has no equivalent in English. "Gelassen," as far as we know, was first introduced into German as an important word and concept by Meister Eckhart, who used it to describe the supreme state of "unbewegliche Abgeschiedenheit," an inflexible aloofness from the things of this world. It was adopted by Angelus Silesius in his *Cherubinischer Wandersmann,* and there becomes a key word referring to a state of renouncement or consent parallel to Meister Eckhart's. "Gelassenheit" is a concept indispensable to mystical thinking, and may be understood as describing an absolute laissez-faire to which the soul attains in depriving itself of all human connection, becoming in this way entirely responsive to God. Rilke had read Meister Eckhart,[25] and that he knew the pregnant connotation of this word is evident from his perfect use of it in a translation of Valéry's *Palme,* where the lines

—Calme, calme, reste calme!
Connais le poids d'une palme
Portant sa profusion!

are rendered by

—Gelassen, bleibe gelassen!
Lerne die Last erfassen
einer Palme, die zahllos trägt!

But Rilke's carrier is of course responsive to the *physical* impulse; her calmness is from the body; she is a version of the tree of sleep. Thus her stance has the heaviness and balance of all physically submissive beings; she submits to, but bears up under, the increasing sleep of maturation, and balanced on her head is the full jug of water like a heavy fruit drawn from the trunk and sap of her body.

There is a further and supreme evocation of the tree of sleep. It is found in the *Sonnets to Orpheus,* and is written for a new Eurydice:

Und fast ein Mädchen wars und ging hervor
aus diesem einigen Glück von Sang und Leier
und glänzte klar durch ihre Frühlingsschleier
und machte sich ein Bett in meinem Ohr.

Und schlief in mir. Und alles war ihr Schlaf.
Die Bäume, die ich je bewundert, diese
fühlbare Ferne, die gefühlte Wiese
und jedes Staunen, das mich selbst betraf.

Sie schlief die Welt. Singender Gott, wie hast
du sie vollendet, dass sie nicht begehrte,
erst wach zu sein? Sieh, sie erstand und schlief.

Wo ist ihr Tod? O, wirst du dies Motiv
erfinden noch, eh sich dein Lied verzehrte?—
Wo sinkt sie hin aus mir? . . . Ein Mädchen fast. . . .*

* "Almost a girl she was, and sallied forth from this united joy of song and lyre, and gleamed bright through her veils of spring, and made herself a bed in my ear.

She slept in me. And all things were her sleep. The trees I wondered at, the sensed distance, the felt meadow, and all the amazement that concerned myself.

How wonderfully applied, in the last stanza, the analogy to direction! The poet conceives this girl to be in that indeterminate splendor between childhood and maturity; he hesitates to call her a girl, "Und fast ein Mädchen," just as he will hesitate in the penultimate sonnet of the series to call her a child, "Du, fast noch Kind." The young girl who has died was a first fruit of Nature not yet confirmed in her maturity by man. Dante, Petrarch, some of the sixteenth and seventeenth century lamenters of the death of virgins, and Novalis are among the few poets who have ventured to describe this moment, the hidden theme of many Renaissance paintings on the Annunciation. The subject, whenever chosen, is picked because of the wish to present a human being whose maturation did not depend on man.

It is the same wish which has inspired Rilke. We note the veil which here, as in "Die Erwachsene," suggests the first veil following physical readiness. But her real veil is her sleep. The theme of sleep is predominant. This girl does not desire to blossom, to wake: "Sieh, sie erstand und schlief." As with the hero and the young dead, the fig tree and the many women figures of Rilke, and as with their love-star Venus, which, as the poet describes it, has no need to ascend very high, but rises shortly only in order to set

> Stern, der schon vollendet untertaucht . . .
> tausendfachen Aufgang überholend
> mit dem reinen Untergang [26] *

so with this young girl: she also is born only to fall into the almost immediate sleep of death or maturity. For early death and maturity, rightly or wrongly, are identified by Rilke as two great types of physical fulfilment. The girl who forgets to blossom and jumps from bud to fruit, from childhood to maturity, the girl in whom the

---

She slept the world. Singing God, how did you perfect her that she did not desire first of all to wake? See, she arose and slept.

Where is her death? O will you have time to invent this theme before your song has consumed you? She sinks from me, whereto? . . . Almost a girl . . ."

* "Already complete star that sets, transcending a brilliant birth by a pure descent."

end of childhood is not felt as a rupture, who, entirely submissive to a physical will, knows an indifference parallel to death—this is Rilke's predominant symbol for the pure physical fruit, the tree of sleep, *the seed growing secretly.*

3

Rilke, in one of his poems, tells of a painter who tries numberless times to paint a certain mountain which, despite his efforts, remains indifferent, huge, impersonal. But all at once, as if it had known this was to occur, the mountain towers up visionary ("wie Erscheinung") from behind the clefts.[27]

Nature's untranslatable concreteness is a common subject and experience among modern artists. The episode might easily refer to Cézanne. Rilke praises Cézanne for the extreme matter-of-factness ("Sachlichkeit") of a vision that will not make a distinction of genre between the human subject and the subject from nature. Before knowing Cézanne Rilke had found the same suspension of the anthropomorphic viewpoint in the art of Rodin, as indeed in all those artifacts which directed him to "a world seen simply and without interpretation as an occasion for things." [28] Rilke not only admired painter and sculptor, he envied them. "Dinge, sag ich, Dinge, Dinge, Dinge!" [29] They can work with symbols closer to the concreteness of nature and less conventional than the ones provided by language. Cézanne painted what he saw, perhaps colors. Rodin molded what he touched, perhaps bodies. Rilke saw with Cézanne, touched with Rodin, but of what did he write? What exactly are the immediate data of sense perception, and to what extent are they representable in poetry?

In Rilke's apperception there is first phenomenality as such, that quality of every perceptible which is its *act of appearance.* The unpainterly mountain will, sooner or later, appear as a visionary thing —*Erscheinung* carries the double sense of "phenomenon" and "apparition." Phenomenality is expressed in the poetry of Rilke by the omnipresent "Siehe." Yet another sign is the equally frequent "Da." The immediate consciousness (Kant's "transcendental") perceives in all things a purposiveness without purpose, though in Rilke this were better described as eventfulness without event. All

things carry with them the mark of a transcendent orientation: "Da
stieg ein Baum. O reine Übersteigung!" *

The tree that stands at the entrance of the *Sonnets to Orpheus*
is witness to a further character of immediate perception. It bears
the letters *auf*. Perhaps no other syllable is so frequent in Rilke's
poetry. *Aufsteigen* and its synonyms indicate the sudden upward
radiation of a thing on entering consciousness. Yet, to be exact, not
every object is perceived to act on the mind on this manner, but
only those seen with the edge of the eyes, momentarily, not brought
into focus, and those on which the eye immediately shuts. There
are, of course, trees and towering things impressing on the mind
the likeness of their shape. These cannot, however, account for
the suddenness. The mountain, equally huge however long it is
looked at, all at once rises up from behind the clefts.

Therefore, that which is common to both phenomenality and
inner radiation is a spontaneity of appearance having its source perhaps in the perceiving mind, perhaps in the thing perceived, perhaps in their contact. This spontaneity does not detach from every
apperception, though in it as possibility. Its occurrence is an event
seemingly independent of the human will. Indeed, though the
mountain be looked at a hundred times, and though each look be
more intense than the previous, the visionary looming occurs but
a single time:

> Einmal
> jedes, nur einmal. Einmal und nichtmehr. Und wir auch
> einmal. Nie wieder. Aber dieses
> einmal gewesen zu sein, wenn auch nur einmal:
> irdisch gewesen zu sein, scheint nicht widerrufbar.[30] †

Let us now look at one such apperception in its entirety: "Und
fast ein Mädchen wars und ging hervor." This girl, the beloved
announced by all creation, appears at the threshold of maturity, in
the phenomenal moment and first short blossoming, almost a girl,

* "A tree ascending there. O pure transcendence!"
† "Once, each thing, only once. Once and no more. And we too only once.
Never again. But to have been this once, if only once: to have been at one with
the earth seems irrevocable."

that is, infinitely near to the unique appearance, like the angel who, announcing to the Virgin her death, "Jetzt wird es Zeit, dass du erscheinst," [31] * comes infinitely near and vanishes as if into her face. The appearance is sudden. There is in the mind an instant of radiation, nothing more, no singular percept; as she rises visionary the mind, before it can awake and before she is viewed in all her qualities, returns to its sleep. But it is a new sleep, for it now holds the possibility of her new and complete emergence.

One marvels. Is nothing, then, immediate in perception save this one unfulfilled moment, no image, no sound, no particular percept? Where is all the boasted concreteness of sense experience— "Wo ist ihr Tod?" Here the senses give no *immediate* sign to consciousness except the one signifying hope, possibility, uniqueness. But only because the girl, as soon as perceived, fell asleep and caused the senses to do likewise. The mind is asleep, but she is nevertheless there in her entirety, in her full sensuous apparel, waiting for a new emergence.

What is the meaning of this sleep that must precede and follow such apperception? It is a readiness of the body and a suspense of the will enabling total reception from the senses. If the poet has been entirely receptive of the event, he may experience its unconscious or involuntary maturing, until the girl appears once more, this time fulfilled:

> Erde ist es nicht dies, was du willst: unsichtbar
> in uns erstehen?—Ist es dein Traum nicht,
> einmal unsichtbar zu sein?—Erde! unsichtbar! [32] †

It remains to be seen how this girl though admitted to the mind in no particular, is admitted in her completeness, and whether such an act of knowledge is representable by poetic means. Not only is it representable, but it constitutes the essential orphic transformation of which all poetry is a shadow. The initial lines of the sonnets to Orpheus herald it with precision: "Da stieg ein Baum. O reine

* "The time is near for your appearance."

† "Earth, is it not this you wish: to arise invisibly within us?—Is not your dream to be some time invisible?—Earth! Invisible!

Übersteigung!/O Orpheus singt! O hoher Baum im Ohr!" So the maiden's lying-in is in the ear, the poetic faculty, and like the tree that Orpheus has built, she too is made of invisible images and inaudible sounds. This may also be phrased as follows: "How does the poet free the mind from the invincible variety and multiplicity of perception in such a way that the original sensuous quality is retained?" Rilke specifies his answer in the last two sonnets of the series. To the question "Wo sinkt sie hin aus mir?" he replies: she is drawn to the "crossroads of the senses," or as it is once called with a pun not producible in English, "die unerhörte Mitte," the unheard and unheard-of center.[33] Can we trace her perhaps involuntary maturing into visibility without image, audibility without sound?

4

It is through an intuition of gestures that the change is accomplished. It was seen previously how the images and, to some extent, the continuity of Rilke's poems rely on certain fundamental gestures; and these may now be noted. They are *stehen* (to stand) and the related *steigen* (to ascend), *gehen* (to go), *springen* (to jump), and finally *tragen* (to bear). Many more particular gestures could, of course, be discovered, and among them such fine examples as this to describe a love conversation: "Sie werden sich hundert neue Namen geben und einander alle wieder abnehmen, leise, wie man einen Ohrring abnimmt." [34] Those listed above do, however, represent the most important ones. We would again point out that *stehen*, etc., are not necessarily gestures of the human body, but qualities whenever and wherever the physical will becomes manifest, and Rilke at times seeks them less in the human body than in certain objects that have acquired for him a value almost sacramental. An enumeration of these is found in the Ninth Elegy: "house, bridge, well, gate, jug, fruit-tree, window—at most: column, tower." Another series, more symbolic, is added in the Tenth Elegy: rider, staff, fruit garland, cradle, way, the burning book, doll, mothers. The problem before us is first to see if these various symbols are consistently derived from or reducible to the basic gestures we have listed; then, to find how these gestures, and the symbols that depend on them, reach the "crossroads of the senses," the imageless vision in which all find their identity.

We shall but touch on *stehen,* having considered it many times. It is a sexual sign, but not restricted to the sexual act. It is the sign indicating adolescence. It is the gesture ingrained in trees and towers. It comes to signify the restless and fatal forward motion of man who must seek his destiny outside of himself, and so uproot himself. Orpheus is characterized by the related verb *steigen,* for his ultimate function as poet and man is to realize experience not as possession but in its character of pure direction, a direction without human or visible end, but direction nevertheless

> Sei immer tot in Eurydike—singender steige,
> preisender steige zurück in den reinen Bezug.[35] *

Only a few uses have here been given, though sufficient to suggest that *stehen* cannot be restricted to any level of being, act, or object, nor is it constant in its linguistic form, appearing either as *stehen* or as one of its compounds, or as *steigen* or *türmen,* or simply in the prefix *auf.*

Gehen and *springen* have a like universality. *Gehen* is the sign of metamorphosis, of pilgrimage, of man's perpetual vagrancy. However simple the context ("Und fast ein Mädchen wars und ging hervor") it conveys a sense of necessary and ceremonious motion. To appreciate all that Rilke felt about *gehen* one should read his lyric descriptions of the "Walker" statues of Rodin. *Gehen* is also in the sound of waters, wells, fountains; it has engraved itself in the stone-motion of bridges; and in bridges and waters it often suggests the related gesture of the jump (*der Sprung, springen*), for Rilke the typical gesture of animal energy, "die Brücken springen wie die Hunde," [36] as also of compulsive or sacrificial action. Stars "go" with steady and circular motion. Hermes is described as "Gott des Ganges und der weiten Botschaft," and the poem in which he appears ("Orpheus. Eurydike. Hermes.") is a pure development of "going," as if these figures, their story, their destiny had grown out of

* "Be always dead in Eurydice—ascend singing, praising, back into pure relation."

this fundamental movement, just as some have claimed that this or that myth has grown out of a veneration of the sun, or of the seasons, or of agriculture. *Gehen,* furthermore, has inumerable combinations—*Aufgang, Untergang, Übergang, Vorgang.*

But *tragen* is the most pervasive of Rilke's gestures, even though it occurs less often as a word, for *tragen* is at the same time the most universal and least visible of signs. While "to go" and "to stand" give the mind an immediate if rough visual image, "to bear" is least suggestive of a stereotype. *Tragen* represents the activity of Eurydice, of woman in general, but also perhaps of man insofar as the body submits entirely to its fate.[37] *Tragen,* as in "Die Erwachsene," is used with all its connotations as the act of simple physical support, of spiritual suffering, and of bringing to birth. It is implied in such symbols as the rider, staff, fruit garland, doll, jug, fruit tree, and of course, mothers. More than any other gesture it attests a physical will which man cannot disturb, and so is present not only in the human body and its motions, or in any single contour and gesture, but in the very material of object, body, and earth.

This material is always represented in terms of weight (*die Schwere*), while the analogy to stone is often employed. As we have emphasized previously, the very text of Rilke is the "body," its weight and balance. There is hardly a metaphor or simile that does not in some way derive from his sense of the physical; he did not have to read Kleist's essay on the puppet theater in order to speculate on the body's center of gravity ("die unerhörte Mitte"!), for this speculation is as essential to him as to the sculptor. His conception of "thing," moreover, tends to negate the generic difference between the objects of nature, man, and art. Whether a tree, a young girl, or a column, Rilke will always understand it as an object in which a physical force has sought a certain kind of weight and balance, so that the contour of visible things is not conceived as static and predetermined, but at the mercy of some perpetual inner fountain which, although achieving momentary balance, continually endangers the object's contour and enclosed nature, liable at any moment to burst forth.[38] Creation seems to be the embodiment of an *élan vital* which has found balance in various forms, fountains of different shapes, and these are comparable to trees whose sap rises and falls according to a principle always the same, indifferent, outside of their power. These same trees "bear" us; nor can we disturb the basic equanimity of Nature by human acts which are inevitably precocious. We are returned once more to the recurrent conception of the pure physical fruit and the tree of sleep:

>   Gibt es denn Bäume, von Engeln beflogen,
> und von verborgenen langsamen Gärtnern so seltsam gezogen,
> dass sie uns tragen, ohne uns zu gehören?
>
> Haben wir niemals vermocht, wir Schatten und Schemen,
> durch unser voreilig reifes und wieder welkes Benehmen
> jener gelassenen Sommer Gleichmut zu stören? [39] *

The symbols of Rilke, then, have their source in certain basic gestures, the intuition of which frees the poet's mind from its obsession with untranslatable concreteness. But these gestures are still more than one. Do they at times actually attain unity at the still center of the senses?

We shall return once more to "Die Erwachsene" and to its image of the water-carrier. One wonders why the poet has chosen the symbol of water-carrier in order to illustrate the gesture *tragen* and the quality *Gelassenheit*.

We have answered in part by saying, that this image seeks to show an act entirely suited to the body; then, that it presents a version of the "tree of sleep," a symbol for the pure physical fruit. We would now go on to show that the image of the water-carrier also suggests the identity of the fundamental gestures we have mentioned, and hints at the identity of several orders of creation represented by the girl herself, the tree, the column and the fountain. The first proposition is obvious: *stehen* and *tragen* are explicit in the theme of the poem as well as in the image; *gehen* is also explicit in the theme as "das Fliegende, Entfliehende, Entfernte" (for *gehen*,

* "Are there trees on which angels alight, and so strangely raised by slow and hidden gardeners that they bear us yet do not belong to us?

Have we never been able, we shadows and phantoms, to disturb the even temper of those calm, indifferent summers with our acts too early ripe, too early decayed?"

as we have seen, serves as a sign for the metamorphosis of life), yet is not at first glance in the image, at least not until we realize that *gehen* and *springen* are signs for the perpetual motion of fountains, and that the figure of the water-carrier may stand for a fountain metamorphosed to flesh or tree or stone.[40] This may at first seem fanciful, but is a very wonderful process of poetic thought, leading to the second proposition, on the identity in the water-carrier of the girl (the physical will in human form), the tree of sleep (the physical will in Nature), the column (the physical will as symbolized by art things), and the fountain (the physical will as such). Though this could be painstakingly documented, we would draw attention only to the simplest resemblances that make such an identification credible.

The water-carrier is conceived as very calm (*gelassen*) and with a full jug on her head. This jug, as has been explained, may suggest a heavy fruit drawn directly from the body's sap risen during adolescence. Thus the water-carrier is transformed into a tree—a tree of sleep, moreover, for this image becomes more effective when we realize that the poet seeks a symbol to express the pure physical fruit, i.e., a fruit sprung directly from the body without need of blossom, so that the full pitcher may be thought of as having assumed the form of a fruit sprung complete from the young girl.

The symbol of the pitcher is not without importance for Rilke. In the *Sonnets to Orpheus* a dancer's act is described in the following manner: transforming transience into continuous motion, she resembles by her final twirl a tree built of movement, imitating the course of the solar year, its crest blooming tranquility, and bearing as its still fruits a pitcher circled into ripening and the even riper vase:

> Aber er trug auch, er trug, dein Baum der Ekstase.
> Sind die nicht seine ruhigen Früchte: der Krug,
> reifend gestreift, und die gereiftere Vase? [41]

Thus the dancer also represents the tree of sleep. After the moment of ecstatic motion in which she transforms transience—just as the girl in our poem endures and is filled with the fleeting, frightening world—*a figure indistinguishable from stillness* springs whole

and without blossom into existence, like the pitcher from the newly
blossomed girl. Nor is it difficult to perceive that this jug, full,
heavy, yet balanced on the head of the girl may resemble the perfect balance of a column's shaft and capital. And to complete the
identity we would recall that Rilke's habitual image of transcendence is a well or a fountain,[42] so that the water-carrier is also, in
the final analysis, a fountain that has penetrated and filled the
pitcher posed on the young girl's head.

We therefore conclude that Rilke has reached the "unheard-of
center" through his recognition of an identity among the orders
of creation represented by column, tree of sleep, fountain, and the
young girl on the point of maturity. But Rilke may also have
reached the "unheard center," the crossroads of the senses, or what
we would call pure vision: visibility without image, audibility without sound.

5

What has been said may be resumed as follows: for Rilke, *the body
becomes a spiritual fact*. Therefore his early attraction to the figure
of the Virgin Mary. "Die Erwachsene" is written with the Virgin
in mind but not for the Virgin. "You are not nearer God than we"
says the angel of the Annunciation. Even when, as in the *Stundenbuch*'s "Book of Poverty," Rilke seeks the true Christian Orpheus,
he finds him not in Christ but in St. Francis, whose bride was not
Mary or Christ but the cross of poverty embraced for the sake of
the earth, the stars, and all the flowering-grounds of Nature:

> Und sie empfingen ihn, den Makellosen
> in ihrem Leib, der ihre Seele war.*

Orpheus and St. Francis are not now live examples. Nature needs
a new interpreter. What Orpheus did by his music and St. Francis
by his life must be done over: creation is once more uninterpreted,
without its soul. The qualities, writes Rilke, are to be taken away
from God, the no longer utterable, and returned to creation, to
love and death.[43] Rilke desires to fashion every experience into

* "And they received him, the immaculate in their womb, who was their
soul."

an image of devotion: "Dein Bild: Ich weih's." Every sense perception is to be valued, stored, understood. He envies, like Wackenroder, Tieck, and Novalis, the medieval artist-artisan the surety of whose interpretations is God. For he, the modern Orpheus, knows nothing but experience and the unmediated force of experience; he is haunted by the hand of the sculptor who works directly and not figuratively with Nature; for what will hold the anthropomorphic and utilitarian word to the truth? The impossibility to create bodies is made into the pain of his own body, causing the persistent effort to experience Nature as sign rather than symbol:

> Hier ist des Säglichen Zeit, hier seine Heimat.
> Sprich und bekenn.[44] *

But how can language be shown as a system of natural rather than divine or conventional signs? Rilke would perceive only with what the French, in contradistinction to "les yeux de l'âme," call "les yeux du corps." Just as the mouths fashioned by Rodin express the mouths of the body, so his own words aim to render the physical rather than historical, social, emotional, or religious connotations. Rilke attempts to create a new idiom which would neglect the anthropomorphic for the physical basis of language. The commonplace sense of words is neglected for their seeming origin as signs signifying weight, direction, and invisibly oriented gesture. Thus Rilke's poetry is made difficult for the foreign reader by the amount of etymological play that restores compound words (*aufstehen, angehen, ertragen*) to the meaning held by the sum of their individual components. This does not mean that ordinary connotations are always neglected or are out of harmony: the word *Auftrag*, for instance, used at two significant points in the Elegies—"Das alles war Auftrag" (First Elegy), "Was, wenn Verwandlung nicht, ist dein drängender Auftrag" (Ninth Elegy)—shows a happy coincidence of commonplace and physical meanings. Such etymological play, not methodic in Rilke, became method in Heidegger and made the logical base of a philosophy. "König, König, das Gewicht wird Geist!"

* "Here is the moment of the utterable, here its home: speak up and acknowledge."

That we do not know the body any more than we know Nature, that we have understood neither love nor the passions, is Rilke's plaint in youth and in maturity. Does Rilke add to our knowledge of these? His work is an expression of the fact that our sense for the vitality of things is stronger than our powers of possession: "Wer lebt es denn? Lebst du es Gott,—das Leben?" The dilemma is slowly given ethical meaning. The will to possession is discounted for the will to experience without hope for possession. Actual sense fulfillment is said to give way before an infinite desire toward everything perceptible.

But why destroy the riddle so carefully built? Rilke's experience moves around two figures needing perpetual interpretation: the tree of sleep and the analogy to stone.

V A L É R Y

LA DORMEUSE

Quels secrets dans son coeur brûle ma jeune amie,
Ame par le doux masque aspirant une fleur?
De quels vains aliments sa naïve chaleur
Fait ce rayonnement d'une femme endormie?

Souffle, songes, silence, invincible accalmie,
Tu triomphes, ô paix plus puissante qu'un pleur,
Quand de ce plein sommeil l'onde grave et l'ampleur
Conspirent sur le sein d'une telle ennemie.

Dormeuse, amas doré d'ombres et d'abandons,
Ton repos redoutable est chargé de tels dons,
O biche avec langueur longue auprès d'une grappe,

Que malgré l'âme absente, occupée aux enfers,
Ta forme au ventre pur qu'un bras fluide drape,
Veille; ta forme veille, et mes yeux sont ouverts.

CHARMES

THE SLEEPER

To what secrets in her heart does my young friend set fire,
Soul breathing in through the sweet mask a flower?
From what vain nourishments may her indwelling warmth
Draw this radiance of a woman fallen asleep?

Breath, dreams, stillness, O invincible calm,
Peace of more power than a tear, yours is the triumph
When the slow wave and ampleness of sleep
Conspire on the breast of such an enemy.

Sleeper, gold mass of shadows and yieldings,
Your redoubtable rest is weighted with such gifts,
O hind with languor long beside a grape cluster,

That, though the soul is absent, busy in the depths,
Your form's pure belly draped by the fluid arm
Is awake; your form is awake, and my eyes are open.

THE POET meditates on a sleeping woman. He wonders at the cause and effect of her repose, one so powerful that, though the soul is hidden, her "form" is awake and perceptible to his open eyes.

The poem has a fine but precarious stability. Each stanza, each verse, each word almost, seems to take a new beginning and exist for its own sake. The straight line of sense is continually suspended by precariousness or beauty of phrase. Most readers will be surprised at the opening verse which, with a rhythm reminiscent of Racine, stops short on *brûle,* suddenly perceived as the verb belonging to *ma jeune amie.* This inversion is the first of many to compel a withholding of the conventional sense of the words. Nothing betrays the meaning of a verse which seems to have emerged from a natural yet nonverbal movement of consciousness. Each line seems to carry the emphasis of the voice as voice, before it has become speech, words, differentiated feeling. We are led to reflect how the single verse with its character of independent, inner equilibrium is joined to the next.

In the first quatrain the soldering is achieved by apposition; also by the assonance of, for example, *amie* and *âme.* But there is also an inner parallelism. The second line of the quatrain is characterized like the first by an inversion ("par le doux masque"), and by a slight continuing of the alexandrine accent from the sixth syllable (*masque*) to the seventh (*aspirant*), a weak syllable, strengthened to this emphasis by its assonance with *masque* and *âme.* Thus, in both lines the predominant accent is found not on the sixth syllable but on both the sixth and seventh; this and inversion give the lines their quality of equilibrium at every point. If we go on to verses three and four we find in addition to assonance of the sixth syllable (*aliments, rayonnement*) that their linking is effected through the verb, suspended at the beginning of verse four, but absolutely without climactic result, for the line is almost at once pulled to the center by the long *rayonnement,* and made finally stable by the double, rising anapest of *d'une femme endormie*. And the first stanza as a whole is of course strongly joined by rhyme and by the parallelism of the two questions.

Apposition, inversion, suspension, assonance, to which in isolation no significance may be attached, are the more evident means ensuring the cohesion not only of the first, but of every stanza. Their mutual effect is to remove the poem as far as possible from the pathos of natural speech, preferring a spontaneity more stable and strange. This may be the spontaneity of a mind in resourceful play with the probabilities of rhythm and word.

For each stanza, like the first, develops out of a sudden verbal gesture or apostrophe promising climactic development (*Quels secrets . . . Souffles, songes, silences . . . Dormeuse*), a gesture that each line shares to a lesser degree; but the promise is deceptive, for equilibrium is at once re-established by the retarding influences of inversion, apposition, and assonance. In the second stanza the tendency toward a free rhythm is so strong that we have one of the rare lines of French poetry composed of three nouns with asyndeton, and in its second part an adjective-noun combination (*invincible accalmie*) with an elision rarely used by Valéry. But the movement is not freed: it subsides as soon as we recognize that all these nouns which seemed independent are mere appositions to "ô paix plus puissante qu'un pleur"; while the stanza concludes with another retarding inversion ("Quand de ce plein sommeil").

Valéry is most sensitive to what he once called the parthenogenesis of the mind. These retardations aim first to render the spontaneous yet equilibrist motion of consciousness, its fundamental yet precarious continuity,[1] then to cause in the reader a withholding of the commonplace sense of the words. Valéry, like Mallarmé, has broken with the French tradition of expository clarity, though he is clear enough in his own way. An initial obscurity is essential to "La Dormeuse." The poet uses every means to retard in us that faculty of the intellect often named induction, by which we are enabled to make a quick or conventional guess at the referent of a phrase.

Fullness of sound that seems to cause a perception of rhythm without a simultaneous perception of the literal sense is additional evi-

dence that we are faced with an amiable conspiracy to retard induction. The suspension of sense by sound seems to increase in
each stanza until we reach the climax of the third: "Dormeuse, amas
doré d'ombres et d'abandons." There is such vocal joy in this verse
that no one would be surprised to find "do-re-mi." Yet to say of
this line "here sense is suspended by sound" is only approximate.
If its sense were merely "do-re-mi" we would not bother about it.
The meaning, though retarded, is finally reinforced by what at first
seems an entirely *arbitrary* effect of sound. These words are given
a surprising resonance as if we heard them echoing not through
the ordinary air, but through an unusual medium, such as water,
though far more mysterious. The idea therefore arises, stimulated
by Valéry himself, that poetry is, by essence, incantation; for, if the
value of poetry lies in the indissolubility of sound and sense, and
if this sound is largely arbitrary to the sense, then the significance
of sound must be of an order other than intellectual—one that could
be called magical.[2] We would recall the fact that "La Dormeuse"
is taken from a collection whose title is *Charmes*.

But with a deal of patience, as indispensable to comprehension
as to analysis, we may render this charm fully accessible to the
understanding. The line beginning "Dormeuse . . ." is characterized by an unusual collocation of metaphor which destroys an
immediate grasp of the literal sense. In what way is the sleeper a
"mass," that is, a lifeless group of elements? Is it not the height
of coldness to call this woman, full of dreams and quiet breathing,
a "gold mass of shadows and yieldings"? This question is, of course,
to a certain extent rhetorical, for the beauty of the sound pro-
tects the line, and *amas* still retains a note of seventeenth-century
préciosité. But the yoking together of visual and spiritual qualities
is strange; the woman is seen almost with a painter's eye as a combination of line and light intimating a purely decorative effect.

Indeed, the mixture is so subtle and the appeal of sound so evident that it may prompt the reader to reverse the usual order of
cognition and instead of seeking the sense first in the general meaning of the words to search for it in the sound. This sound is more
than a fine variation of similar elements forming the basis of all
aesthetic charm.

French poetry since the appearance of romance intonation has had to both fight against and capitalize on the excessive lilt of its language. The classical alexandrine which Valéry modifies brings one solution, for in it, as opposed to that alexandrine which Ronsard found prosy, spineless, and without nerve,[3] the upward movement is severely curtailed by a caesura, and by placing the main accents on the sixth and twelfth syllables, so that while the line wishes to fly away with the natural impulse of French speech, it gains order and intensity by the knowledge of a new commencement at the point of highest pitch. But when we read, "Dormeuse, amas doré d'ombres et d'abandons," a further development is felt. This line has, like most of Valéry's verse, a marvelous stability making it difficult to pick out the main accents of intensity. Every word seems so charged that the line affects us like a pattern of musical syllables, purified of the arbitrary emphases of speech, but not deprived of its own general and intense accent. In this line, and in the poem as a whole, there is an attempt at what may be called continuity by syllabic sound.

Valéry, in other words, evolves a poetic line truly both "poetic" and "line," that is to say, one whose rhythm, sound, and accent are continuous and stable, with the same continuity and the same stability as the melodic line of Gluck,[4] where in spite of passion the only sign of it is in the sustained beauty of the voice's course, and the only sign of discontinuity is in the poignant vibrato of the voice that sings. But how can it occur in language that a syllable (i.e., a fragment of sound without sense except in a word) and a succession of syllables free themselves from that unit of sense we call a word and proceed to carry and perhaps determine meaning? Here, however, we arrive at a most general problem of verse, for Valéry has only made extreme use of poetry's general tendency to endow the sound of a word with a meaning independent of that word's ordinary signification.

The apparently arbitrary relation between the sound of a word and its sense intrigued Valéry. He reflected on it continuously, and this concern parallels his wish to retard the mind's conventional responses to language. Not by caprice, dandyism, or philosophical prejudice does he inveigh against the commonplace, but because he feels to an extreme degree the arbitrary nature of all conventional signs. He therefore insists on drawing attention to the fortuitous and indefinite character of signs in which we often see inherent significance or which we take on trust; and the highest praise he knows is to say of someone (as he did of Mallarmé) that this poet used language as if he had invented it. Can the connection between the sound of words and their sense, between conventional signs and their referents, be shown as more than arbitrary, since it is, no doubt, a more than arbitrary process that brought it, and still brings it, into being?

"La Dormeuse" gives an example of how an arbitrary yet necessary and perhaps even at base natural relation is constructed between sound and sense. One is impressed on reading the poem by the importance of the vowel *a* and its combinations. To list those more evident: *amie,* followed by *âme* and *aspirant; naïve chaleur; grave et l'ampleur; amas; âme, absente.* It is also difficult to distinguish between a shorter and a longer *a,* their length being equal because of the equilibrium and inner tension of the line. One may therefore find that the poem causes a fusion in the mind between the *am* of *âme* and the *am* of *amas,* probably aided by the association of the vowel *a* with the idea of *aspirant,* and of the consonant *m* with the idea of repose as in *femme endormie, sommeil,* and *ampleur,* so that on reaching the *amas* of stanza three the reader feels the tranquil breath of the sleeper. But though such single vowel or consonant effects are found always anywhere in poetry and are too delicate to isolate, the decontexualization of *am* as a sound unit is made possible by the verses' prompting of what has been called syllabic continuity. And coming to *amas,* we find that *âme* is present, simply through a sound syllable *am* that has, so to say, migrated.

But supposing this to be correct, that contained in *amas* is the meaning of *âme,* then we have found, by attention to sound, the persistent theme of the poem which at first resists logical analysis. For the indeterminate sense of *amas* leads us to the poem's fundamental theme: that the beauty of things is independent of our sense for what is human, the sleeper affecting not by her soul (*âme*), here hidden by sleep, and perhaps if genuine, always hidden, but by her quality to sheer sight, the word *amas* then denoting the in-difference of the eyes to the human appeal of the subject.

Just as the poet withdraws words from common currency, and charms us into a retarding of their conventional sense, so the soul itself is withdrawn, and we are shown its secret influence not as a simple, commonplace, and sentimental object (as in Mme de Staël's "chantez votre âme"), but as something most beautiful when almost inhuman, affecting most powerfully when most unconscious or deprived of its displayed human sense, the object not of the mediate and sentimental, but of the immediate and aesthetic vision. In the impressionist and abstract painters the rendering of a human figure as human is no longer a pictorial value. In Valéry the rendering of a human figure as human is no longer a poetic value. Despite *âme*, the sleeping woman affects as *amas*, and it is this dehumaniza-tion as a result of which a thing or a person is seen only in terms of light, line, or visual quality, that gives the beauty of such lines as "Dormeuse, amas doré d'ombres et d'abandons" and "O biche avec langueur longue auprès d'une grappe."

Though we have approached this meaning by an analysis of rhythm and sound, it is there also and very strictly in the logical development. The unity of theme and style rests on a withholding from view of all human, that is to say, of all immediately moral, emotional, or sensual, attributes, and it is precisely this kind of retardation which is often termed aesthetic. The "burning" of the first quatrain, for example, does not produce heat but light (*ray-onnement*); in "l'onde grave" a moral attribute is employed in its formalistic sense, and in "biche avec langueur longue" a sensuous quality delimited by a formal adjective.

Indeed, everything tends to this quality named in the last line "form." This is the thing that endures and remains awake in the sleeping woman, even though the soul is hidden and busied with a strange alchemy. What is "form"? It is evidently that which sus-pends hasty rationality or commonplace recognition, and which grants what may be called pure visibility. There is no doubt that the poem deals with a concrete and very sensuous experience, but the senses are touched as if they all had the objective and luminous vision of the eyes: "ta forme veille et mes yeux sont ouverts." The poem is concerned with the nature of contemplation, and probably aesthetic contemplation; the girl is revealed in the form of her body —"ta forme au ventre pur qu'un bras fluide drape"—yet this form does not express the organic reason of the body, but one touching the mind with the directness, luminosity, and coolness of a sight touching the eyes. The result is repose: neither sexual nor mental avidity but an indefinite suspension of the act of knowledge in favor of sheer visibility.

2

There is in Valéry's work an exceptional permanence of theme to which "La Dormeuse" gives only a single, if perfect, expression. We may choose works from any period of the poet's life—of the earliest poems such as "Été" (*Album de vers anciens*), or later ones like *La Jeune Parque* (1917), "Le Cimetière marin" (*Charmes* 1922), the *Cantate de Narcisse* (1938), or the fragments of crude poetry (*poésie brute*) stemming from various dates and found in *Mélanges*—the result is the same: every major poem presents the same experience, namely of a type of contemplation in which all knowledge about things is suspended, only their "form" remaining as the object of knowledge. We shall now define the nature of this contemplation, and of "form," its sole immediate object.

Each poem represents a conflict between the appeal of sensuous beauty as an image of fertility and its appeal as an image of self-sufficient purity. Let us take first the poem "Été," then "Le Cimetière marin," and finally *La Jeune Parque*. In "Été" the perfume of summertime is said to be as heavy as rock yet as pure as a rock of air, while the drowsy rumor of the sea is likened to that of a hive of busy bees. These comparisons, and the rest of the poem, both in sound and image, show the poet regarding summer as indistinguishably a figure for fertility and a figure for a luminous, self-sufficient beauty:

> Été, roche d'air pur, et toi, ardente ruche,
> O mer! Eparpillée en mille mouches sur

Les touffes d'une chair fraîche comme une cruche,
Et jusque dans la bouche où bourdonne l'azur.*

In the "Graveyard by the Sea" the image of fertility which
haunted Valéry in his youth is now generalized as the image of an
experience that the mind cannot satisfy by contemplation, the
emprakton of Pindar.[5] There is a restatement of the conflict between the active and the contemplative life. The sea—that changer,
bitch, resounding whore! [6]—suggests by its perpetual motion both
the renewal at the source of perception which is the mark of the
active life, and the repetitive sameness which is the fate of the
thinker who would forestall experience by systematic thought. "La
mer, la mer, toujours recommencée." †

As for *La Jeune Parque,* this poem has for its subject a mysterious person of almost indifferent gender (we shall simply call her JP)
who reflects on the conflicting purposes of her body, a figure for
love, fertility, and experience as well as a figure for contemplation,
self-sufficient purity, and narcissim. The opening verses

Qui pleure là, sinon le vent simple, à cette heure
Seule avec diamants extrêmes? . . . Mais qui pleure,
Si proche de moi-même au moment de pleurer? ‡

already contain in full the theme and magic of the entire poem.
JP wakes to hear a cry and to perceive light in that twilight moment
of the birth of consciousness which Valéry delights to picture. It
is actually JP who has just cried beneath the bite of the serpent,
but her body with its breath and tears is felt as a strange body:
perhaps it was the wind that cried, and perhaps her tears, the "extreme diamonds," are really stars, "extreme" because set far away
in the sky, or shining at the extreme surface of her body, in her
eyes. Here again is that distancing effect also found in "La Dormeuse," the dehumanization of the body by means of a purely visual

* "Summer, rock of pure air, and you, ardent hive, o sea! scattered like a
thousand flies upon the tufts of a flesh cool as a pitcher, and even into the
mouth where hums the azure."
    † "The sea, the sea, always re-starting."
    ‡ "Who weeps there, if not the simple wind, at this hour alone with extreme
diamonds? . . . But who weeps so close to myself at the moment of weeping?"

perspective that will not recognize the evident organic structure of movement and life. So the poem as a whole may be considered the Odyssey of Consciousness in search of its true body.

JP is met on her way by many temptations that would persuade her to consider her own body as she consider the body of others, i.e., as a sensual and practical thing with no other purpose than life or fertility. These temptations are the bite of the snake, betokening sensual self-knowledge; memories of childhood and spring; the flesh itself and its lassitude; and finally, the sea's sharp call for rebirth. But consciousness, in love with the impersonal beauty of a body moving in space, overcomes every temptation until the very end of the poem, where there is an ambiguous and forced gesture toward an experience of things beyond contemplation and outside of the original body, an "il faut tenter de vivre."

Thus the body perceived under the sign of contemplation is contrasted to the body under the sign of experience or fertility. And there is always one quality through which physical beauty is enabled to become the object of a purely visual contemplation, and which Valéry describes as *clair* or *lumineux*. That phenomenon which Descartes made a quality of adequate ideas is made by Valéry into the quality of fully perceptible bodies. His entire output of verse gives the effect of being a continual meditation on the nature of space and the distribution of light. Everything appears to have *éclat de matière*, "brightness of matter." Even the air, space, *Cher Espace*, is felt as incandescent. We see midday as alchemist in "Le Cimetière marin," and one of its stanzas uses the term "immaterial fire" in description of the graveyard: "Fermé, sacré, plein d'un feu sans matière/Fragment terrestre offert à la lumière" (stanza X). Now the sleeping woman's body was also termed luminous, and form represented as the result of a special burning. It is described as *rayonnement* and seems to affect the eyes alone, insofar as these are the luminous sense. Indeed, form as the immediate object of Valéry's special contemplation is not distinguishable from the sensation of radiance. The phenomenon of radiance as a constant of perception has only recently become a subject for empirical study by the eidetic school; but Valéry practised the phenomenological method as a matter of course, and is unafraid to base his poetry on simple psycho-physical observations. So the radiance in question is at origin a physical light, not Milton's "before the Sun/Before the Heavens thou wert." It results from this physical law, that we perceive the outgoing light of another body, but not of our own. Yet our own eyes surely have the outgoing light, even if we cannot perceive it. Valéry knew of this intuitively. The constituent character of that special contemplation the experience of which he seeks to express is that it causes the eyes and the intense mind to become aware of their emergent light, to desire its pure reflection by the thing about to be perceived.[7] So Valéry goes in search of that material thing which might in fact show the desired quality of pure reflection; and almost finds it in the burning gulf of the cemetery, reflecting the zenith light of a southern noon:

> L'âme exposée aux torches du solstice,
> Je te soutiens, admirable justice
> De la lumière aux armes sans pitié!
> Je te rends pure à ta place première:
> Regarde toi! *

Is not Valéry in search of a body having the quality of pure or total reflection? For the image that he pursues is not for him a Platonic abstraction but a perfectly perceptible, and therefore intuitable, body, not an *eidos* simply, but also an *eidolon*. The poet of "Le Cimetière marin" stands in the same relation to the light as the sleeper's radiant body in "La Dormeuse" stood to his eyes. The torches of the solstice seek a being that would return their light as purely and strongly as it came; the poet sought a body that would answer entirely to the notion of his eyes. Valéry's reaction to the light is "Je te rends pure à ta place première: Regarde toi," and the form of the sleeping woman seems also to suggest "Regarde-toi," for he tells us not that he has understood the function of her beauty, but merely, "Your form is luminous, awake; my eyes are open." Just as the poet ideally returns the light to its source, and the sleeper the light to his eyes, so form is that which by some

* "My soul exposed to the torches of the solstice, I bear up under you, admirable justice of a light whose arms are merciless! I give you back, pure, to your original place. Look at yourself! . . ."

quality of pure reflection returns to Valéry the image of his mind.

The poet of course never finds the magical body of his quest. But he is always on the point of finding it: "ta forme fraîche, et cette claire écorce . . . Oh! te saisir enfin . . . Plus pur que d'une femme et non formé de fruits." * The form sought by Valéry in the special contemplation is always almost visible, and "visible" must be understood in an absolute sense; it is the very same thing that Narcissus looks for, the always potential embodiment of the mind. Just as this contemplation, which perceives a radiance that cannot be perceived except in an almost unlighted mirror, which suspends every suggestion of the fertility or use of an object, is only virtual, never actual, so its object also is only virtual and never more than possible. Sight is experienced by Valéry as an unfulfilled condition, as *visibility*, and the object of sight as an unfulfilled existent, as *possibility*. And in order to convey the virtual quality of consciousness Valéry uses a specific method of style.

Few writers neglect so systematically the commonplace and sentimental quality of words, and combine such incongruous images as Valéry in his mixtures of metaphor. The technique which generally leaves in the mind a sensation of brilliance may be named the *metamorphosis* of metaphor: Valéry refuses to take any one image or metaphor seriously: the shimmering waves suggest mysterious sheep, a white flock of tranquil tombs, a swarm of doves, inquisitive angels. Such metamorphosis is also found on the level of sound; here it could be called modulation. But since we have to do with poetry and not music, we should find a term adequate to the fact that poetic sound never attains the freedom of the note, being limited by signs having direct referents in experience. The metamorphosis of metaphor, on the level of sound, is syllabic continuity.

An important example of syllabic continuity was suggested in our analysis in "La Dormeuse" of *âme* and *amas*. Now the syllables which in Valéry construct meaning through sound are not unlimited; there is in fact only one principal series, and this series may be considered as modulated from the root sound of *am*.[8]

* "Your cool form and this light-colored bark . . . Oh! if at last I could seize you! . . . Purer than a woman's and not formed of fruits."

A first variation of *am* is that of *aime, même, extrême.* The couplet *même: extrême,* in particular, parallels the meaning of *âme: amas.* But the major variation of *am,* the fundamental, the most persistent, is that of *amer, mer, air, or,* etc. It could also simply be looked at as a modulation of a vowel-plus-*r.*

We remember the beginning of "Été": "Été, roche d'air pur, et toi, ardente ruche/O mer. . . ." One can make an impressive list of all the words ending in a vowel-plus-*r* that are found in this poem. *Air, pur, mer, sur, chair, azur, cher, perd, mer, odeur, purs, matière, lumière, hennir, pleurs, perd, amour, purs, l'or, éphémère, chair, splendeur amère, miroir, préfère, amour, l'heure, futur, sacrificateur, jour, azur, dur, autour, obscur, mer, jour, dore, air.*

The length even of this list makes it improbable that the variation is merely part of the aesthetic charm to be found in any poem. Our ear is haunted by syllables in vowel-plus-*r* until we tend to neglect continuity by word and sense for continuity by syllable and sound. Is there here a construction of meaning through sound similar to that found in "La Dormeuse"? We may safely say that a subtle identity is gradually induced between the concepts corresponding to the sound of *air, mer,* and that corresponding to the sound of *or.*

Thematic evidence may be added. A wave spilling onto sand is described as "a power, losing as tears all its diamonds." [9] We are reminded of the "peace more powerful than a tear" invoked in "La Dormeuse." *La Jeune Parque* commences with "Qui pleure là" and includes the beautiful canticle of the tear. *Pleur* is one of the vowels-plus-*r* that echo through many of Valéry's poems. Nor is the poet's admiration for the tear an eccentric interest; it has a long literary tradition going back to the blazon of the Renaissance. Why is Valéry so concerned with weeping?

He is concerned because a tear is grief or passion made visible and therefore powerful, for nothing, according to Valéry, has power unless it also has visibility. But though the tear is compared to a diamond, it is less powerful than the simple imminence of grief, for its appearance already signifies a passing into act of what was in the highest degree virtual. That is also why the repose emanating from the sleeping woman is described as more powerful than a tear, because it is more virtual. In all things Valéry seeks this quality of the virtual, one recalling the emergent yet unrealizable character of consciousness, a state where intense expectation is not as yet betrayed by event.

The tear, then, has power insofar as it has visibility, but its very appearance already suggests the passing of this power. By emerging from the depth of invisible feeling or the depth of the unlit sea, tear and wave become visible and brilliant like a diamond. This act of gradual emergence parallels the gliding of vowel and concept between *mer* and *or:* gold, or rather, gold purified, gilt, representing what is most precious to sight. And the last line of the poem hints at the transmutation of even *air* into *or*—"Toute la peau dore les treilles d'air."

Thus gilt is taken as the property of everything that has become —like wave, tear, air and skin—visible, significant to sight. Numerous examples could be adduced to show this Midas touch of the eye, its gold-radiation:

> Je me voyais me voir, sinueuse, et dorais
> De regards en regards, mes profondes forêts.*

Indeed, in one stanza of "Le Cimetière marin" this gold-glance of the eye is the actual subject, and its magnificent last line expresses the paradox of the instantaneous look understanding discontinuously and ever anew the moving sea—an analogue of the moving and ever-changing world as well as of the perceiving eye:

> Stable trésor, temple simple à Minerve,
> Masse de calme, et visible réserve,
> Eau sourcilleuse, Œil qui gardes en toi
> Tant de sommeil sous un voile de flamme,
> O mon silence! . . . Édifice dans l'âme
> Mais comble d'or aux mille tuiles, Toit! †

* "Sinuous, I saw myself seeing myself, and gilded with glance after glance my deep woods."

† "Stable treasure, simple temple to Minerva, mass of calm, and reticence that can bé seen; lidded water, Eye that keeps hidden under its veil of flame so much sleep—O my silence! . . . Mansion in the soul yet Roof with a thousand-tiled climax of gold!"

The exclamation "O mon silence!" informs us how intimately this stanza bears on Valéry's experience as poet. Its every image is a bead on the same string. The sea appears as a visible reserve or reservoir of visibility, as an eye sheathed in light yet dark and inexhaustible within, as the invisible and indivisible edifice of the soul revealed as a resplendent but splintered surface. All these metamorphosed metaphors are but analogues to the poet's famed silence, and this silence itself is but a synonym for Valéry's primary experience, of *possibility as such:* of the mind insofar as it forms only imminent desires, of the body insofar as its power seems greatest when still potential, of both mind and body insofar as visibility is their ideal fulfillment and certain betrayal.

But another analogue to this silence striving for expression, this power of sight unrealized under its veil of light, this gold-spotted sea calm and inexhaustible in the depths, is the sleeping woman's invincible and radiant calm:

Dormeuse, amas doré d'ombres et d'abandons!

At the heart of "La Dormeuse" is the fusion of *dor*mir and *dor*er. For Valéry's desire is to have this repose, common to body and mind at the height of power before the act, made visible, and gilt is the poet's major image of a transformation causing visibility without loss of purity—"It is, in fact, the most abstract agent that exists, after thought: while thought may metamorphose and envelop only images, gold has the power to excite and favor the transmutation of all real things, changing one into the other; and yet it remains incorruptible and, passing through all hands, pure." [10]

Valéry shares in the general crisis of the aesthetic consciousness which would suspend all relational knowledge of things in order to know the indefinite moment between possibility and act, but knows only the dispossession of a mind for which no visible form is visible enough.

3

O moment, diamant du Temps . . . Contemplation in which time flashes like the diamond sea (and revery is indistinguishable from knowledge) is a rare experience, or else is swiftly lost among utili-

tarian thoughts. Valéry's special contemplation is all the more
strange for having not God as its transcendent object, but any
phenomenon of consciousness as such. What is found in consciousness cannot therefore be referred to anything but consciousness or
itself. Valéry encounters the same problem as Rilke concerning
the possibility of symbols. For the objects of perception cannot be
represented in terms other than those directly given in perception.
The body speaks its own language. Do "La Dormeuse" and the
other poems of Valéry give evidence of a reflection on the possibility
of symbols?

Two types of disproportionate movement are often represented
by Valéry: that of the body to thought, that of the object to the
eye. To illustrate these we could quote once more the stanza from
"Le Cimetière marin" beginning "Stable trésor." Here are two
other examples, from *La Jeune Parque:*

> Cette main, sur mes traits qu'elle rêve effleurer,
> Distraitement docile à quelque fin profonde *

> Reptile, o vifs détours tout courus de caresses

> . . .

> Coule vers d'autres lits tes robes successives.†

In such verses movement is represented as complete though still
in progress, the static position is noted before the motion, or there
is an almost immediate dissociation of living, organic things, like
the snake, into a pattern of discrete acts moved by a cause indistinguishable from movement. To such effects may be given the
collective name of prolepsis or anticipation.

Prolepsis is difficult to define as a feature of style; in general
practice it is used only to refer to a special use of the adjective, a
famous instance being Keats' "So the two brothers and their *mur-
der'd* man." No afterthought in Keats, prolepsis is used merely to
heighten a narrative style. In Valéry, however, his frequent adjec-

* "This hand, distracted and docile toward some profound end, on my features which it dreams of caressing."

† "Reptile, o swift turnings ashiver with caresses. . . . let your successive
robes flow toward other beds."

tival use—"Mais je sais ce que voit mon regard *disparu*"—is only
an instance of a larger pattern. Extreme prolepsis may of course do
away with a good deal of grammatical and logical subordination,
the very effects peculiar to language. At times there is an obvious
flaw, as when the poet causes an appositional phrase to precede
the main clause solely because of metrical embarrassment. But
most of the time, even though inversion and suspension be as great
as

> Quel éclat sur mes cils aveuglément dorée,
> O paupières qu'opprime une nuit de trésor,
> Je priais à tâtons dans vos ténèbres d'or!
> (*La Jeune Parque*)

the various uses of prolepsis may be justified as an expression that
the immediate object of perception is a visual surface, or more radically, that "substance," "essence," "soul" are but a succession of
surfaces.

Now it is evident that this proposition stands close to painting,
and especially modern painting, which recognizes plot, character,
and movement only as a function of visual surfaces. And it may in
general be said that prolepsis is the constitutive metaphor of painting, since painting is essentially anticipation: of action through
positioned bodies, of these bodies through the effects of surface and
light, of surface through the relations of line and color.

Yet the proposition "Substance is but a succession of surfaces"
is evidently a paradox, the same one we find throughout the work
of Valéry. Succession indicates a continuous series. How are surfaces continuous? Here is a girl: she moves, she has moved, she is
about to move. What is at all times the line of her hands, feet, and
face with that of her body, the line of her body with that of her
surroundings? Is there one exhaustive line which, like a mathematical formula, could circumscribe the actual and implicit motion
which all her surface makes with all other surfaces? "That woman
who was just now there has been devoured by countless forms." [11]
Painting must seize this line, impossibly complex, but not by succession. It is given one moment only, one surface. It must render
the essential by a simultaneity of surfaces. Poetry cannot pretend
simultaneity, only succession; and then a succession not of *surfaces*

but of *sounds* (which do not have a direct referent in sight), or *words* (which rarely have a complete referent in sight). To conceive substance as a succession of surfaces is so paradoxical that neither of these arts, nor music, may do it justice.

But Valéry does work toward an imaginative solution. In one of his books a figure appears which ends the race in which body is always swifter than thought or eyes, realizing an organic equation of infinite line, a total surfacing of the soul:

> *Socrates:* It is the supreme attempt . . . She turns, and all that is visible detaches itself from her soul . . . men and things will form around her a shapeless and circular dough . . . She turns . . . A body by its simple force, and by its act is strong enough to alter more profoundly the nature of things than the mind ever could in its thoughts and wildest dreams. . . . She could die like this. . . .
>
> *Eryximachus:* Sleep, perhaps, fall asleep with a magic sleep. . . .
>
> *Socrates:* She will rest motionless at the very center of her movement. Isolated, isolated, like the axis of the world. . . .
>
> *Athikté:* Shelter, shelter, O my shelter, O Whirlwind—I was within you, O movement, outside of all things. . . .[12]

The book is *L'Âme et la danse,* and the figure is Athikté the dancer.

The allusion to her magic sleep reminds us of "La Dormeuse," for the sleeping woman of 1922 is probably an anticipation of the dancer of 1923. Both figures result from speculation on the immediate objects of sense experience. Both present an imaginative victory over prolepsis, if prolepsis is defined as that shortcoming in symbolic representation which forces us to consider movement or soul or understanding as a succession of discrete events. But they are equally symbols for "metamorphosis overcome," if metamorphosis is defined as that shortcoming in symbolic representation which forces us to show continuity (soul, movement, understanding) where there is only a "diamant du Temps." In Athikté movement, soul, and body become entirely surface, entirely visible, even though she rests at the still center of motion; and in the sleeping woman the body and its secret dimension are viewed only as visible surface, as form, while this form is neither a momentary and discontinuous apparition nor an enduring quality, but perpetually virtual to the eyes.

Now Athikté acts as the explicit representative of the art of dance, even as Eupalinos is a representative of architecture, and Amphion of music. But what does the sleeper represent? The example of Athikté affirms the possibility that the body may be known in itself and with no intermediary other than the act of dance. The example of Eupalinos affirms the possibility that the mind may be known in itself without intermediary except the act of construction. But the "Dormeuse" is an example of the "body of the world" as poet and painter try to know it. The latter knows it only in terms offered by the object itself—conventional terms like color, line, concept, image, and word—not, as dancer, musician, and architect know it, in terms almost negligible as intermediates, terms which provide an almost direct intuition of universal forms. "A beautiful body makes itself be looked at for its own sake" writes Valéry, and adds "But music and architecture make us think of something quite different from themselves . . . It was the symphony itself that made me forget my sense of hearing. It changed so promptly, so exactly into souled truths and universal adventures or even into abstract combinations, that I no longer perceived the sensuous intermediary, sound [que je n'avais plus connaissance de l'intermédiaire sensible, le son]." [13]

Poetry, then, perhaps painting also, differs from the other arts by a use of symbols which retain inevitable referents in conventional speech and image, and cannot therefore represent mind and body or consciousness of mind and body in a direct way. "La Dormeuse" tells us of the poet's impossible attempt to understand the body as if it did not need mediation; his desire to know reality without the aid of symbol and by sheer contemplation. And the last words of the poem, *mes yeux sont ouverts,* express this dilemma exactly, suggesting that the eyes are open by nature and necessity in endless anticipation and as a physical figure for an unrealized spiritual power. The intellectual pursuit of Valéry is to this end, that the body may be seen as what it virtually is, a magnificent revelation and instrument of the soul. Could it be viewed as such, the eyes would not be symbol, but reality.

4

We have talked about the aesthetic consciousness, but Valéry makes no distinction between the aesthetic and other kinds of consciousness. In his very first essay, on the method of Leonardo da Vinci, he insists that artistic and scientific minds work toward the same end, the discovery of a fundamental law of continuity. Valéry is evidently oppressed by the modern multiplication of the modes of knowledge, and he would like to discover that method of intellectual construction which stands at the unitary base of mental endeavor. He even suggests in his essay on Poe's *Eureka* that the modern world needs a poet who would take his materials from the sciences: "We have no poets of Knowledge [poètes de la connaissance] among us, absolutely none. Perhaps this is because we have so strong a feeling for the distinction of genres, that is to say, for the independence of the divers movements of the mind, that we do not accept those works which combine them." [14] Not only is Valéry haunted by the idea of a *mathesis universalis,* but he develops a highly conscious *method* of symbolic construction in order to unify various modes of apprehension, including the scientific. We shall now consider the character of this method and, finally, show it operative in his poetry.

At Valéry's appearance the concept of causality, criticized by Hume and Kant, had lost much of its intellectual attractiveness, and had been put more and more on a par with metaphysical curiosities like radical heat, occult essence, etc. Knowledge and perception had become the inexplicable, central facts. For Valéry there is on the one hand consciousness, on the other, mere events governed by the "laws" of chance. Between consciousness and the fortuitous object lies perception and the mystery of perception. From the beginning he found himself attracted to two major phenomena, air and sea. The sea demonstrates most forcefully the operation of chance: "Foam lights up from *time to time,* on the field of the sea, and these *times* are created by chance." [15] Or, "Here, the sea gathers, takes back into itself its innumerable dice, throws them once more." [16] If the sea represents events governed by chance, air is the analogue of consciousness, the element of possibility, the lumi-

nous void. To cite here even one supporting quotation would belie
the richness of all—"L'Air immense ouvre et referme mon livre."
What under these conditions is the image for an act of perception
or of knowledge? The answer is the fact of visibility, the action of
one thing upon another from a distance, induction—"Could the
inexplicable . . . have for its image *distance?* Action from a distance, induction, etc.?" [17]

As early as the *Essai sur la méthode de Léonard de Vinci* Valéry
is concerned with "action à distance." The essay holds that invention results from the discovery of a law of continuity for objects not
yet subsumed under such a law. All speculation is said to have as
its end the extension of continuity by means of metaphor, abstraction, and language. Action from the distance is an unimaginable
thing. Great men of science like Faraday (discoverer of electro-
magnetic waves) came to their ideas through an attempt to fill the
void, a purpose also evident in da Vinci, of whom the following
passage is quoted:

> The air is full of an infinite number of straight and radiating
> lines that intersect and interlace without any one ever taking
> the trajectory of any other; and they represent for each object
> the true *form* of its being.[18]

It is clear that the poet also thinks of continuity as visual in nature. If the concept of visual continuity is kept in mind, many ob-
scure images are clarified. "Été," for example, tells of the skin that
gilds the vine-arbors of the air: "Toute la peau dore les treilles
d'air." This surely refers to that network of visual or potential rays
described by Leonardo, here represented as a luminous, life-giving,
bacchic vine.

But the thoughts of the essay on Leonardo are still germinal. Two
concepts touched upon, that of construction and that of substitution, receive fuller development in the poet's later work, and especially in *Eupalinos*. Both methods require a supreme play of ideas
("un jeu suprême d'idées") neglecting the material nature of the
objects reflected on: "One order is substituted for another the initial
one. . . . Stones, colors, words, concepts, men, etc., their particular nature does not change the general condition of this sort of

music in which they play only the role of timbre." [19] Now these
ideas, if taken seriously, must evidently derive from a theory of
space and thought as homogeneous, i.e., uninterrupted by the bodies
in it. And the imaginary space of Valéry is indeed a mathematical
rather than a physical continuum, a locus of action which, though
it does have three dimensions, is uninterrupted by the bodies it
contains, and presents these as arabesques or as a succession of surfaces:

> Reptile, o vifs détours tout courus de caresses
>
>   .   .   .
>
> Coule vers d'autres lits tes robes successives.

If thought and space, then, are homogeneous, objects of thought
(man, stone, word, color) are indifferent to the nature of thought,
exerting no modifying influence; and the operations of the mind
are reversible and indefinitely repeatable. The first proposition
is already expressed in 1894 and the term "homogeneity" used,[20]
though the concept is best explained in a later addition to the
Leonardo essay as "Color and pain; memories, expectation and
surprise; this tree and the waving of its leaves, its annual variation,
its shadow just like its substance, its accidents of shape and position, the far-away thoughts which it recalls to the distracted mind—
all this comes to the same. . . . All things are interchangeable—
might not this be the definition of *things?*" [21] The second proposition may be given the name which Valéry borrows from Henri
Poincaré,[22] reasoning by recurrence, but Valéry immediately lifts
it from the sphere of pure intellect in order to make it a principle
valid for all knowledge, whether through body or mind: "the conscious imitation of my act is a new act which comprises all the possible adaptations of the former." [23]

Now Valéry's method of symbolic construction depends on a
view of mind and space as homogeneous, together with the two consequences thereof, *the endless possibility of substitution and the
indefinite repetition of the same act of knowledge.* To illustrate
this method in operation we need only two verses, for Valéry has
the power, a consequence of his method, to complete his entire
thought over and over again in this short space.

Let us consider the following from "Été":

Et toi maison brûlante, Espace, cher Espace
Tranquille, ou l'arbre fume et perd quelques oiseaux.*

A first interpretation of this "tree that smokes and loses several birds" is that the poet describes the mist around it, and some birds by chance flying away. Valéry is far from insensitive to such moments of natural magic, especially when the event, as here, is of the essence of chance. Indeed, it is necessary to understand it first as such. But the wonderful accent on *perd,* the restraint of *quelques,* and the surrealistic touch of *fume,* may also suggest much more. *Sfumato* or chiaroscuro is that condition which, according to Leonardo, grants full visibility. *Perdre* returns a few stanzas later in description of the wave flowing onto sand, "Où sa puissance en pleurs perd tous ses diamants." In both cases, of tree and wave, what is described is a yielding of the materiality of matter to the brightness of burning space; and perhaps the only pathos to be found in Valéry concerns a loss of visibility even in the most ordinary circumstance—as here perhaps, where the poet tries to render the impression of mist or leaves fading into the brightness of the air. Whether bird or mist or leaf does not really matter, the impression on the homogeneous mind remains the same—"this tree and the waving of its leaves, its shadow just like its substance, its accidents of shape and position, the far-away thoughts which it recalls—*tout cela est égal."*

The possibilities of such substitution (bird for leaf, leaf for bird) are, of course, many; the charm of the verse results from its suggestion of a twilight consciousness which perceives all things in terms of almost abstract motion and proportion; and it needs no special effort to see that this couplet is also a reflection on the nature of contour. What is the line that keeps this tree from spreading over the air, or this air from burning the tree? In Leonardo's notebooks, which Valéry knew very well, we find the following typical notation:

When the sun is in the east, the trees in that quarter are dark toward the center and their edges are in light.[24]

* "And you, burning House of Space, dear tranquil Space, where the tree smokes and loses several birds."

Here then is another "arbre fumant"; it is evident that Valéry often borrows the cleared vision of the painter, wishing, somewhat like the impressionists, to see objects with the unprejudiced splendor of the eye.

Now the geometer, fundamentally, has the same problem as the painter; he also speculates on contour, wanting to define a line without breadth and a point without extension, so as to make "bodies" entirely intuitive. But while the geometer must suppose a world of ideal and impermutable solids, a world of interior bodies, the painter works with exterior bodies, actual trees in real space. Valéry, like the painter, also thinks of exterior bodies; yet he is also in accord with the geometer, for he knows that however exterior objects are, they affect the mind only insofar as interior. And this is specifically expressed in a stanza from "Anne" (*Album de vers anciens*), where another house of burning space and another smoking tree and another bird appear:

> Mais suave, de l'arbre extérieur, la palme
> Vaporeuse remue au delà du remords,
> Et dans le feu, parmi trois feuilles, l'oiseau calme
> Commence le chant seul qui réprime les morts.*

The bright and inevitable calm opposed to the perceiving consciousness by whatever object is perceived has rarely been more perfectly rendered.

But after the painter and the geometer we may venture to add yet another view, that of the scientist. "Burning" and "smoking" are used in many ways by Valéry including that which signifies a change of state, the not quite explainable phenomenon in physics occurring when, increased energy being brought to bear on an object, not its temperature but its form changes. So ice becomes water and water, steam. It is in fact a kind of physical displacement that can be measured by the eyes; what is again important is the visibility of an object that changes its form—"The burning incense exhales an endless form" (*La Jeune Parque*). In Valéry, everything—flesh,

---

* "But suave, the palm of the external tree stirs mistily beyond remorse, and in the fire, amidst three leaves, the calm bird begins its lonely, death-repressing song."

time, soul—tends toward this change of state, going always from heavy to rarified, from less visible to more visible, finally to be lost in the overbright and burning house of space: [25]

> De sa profonde mère, encore froide et fumante,
> Voici qu'au seuil battu de tempêtes, la chair
> Amèrement vomie au soleil par la mer,
> Se délivre des diamants de la tourmente.*
>   (*Naissance de Vénus*)

> Aspire cet encens d'âme et de fumée † (*Semiramis*)

> Je hume ici ma future fumée ‡ ("Le Cimetière marin")

This poetry is also an allegory on change of state, from heavy to rarified, all things seeking to reveal themselves by a change into light and air, but as they do, dying into the greater brilliance of the air (cf. "La Fileuse"). Therefore his apostrophe to space, full both of affection and of despair:

> Et toi, maison brûlante, Espace, cher Espace
> Tranquille, où l'arbre fume et perd quelques oiseaux.

Valéry's charm and logic are thus seen to depend on the substitutions of the homogeneous mind which perceives the outside world in terms of pure visibility, allowing no ideas of the reasoning reason and no impressions of materiality to stand between it and a direct visual effect. We would only add that such condensation of meaning in so small a space, thought being as complete almost in every couplet as in the whole poem, is due to the second quality of the homogeneous mind, its endless variation of the same act of knowledge, completed again and again in the shortest unit of sense.

5

The various interpretations here given center on one theme, *sheer visibility*, Valéry's desire to intuit the visible form and virtual idea

---

* "From its deep, still cold, and vaporous mother, look where on the threshold lashed by tempests, vomited bitterly by the sea into the sun, the flesh frees itself from diamonds of torment."

† "Inhale this incense of soul and smoke."

‡ "I breathe here my future's smoke."

of an object by a coincident movement of the naked eye and of the unconditioned, a priori consciousness. "La Dormeuse" is a meditation on how an image before the eye becomes an idea in the mind. It forms part of that incessant epistemological quest, common to poet and philosopher alike, which seeks the way from εἴδη to εἶδος.

Valéry completes the de-rationalization of sight begun by Hugo and furthered by the French symbolist poets. His vision dispenses with innate, sentimental, and acquired ideas, yet does not therefore admit the formative influence of the visible world. Sight, for him, is that luminous and perpetual limbo between perception and the unexplainably fixed idea: the gradual and endless inductions of the aesthetic consciousness. In his Leonardo essay of 1894 he has already formulated a theory of gradual induction:

> the surest method of judging a painting is to recognize nothing at first, and to pursue step by step the series of inductions which a simultaneous presence of colored patches in a limited area makes necessary, in order to raise oneself from metaphor to metaphor, from supposition to supposition, and so to an intelligence of the subject.[26]

This method parallels that of "substitution" which is operative in his poetry. His metaphors depend on it. In the Leonardo essay, again, Valéry gives a definition of metaphor as of imaginative logic in general: "All things move in the imagination from degree to degree."[27] It is the function of metaphor and of analogy to extend to the utmost this continuous play of the visual and abstracting imagination, which we have previously characterized as the metamorphosis of metaphor, and, on the level of sound, as modulation. "Le Cimetière marin," for instance, is rather hard to explain without an understanding of Valéry's special use of metaphor. In Gustave Cohen's *Explication du Cimetière marin*[28] one finds the following about the first line of the poem: "No one will doubt that the doves are the white sails of the fishermen of Sète," and when the word "doves" recurs in stanza nine, a note in fine print is added: "This no longer refers to the boats of stanza I." But one thought there was no doubt about the matter! What *do* the doves refer to? Cohen goes on to suggest that they are now the doves of the Holy

Ghost, "a consolation which Faith offers to believers prostrate before their icons."

The critic is not absolutely wrong, but he has not understood that the concept of dove is in Valéry subordinate to a visual idea which never submits to complete conceptualization or, conversely, to an idea that desires but never attains visibility. This fact forces the poet to a continual change of metaphor. The sails are now doves and now sails, now perhaps the saucers of sunlight on the palpitating sea, now the whiteness of marble trembling in the shaded graveyard, now mysterious sheep, vain thoughts, inquisitive angels. It is the play that matters, "le jeu suprême" of a mind haunted by an inexhaustible visual desire.

If "Le Cimetière marin" renders the gradual process of induction that begins with sheer sight, then a poem like "Été, roche d'air pur . . ." may be said to render also the gradual process of induction starting in a modulated sound, the vowel-plus-*r*. In each case the true persistent subject is not originally or ultimately summer or a graveyard by the sea—themes more or less fortuitous—but induction and retroduction. *"Rendre purement possible ce qui existe; reduire ce qui se voit au purement visible,* telle est l'oeuvre profonde." [29] * "La Dormeuse" is the perfect representation of an act of knowledge, proceeding from sight and sound, proceeding from the imminent powers of consciousness, but always and truly virtual.

* *"To return what exists to pure possibility; to reduce what is seen to pure visibility;* that is the deep, the hidden work."

CONCLUSION

PURE REPRESENTATION

V ALÉRY once declared that truth in the raw state is more false than falsity. But having lingered with the poets in the foothills and between the fences of truth, we now face a peak that cannot be scaled except by a frontal assault.

This statement may be ventured as one of the few empirical truths concerning perception: the eye is the predominant (we do not say most essential) organ through which perception takes place. The eye, Plato writes, is of all the sense-organs the one that holds most sun.[1]

It is common experience that the faculty of sight is both the most oppressive and the most enlightening. Does the mind have any greater desire than to perceive with the directness and splendor of the eyes? But is the mind not sick with the multiplicity and irreducibility of phenomena entering by the eyes? "O dark, dark, dark, amid the blaze of noon"!

Now symbols may be described as signs having the power to release the mind from the tyranny of the eye, as from all singular impressions. But the mind cannot ultimately distinguish symbol and sign according to kind: signs become symbols in its continuous context and insofar as the mind is not divided against itself. We say "hair" is a sign, but who is interested in "hair"? It is a discrete sign, it does not stimulate that *motus animi continuus* which gave Cicero his greatest human pleasure. Yet when Milton, in *Samson Agonistes,* writes "the fatal harvest of his head," the life of Samson is suddenly and in its entirety before the mind. Both sign and symbol, nevertheless, depend on something perceived through the senses, and especially the eyes.

Thus while the sign does not release the mind from visual perplexity—unless we are like a man suffering from extreme thirst who cries water, water and finds nothing but the image of water before his eyes—the symbol restores the mind to its paradise of motioned rest. To this end also the symbol often mobilizes other senses or relics of sense experience against the eye, until the mind's continuity is re-established.

How is one to describe the nature of this continuity assured by symbols to the mind? Critics rush in where poets fear to tread. One could say that it prefers chance to emptiness, event to chance, and emptiness to event; that it is a light which illumines without self-division or decrease, a power for which everything, beginning or result, seems fortuitous, but ultimately a game the reality of which rests beyond the player.

Yet the symbols which poetry has at its disposal are less immediate and unique than those of the other arts. A musical phrase may be heard without a distinct image forming in the mind, but a verse containing the word "tree" cannot be heard without the formation, however fleetingly, of the image of a tree. The composer works directly with signs that have a highly arbitrary relation to the things they perhaps represent: sound answers to sound, and in many painters, color to color; but the poet, though he will treasure words, must respect the things they conventionally represent, and cannot use his signs as if they spoke directly or exclusively to ear and eye. Words do not answer to words.

If poetry cannot escape, if a good part of its power, even, stems from distinct representations, how may poetic symbols induce the unconditioned continuity of the mind? The poet will accept representation, but only for its own sake, desiring what may be called a *pure representation*. In pure representation, the poet represents the mind as knowing without a cause from perception, and so in and from itself; or he will represent the mind as no less real than the objects of its perceiving. For the mind that perceives, and accepts this fact, since it can never know the objects of perception entirely in themselves, would know itself in itself—free of the irreducible, objective, and inevitable cause of perception. However, since it can never know itself entirely in itself, it is seized by an infinite desire for the very externality perceived.

The mind, therefore, being most keenly aware through the dominant eye of that which is the cause of perception, pure representation will, at base, be the urge to construct that ideal system of symbols which relieves consciousness of the eyes' oppression but assures it of the eyes' luminosity. Is it necessary to say more? Valéry, working on *La Jeune Parque*, draws up a mock questionnaire, the seventh problem of which is

> What is to be thought of this custom: Piercing the eyes of a bird so that it may sing better. Explain and develop (3 pages).[2]

The four poets here studied are united by their common striving for pure representation, which we have sometimes called the imageless vision; for poetry is at one with the other arts in seeking, though by varying means, visibility without image, audibility without sound, perception without percepts. In modern poetry, which relies much more on the immediate significance of sense perception, the theme of sight is often a conscious theme, and a work may be written to get rid of the tyranny, or realize the beauty of the bodily eye. We shall now examine each poet, his individual problem and solution; perhaps we can in this way gain an insight into the nature of the mind and of symbolic process, for it is difficult not to acknowledge that the perplexity of the eyes does not in some sense stand for a deeper and metaphysical perplexity. *Cur aliquid vidi?*

We know from "Tintern Abbey" that in the mystical moment the eye, owing to the power of harmony, is quiet. But Book XII of *The Prelude* relates that the tyranny of sight was, as well as "almost inherent in the creature," especially oppressive at a particular point in Wordsworth's life. This time coincided with an excessive sitting in judgment and may safely be identified with the period when the poet, disillusioned by the French Revolution and with Godwin sought formal proof in everything, till "yielding up moral questions in despair":

> I speak in recollection of a time
> When the bodily eye, in every stage of life
> The most despotic of our senses, gained
> Such strength in *me* as often held my mind
> In absolute dominion. (XII, 127 ff.)

He refuses to enter upon abstruse argument to show how Nature
thwarted such despotism by summoning all the senses to counteract each other; but his reflections lead him somewhat later in the
same book to think of those "spots of time" which preserved and
renovated him. One of them is the famous episode of the young
boy, separated from his companion on a ride in the hills, dismount-
ing out of fear and stumbling onto a murderer's gibbet, mouldered
down, and of which nothing remained except the murderer's name
carved nearby and kept clean because of local superstition:

> The grass is cleared away, and to this hour
> The characters are fresh and visible:
> A casual glance had shown them, and I fled,
> Faltering and faint, and ignorant of the road:
> Then, reascending the bare common, saw
> A naked pool that lay beneath the hills,
> The beacon on the summit, and, more near,
> A girl, who bore a pitcher on her head,
> And seemed with difficult steps to force her way
> Against the blowing wind. It was, in truth,
> An ordinary sight. . . . (XII, 244 ff.)

The nudity of such scenes has often been remarked and various
hypotheses invented, for example that Wordsworth lacked sexual
sensibility, saw in Nature a father substitute, etc. But a correct
detailing of the characteristics of this moment would have to note
first the cause of the faltering and fleeing, which is not so much
the mouldered gibbet as the fresh and visible characters engraved
by an unknown hand. The name evidently doesn't matter, only the
characters as characters, and the effect on the boy is swift and out
of proportion to the simple sight, a casual glance sufficing. Suggested first, we would say, is an indestructibility of human consciousness, exemplified by the new characters, and after that the
indestructibility of a consciousness in Nature, figured in the skel-
etal characters of a scene denuded of all color, sketched in a per-
manent black and white, yet capable of immense physical impact.
The mystical chord is touched, and the eye overpowered by an
intuition of characters affecting no single sense but compelling a

comparison between the indestructibility of human consciousness and a physical indestructibility. The same effect will be found suggested in the second of the spots of time:

> I sate half-sheltered by a naked wall;
> Upon my right hand couched a single sheep,
> Upon my left a blasted hawthorn stood; (XII, 299 ff.)

and the description of the characters of the great Apocalypse likewise starts with an intuition of indestructibility:

> the immeasurable height
> Of woods decaying, never to be decayed (VI, 623 ff.)

This, moreover, is coupled with a hint of the Last Judgment in the trumpeting of waterfalls that to the eye seem to possess the rigidity of rock,

> The stationary blasts of waterfalls.

But before reaching a conclusion we should consider one more event, the most significant perhaps that enters through, yet overpowers, the eye. Wandering among London crowds the poet is smitten

> Abruptly, with the view (a sight not rare)
> Of a blind Beggar, who, with upright face,
> Stood, propped against a wall, upon his chest
> Wearing a written paper, to explain
> His story, whence he came, and who he was.
> Caught by the spectacle my mind turned round
> As with the might of waters; and apt type
> This label seemed of the utmost we can know,
> Both of ourselves and of the universe;
> And, on the shape of that unmoving man,
> His steadfast face and sightless eyes, I gazed,
> As if admonished from another world. (VII, 638 ff.)

As in the gibbet scene, the poet emphasizes that the sight was ordinary and sudden, that is, having no intrinsic claim on the mind, nor worked up by meditation. But a greater similarity obtains between

the two, though it is by no means complete. Both events focus on
a label written by an impersonal hand. But whereas the characters
in the one case seem indestructible, here the label is a sign of human impotence. Yet the superficial label clearly points to a set of
deeper and indestructible characters, for the suggestion is that
the lost eyes of the beggar were only like a piece of paper, a visual
surface, and that, being removed, they leave the man more stead-
fast, fixed, eternal. We rediscover Wordsworth's constant concern
with denudation, stemming from both a fear of visual reality and
a desire for physical indestructibility. And the fine image of the
mind turned by the spectacle as if with the might of waters, refers
to that vast identity established throughout the poems of Wordsworth, an identity against sight, its fever and triviality, and making
all things tend to the sound of universal waters; subduing the eyes
by a power of harmony, and the reason by the suggestion of a Final
Judgment which is God's alone. The intuition of indestructibility
in the midst of decay, and the identity of the power in light with
the power of sound ("by form or image unprofaned") [3] are the two
modes of a vision in which the mind knows itself almost without
exterior cause or else as no less real, here, no less indestructible than
the object of its perceptions.

Hopkins, like Wordsworth, passed through an acute stage of
the tyranny of sight, and there is evidence that he joined the Catho-
lic church not only through a motive of faith but also through a
compulsion of the bodily eye: "You will no doubt understand," he
writes to a friend in 1865, "what I mean by saying that the *sordidness* of things, which one is compelled perpetually to feel, is perhaps . . . the most unmixedly painful thing one knows of; and
this is (objectively) intensified and (subjectively) destroyed by
Catholicism." [4] The paradoxical justification of God by the sordidness of his creation will continue in much of his poetry; and compared to Wordsworth he has little sense for beauty, unless the meaning of the word is overworked. His mind does not rest on things,
but these flare against him with "the fire of stress." In a sonnet from
the last year of his life that disconcerts by its despair and has been
without reason placed by his editors among the unfinished poems,

this early sense of sordidness breaks through when, crying for "the horror and the havoc and the glory" which all creation except man seems to possess, he sees himself imprisoned in a life of trivial observations: "in smooth spoons spy life's masque mirrored." [5] Such despair is not a "moment of cynicism." It is the continuous dilemma of an artist, a religious artist who, trying to understand creation by the naked eye, is struck by the ambivalence which tells him both of undeniable powers in the external world and of their impotence vis-à-vis the human observer, because reflected with equal success in smooth spoon or living eye.

To free himself from this indifference of the eye, Hopkins begins to represent perception as the result of actual physical stress. There is a "stem of stress" between us and things, which is their physical recalcitrance and resilience, whether to the wearing down of sight or of feet, and it informs us not of their soul or essence, but of their simple, mechanical, particular, and durable existence. The eye is made into an organ totally physical, possessing the immediacy and shock of the other senses, or endowed with the radical sense of the body as nerve and source of sensing. Sight may therefore be represented as a physical compulsion; but the body is not apprehended for its own sake, for joy and lust. It is considered as the only principle of compulsion toward Christ and imitation of Christ; for the mind being, like the eye, essentially indifferent and incapable of self-imposed suffering, only the body can truly suffer and offer sacrifice. And so an identity suggests itself to Hopkins between the body of man and the body of Christ, one that would thwart the indifference of the eye and the impotence of the mind:

> I leave it to you, brethren, then to picture him, in whom the fulness of the godhead dwelt bodily, in his bearing how majestic, how strong and yet how lovely and lissome in his limbs, in his look how earnest, grave but kind. In his Passion all the strength was spent, this lissomeness crippled, this beauty wrecked, this majesty beaten down. But now it is more than restored, and for myself I make no secret I look forward with eager desire to seeing the matchless beauty of Christ's body in the heavenly light.[6]

While Wordsworth, then, tends to represent a consciousness as the only indestructible thing in man, Hopkins, as he goes toward his pure vision, represents the eye itself as the physical, and the body itself as the finally indestructible reality. But the second tendency, bearing more on the nature of symbols, is also present. In the final analysis Hopkins may be said to move toward an ideal view denying the external world as cause or modifier of his perceptions, insisting that speech has its own laws parallel to those of organic creation. Just as Wordsworth identifies the power in light with the power of sound, so Hopkins sees an identity between the law of organic growth and the law of speech. This should be evident on reading his poetry aloud, the final meaning of which is not to any single sense, nor to the reasoning reason, but to the unclassified faculty of speech itself, its explosiveness, its sinew, its shifting accent. Speech becomes, as it were, a fruit of the body. "Poetry," he writes, "is in fact speech only employed to carry the inscape of speech for the inscape's sake—and therefore the inscape must be dwelled on." [7] And we may add the following passage from the notebooks in which "word" becomes a verb signifying an act of organic growth:

> Young elm leaves lash and lip the sprays. This has been a very beautiful day—fields about us deep green lighted underneath with white daisies, yellower fresh green of leaves above which bathes the skirts of the elms, and their tops are touched and worded with leaf too.[8]

Few poets have undergone the temptation of the eye with such will and force as Rilke. Nor was there any hope, in his case, of finding refuge in one of the other senses, or in their combined "long et immense déréglement," for the other senses but intensify his obsession with an invincible exterior reality. Rilke, moreover, is aware that in submitting to sense experience he follows a long line of literary precursors who sought a modern descent into hell. The myth of this descent may be said to start with Novalis, reaching its climax in French symbolism—Nerval, Baudelaire, Rimbaud—and its conclusion in Rilke, although Thomas Mann will still concern himself with it.

The nature of this descent is explained in a letter to Clara Rilke of October, 1907, Rilke being in the full flush of his enthusiasm over Cézanne, whose work he had just viewed in the "Salon d'Automne." Cézanne's new objective style, he writes, would have been impossible without Baudelaire and his poem "La Charogne" or Flaubert and "Saint-Julien l'hospitalier." These works of art show that aesthetic contemplation overcame itself to such an extent that it was able to discover and accept the essential reality of the horrible and the repulsive, and to do this without any choice or refusal.[9]

The descent into hell is the total acceptance within art of everyday reality. We are now very far from the classical "L'Art est la Vérité choisie." Did not Henry James say of Balzac that he wound reality around him like a huge serpent? For Balzac, Nerval, Baudelaire, and, as it happened, for Rilke also, hell, at least the inner circle, was Paris. It was the experience of Paris that led to the writing of *Malte Laurids Brigge.* What does the experience of Malte signify? "And suddenly (and for the first time)," continues Rilke in his letter of October, 1907, "I understand the fate of Malte Laurids. Is it not that this temptation and trial transcended him, that he did not pass the test of reality, although so convinced of its necessity as an Idea that he sought it intensely and instinctively till it caught hold and never left him?" [10] Novalis, in a fragment written a century earlier, foresees the kind of modern and frightening fairy tale represented by *Malte Laurids Brigge,* if we interpret the sickness of which Novalis speaks as that of the senses, and the evil as that of existential reality:

> Significant trait in many fairy tales . . . that when a man conquers himself, he also at the same time conquers Nature—and a miracle occurs . . . e.g., the transformation of the Bear into a Prince, the moment that the Bear was loved . . . Perhaps a similar transformation would occur if man would come to love the ills of the world—the very moment that a man began to love his illness or his pain, the most intense delight would

lie in his arms—the highest positive energy would run through him. Could illness not become the means toward a higher synthesis? [11]

We shall see these words of Novalis, that sickness may become a means of transcendence, turning real in the work of Rilke.

It is a sickness of the senses and a fever of the whole body. It starts with the bodily eye unguided by any plan of action and left to the confusion of a swarming city:

> I saw a man somewhere, pushing a cart-load of vegetables. He shouted: Chou-fleur, Chou-fleur, the "fleur" with a curious dull *eu*. An angular, ugly woman walked beside him and nudged him from time to time. And whenever she nudged him, he shouted. Sometimes he also shouted of his own accord, but then he had done it in vain, and had immediately to shout again, because he had reached a house where people wanted to buy. Have I told you that he was blind? No? Well, then, he was blind. He was blind and shouted. I'm falsifying when I say this, I overlook the cart, I pretend not to notice that he is offering cauliflower for sale. But is all this essential? And if it were essential, would it not rather be a matter of what the whole thing meant for me? I have seen an old man who was blind and who shouted. That is what I have seen. Seen.[12]

This man is blind and he shouts. Rilke repeats that he is blind and that he shouts. And that he has seen this, seen this, an old man who was blind and who shouted. Does not Malte expect the simple act of sight to be fated? He, Malte, has seen this man, at a particular moment in a particular circumstance, and this must have bearing on his destiny. The book begins with the act and word "Gesehen": "11 September, rue Toullier. . . . Ich habe gesehen: Hospitäler. Ich habe einen Menschen gesehen. . . . Ich habe eine schwangere Frau gesehen. . . ." Rilke like Malte is beset by the contingency of experience and the inevitability of the eye. He is haunted by accident and by the unmediated vision. These are the basic experiences from which he will try to free himself through representation.

A first way in which Rilke releases himself from the oppression

of eye and accident is through the symbol of the pure cry. At first
Malte forgets to tell us that the huckster crying chou-fleur, chou-
fleur is blind. His attention is caught by the cry itself, with its curious dull *eu*, and all the other circumstances that make it an automatic, repetitive, senseless cry. But then Malte remembers. "Have
I said that he was blind? No? Well then, he was blind. He was blind
and shouted." What Malte has really remembered is that this man
still cries out, though blind and absurd, but that he, who is far
from blind, does not cry. "I have seen an old man who was blind
and who shouted. That is what I have seen. Seen." The connection
Malte makes between himself and the blind man is quite illogical
and has the force of the illogical. The episode shows the poet's
prevoyance of a cry, but a sublime not a "cauliflower" cry, pure
of all accident and preceding every cause.

Are not the *Elegies* an attempt to formulate this pure cry? In
the first elegy, "Wer, wenn ich schrie, hörte mich denn aus der
Engel/Ordnungen?" * the futility of an appeal to the divine is
made evident. In the seventh elegy, "Werbung nicht mehr, nicht
Werbung, entwachsene Stimme/ sei deines Schreies Natur; zwar
schrieest du rein wie der Vogel" † the futility of both divine and
human appeal is made evident. The human cry remains only as
possibility, at the extreme point of yearning but never irrevocable,
neither calling nor yet not calling. But it is different in the animal
creation. Rilke explains the significance of the bird's cry in the
twenty-sixth poem of the second part of the *Sonnets to Orpheus:*

> Wie ergreift uns der Vogelschrei . . .
> Irgend ein einmal erschaffenes Schreien.‡

The cry of a bird pierces because it has the quality of undivided
consciousness, purpose, life. We, already as children, can only
waste the voice: "Schreien den Zufall." The blind man's cry ap-
pealed because it had the monotony and entirety of a bird's. But
it was still accident, absurd, "acte gratuit." Rilke desires a consum-

---

* "Who if I cried would hear me among the angelic orders?"
† "No longer wooing, not wooing, voice that has outgrown it, be the nature
of your cry, though your cry be pure as a bird's."
‡ "How the cry of a bird seizes us . . . A unique and once-created cry."

ing cry greater than any cause. His work often gives the image of
the glass that breaks itself in one spasm, and he invokes Orpheus
with the cry "Ordne die Schreier, singender Gott!"

A second symbol by means of which Rilke frees himself from the
tyranny of sense and accident is that of the body as fate. Malte is
not repelled by what he sees and smells, he accepts it, accepts it
totally, with a fatalism that has no reason except the simple fact
of existence: "Das Kind schlief, der Mund war offen, atmete Jodo-
form, Pommes frites, Angst. Das war nun mal so. Die Hauptsache
war, dass man lebte. Das war die Hauptsache." [13] * It is curious
how this tone anticipates so many more recent works, such as
L'Etranger by Camus. At its base is what Rilke thought he could
see in Cézanne, Baudelaire, and Flaubert, a full acceptance of everyday reality, of *Dasein*. This mood is so deeply present in Rilke that
it may be discovered to precede his thought in the same way as
rhythm precedes the realization of a poem. So the first stanza of
"Die Erwachsene," through its one sweeping sentence and recurrent central verb—"Das alles stand auf ihr . . . wie auf ein Volk
gestellt"—conveys to the sensitive reader a feeling of circular motion, the most typical rhythm of Rilke's poetry, one which he named
Kreislauf:

> Das alles stand auf ihr und war die Welt
> und stand auf ihr mit allem, Angst und Gnade,
> wie Bäume stehen, wachsend und gerade
> und feierlich, wie auf ein Volk gestellt.

Is not this the rhythm of maturation, of the earth, of the eternal
return of the seasons, of any mighty force that turns perpetually
around a center of gravity, of *Dasein?* In the second poem of the
Stundenbuch it becomes a symbol for man's inconceivable orientation toward God:

> Ich kreise um Gott, um den uralten Turm,
> und ich kreise jahrtausende lang;

* "The child slept, its mouth was open, exhaled Iodoform, fried potatoes,
fear. That's how it was. The main thing was that one lived. That was the main
thing."

und ich weiss noch nicht: bin ich ein Falke, ein Sturm
oder ein grosser Gesang.*

Three years later Rilke writes what is perhaps the earliest poem
of the *Neue Gedichte,* "Der Panther," taking its inspiration from
a visit to the Zoo but also from a small Rodin statue:

Der weiche Gang geschmeidig starker Schritte,
der sich im allerkleinsten Kreise dreht,
ist wie ein Tanz von Kraft um eine Mitte,
in der betäubt ein grosser Wille steht.

Nur manchmal schiebt der Vorhang der Pupille
sich lautlos auf—. Dann geht ein Bild hinein,
geht durch der Glieder angespannte Stille
und hört im Herzen auf zu sein.†

We emphasize the rhythm and theme of the gravitational circle
because it is the most subtle and complete symbol for Rilke's feeling of simple presence (*Dasein*), a key mood of modern literature
that may be traced as far back as Wordsworth. One of Wordsworth's
most effective and puzzling poems is "A slumber did my spirits
seal," a kind of epitaph on Lucy, in which the poet expresses an
ambivalent attitude toward death very similar to his feelings about
the blind beggar: death being the absolute denudation of sense,
but also a return to the only immanent and truly physical force,
that which resides in the motion of the earth:

No motion has she now, no force;
She neither hears nor sees;
Rolled round in earth's diurnal course,
With rocks, and stones, and trees.

* "I move in circles around God, the ancient tower, and I have been circling
thousands of years, and yet I do not know whether I am a falcon, a storm, or a
mighty song."

† "The velvet pace of steps, supple and strong, turning in the very smallest
circle, is like a dance of power around a center in which a great will stands
stunned.

The curtain of the pupil opens but infrequently and without sound. Then
an image enters, passes through the tense stillness of the limbs and, in the heart,
ceases to be."

Now it is surely more than accident that a hint of a similar denudation of the external sense is found in both "Die Erwachsene" and
"Der Panther." The visual image that enters the circling panther's
eye, ceases in the heart. And in "Die Erwachsene" the curious line
"Ganz Bild und bildlos wie die Bundeslade" occurs, one which, if
it means anything, can only be explained by the following hypothesis: the girl, like the panther, is so immanently a part of nature,
and subject to a great but stunned will, that the external world in
the period of maturation is a subsuming but imageless impression,
like God who, as symbolized by the Ark of the Covenant, is also
a subsuming but imageless presence. We therefore return by a
strange route to our concern with the pure or imageless vision:
effortless or subconscious perception is here advanced over that
of the eye as a mediate sense. The constant of Rilke's mystical experiences is that the eyes are forgotten and the body itself made one
subsuming penetrable sense to accommodate the earth and to make
it invisible:

> He remembered the hour in that other southern garden [Ca-
> pri], when, both outside and within him, the cry of a bird was
> correspondingly present, did not, so to speak, break upon the
> barriers of his body, but gathered inner and outer together
> into one uninterrupted space, in which, mysteriously pro-
> tected, only one single spot of purest, deepest consciousness re-
> mained. That time he had shut his eyes, so as not to be confused
> in so generous an experience by the contour of his body, and
> the infinite passed into him so intimately from every side, that
> he could believe he felt the light reposing of the already ap-
> pearing stars within his breast.[14]

In summary, then, we can point out in Rilke, as in the case of
Wordsworth and Hopkins, two main modes of pure representation,
not strictly separate, but distinguishable. His desire for the pure
cry is for an expression that does not have its cause in the perplexed
eyes, and so the liturgy of gestures which he represents seems to
arise from the body alone. Yet the poet is also haunted by the contingency of sound, and would imagine a world "before the creation
of sound," or, more exactly, the temple of music built by Or-

pheus, in which sound is not perceived as sound ("Brüllen, Schrei, Geröhr") but as the sensation of listening, as pure audibility. On the other hand, Rilke affirms the invincible concreteness of things, submitting himself entirely to a fate and will unperceived through any mediate sense, residing in the body as such, and realized by the simple fact of being present in the same way that the earth, the stars, and nature in general are present, assenting like them to every experience, and assured by the same force that guides and assures them: "Gesang ist Dasein." The ultimate indestructible reality is for him the body of the earth itself or the fertile and physical will that empowers it.

Physical decay, therefore, is not a tragic thing; by means of it the human body feels or returns to a greater physical force: and Rilke's strong rendition of physical decay in *Malte Laurids Brigge* is made possible by the fact that he does not view the inevitable corruption of the flesh as a sign of evil or of human frailty, but, on the contrary, as a means of transcendence. Rilke remembers the sensation of childhood fever in which the body seems inhabited by a greater and more intense physical being, *Das Grosse:* "It was there, present like a huge, dead animal, that at one time, while still alive, had been my hand or my arm . . . And my blood went through me and through it as through one and the same body." [15] And in this way Novalis' intuition that sickness may become a means of transcendence is realized—as it is more than once in modern literature.

Valéry, like each of the poets here studied, passed through a crisis involving perception. He avows that his ideas were formed between the age of twenty-one and twenty-four,[16] and his future thought does indeed seem to be germinally present in the two works of this period, *Monsieur Teste* and the *Introduction à la méthode de Léonard de Vinci*. Both testify to the poet's refusal to accept the disorder perceived by the eye as the result of mere chance. Everything for him is equally chance before the event and law after it. This law, moreover, is discoverable to the eyes acting without aid from other senses or media of knowledge, except insofar as conditional on the eye. The fans which M. Teste and the author spot in a theater appear as independent agents, governed by their own law of motion: "A number of detached fans were living their own lives in the crowd that foamed up, dim and clear, to the level of the top lights." [17] (Even a casual vignette like this one, has for its submerged metaphor the sea, Valéry's major analogon for events governed by the laws of chance). The hypothetical Leonardo of the *Introduction* intuits space itself, divining "the wave a bird engenders in its flight, the curve on which the hurled stone glides, the surfaces which define gestures, extraordinary tearings, fluid arabesques, unformed rooms increate in a network that penetrates all things, to the grimacing course of an insect's trembling, the roll of a tree, wheels, the human smile, the tide." [18]

This technique of synopsis, in which events from the most un-related areas of experience are brought together, is a common tech-nique in Valéry, and clearly denotes his perceptional crisis, the loss of genre that occurs when all things are perceived equally present to the eye. For life, according to Valéry, is played out on a single stage, that of space, and dependent on at least a single constant: "Nothing can be born, die, or exist in any degree, or have time, place, form, or meaning, except on this stage which the fates have circumscribed, and . . . have opposed and subordinated to the condition of *being seen*." [19]

Valéry, then, seeks laws that speak to the eye, and to that alone. Modern abstract art may also be considered from this point of view, for it, like this poet, withholds from the canvas all ideas which can-not be reduced to sheer sight. Thus even the body's plastic nature, Valéry's unending delight, is neither by Valéry nor by modern art accepted as a simple visual idea. A surprising concordance is found between the development of Picasso and that of Valéry, each trying to deprive the mind of all concepts and associations not given di-rectly in sight. But what, exactly, does the poet learn from the eyes?

A first intuition bears on the affinity of the law of visual space to a law of the mind. "Law," as applied to the mind, is not used here in a metaphorical way, but in the strict sense of a determined and predictable course of behavior, differing from "law" as applied to the material world insofar as the course of behavior it indicates is not inevitable, but only so as a means to perfection. This first law is that *just as all things are reduced to visibility by space, so all things are returned to possibility by the mind.*[20]

Kant considered space as a form of sensibility preceding in the observer all the actual impressions through which he is affected by objects. But this type of space-perception, which Kant describes as a function of the Pure Reason, Valéry describes as a direct, not mediate, function of the eye, implicit in the eyes' perpetual absence-presence. There is a small, gem-like poem which may be quoted here. It is entitled "Intérieur":

> Une esclave aux longs yeux chargés de molles chaînes
> Change l'eau de mes fleurs, plonge aux glaces prochaines,
> Au lit mystérieux prodigue ses doigts purs;
> Elle met une femme au milieu de ces murs
> Qui, dans ma rêverie errant avec décence,
> Passe entre mes regards sans briser leur absence,
> Comme passe le verre au travers du soleil,
> Et de la raison pure épargne l'appareil.*

This moment of luminous clarity in which a thing, though fully seen, affects the eye no more than a glass passing across a beam of light—one is reminded of the many painters who include among the solid forms and fruits of a still life a decanter pure or filled with transparent wine—is another example of the reduction to visibility without image. The act is not complete, for it still needs the presence of the woman. Valéry describes a similar act more explicitly in *Mon Faust,* when Faust at the summit of his reflections demands the meaning of that which he sees, and answers:

> To see is enough, and to know that one is seeing. Therein lies a whole science. I see that pine tree. And what does that pine tree itself mean? Couldn't it just as well be an oak? I would

---

* "A slave with slant eyes weighed down by subtle chains
Changes my flowers' water, swims across nearby mirrors,
Lavishes her pure fingers on the mysterious bed;
She brings a woman into these walls
Who, wandering chastely through my dream,
Moves across my glances without breaking their absence,
Like a glass that moves across the sunlight,
And does away with the apparatus of pure reason."

see it just the same. And that roof of gleaming slate might just
as well be a mirror of calm water. I would see that. . . . To
see is then, as well, to see something else; to see what is possible as well as what is. And what then are these extraordinary
visions which the ascetics seek compared with this prodigy of
seeing whatever it may be? The soul is a beggarwoman.[21]

The image of the roof of gleaming slate that could also be a mirror
of calm water betrays the secret affinity of this meditation to "Le
Cimetière marin": "Ce toit tranquille." Each image here, where
things are seen but not as things, suggests the possibility of endless
substitution toward pure visibility.

Just as the eyes reduce all things to visibility, so the mind returns
them to possibility. The relation is suggested, but left unexplained.
On the height of the cemetery, looking down on the blinding sea,
situated between the immense vacuum of death and the unbeara-
ble vacuum of burning space, Valéry, deploring the impurity of
life to thought and of thought to itself, conceives a symbol denoting pure possibility, and transcending all his other images of the
monotonous circle or of the snake biting its own tail. It is a view of
the southern sun motionless at noon:

> Midi là-haut, Midi sans mouvement
> En soi se pense et convient à soi-même . . .
> Tête complète et parfait diadème,
> Je suis en toi le secret changement.*

And a few stanzas later, at the poem's climax, the poet confirms the
relation of the law of visual space with a law of the mind in his
apostrophe to Zeno which again evokes the still point between
potency and act, though this time with yet greater despair. For the
arrow of possibility, "that quivers, flies yet does not fly," is, like
the vastness of space, the nothingness of death, and the endlessness
of thought itself, too cruel for thought. "Il faut tenter de vivre."
The mind has overcome its temptation, but also perhaps its per-

---

* "Noon up there, motionless Noon, brooding on itself and self-sufficient
. . . Faultless head and perfect diadem, I am in you the thing that changes
secretly."

fection, in refusing to know itself unconditioned by all act, image, or external cause.

To this first law or means of attaining perfect knowledge, whereby the eye reduces all things to visibility while the mind returns them to possibility, the name of *retroduction* may be given. But there exists also a second law just as necessary to complete understanding. While often in contemporary philosophy given the name of *induction* and identified with a law concerning the association of ideas, it is recognized in earlier philosophy as a principle of spontaneous attribution, and has always been at the source of the religious experience whenever indistinguishable from the act of expression. "Il est manifeste, par une lumière qui est naturellement en nos âmes, que le néant n'a aucunes qualités ni propriétés qui lui appartiennent et qu'où nous en apercevons quelques-unes il se doit trouver nécéssairement une chose ou substance dont elles dependent" (Descartes, *Principes de la philosophie, 1, 2*). "While I live will I praise the Lord: I will sing praises unto my God while I have any being" (Psalms).

Induction, should the eye be the dominant organ of sense perception, is to rise from visual impressions to more than visual ideas. Yet we are not even sure about the immediate data of sense perception. What the eye in its purity gives, is not, as we have seen, the notion or detail of concreteness, but visibility inexplicably and at once interpreted by the mind as possibility. That which speaks to us, whatever it may be in itself, speaks to us first and most purely in terms of possibility.

But the soul is a beggarwoman, and what it begs is sensuous beauty, externality. It conceives such infinite envy of visible and tangible offspring as only poets can represent. Potency must pass into act. Act presupposes something acted upon, for act without motive, the pure act, like representation without image, the pure representation, is never more than desire or possibility. Yet a something acted for must itself repose on an idea of concreteness or externality. Whence comes this idea, that does not arise from either soul or eyes?

It may be said to derive from another sense, like the touch; but what we then mean by touch is not a property restricted to the hands or to the surface of the body, but something that, when it is in the hands, is already in the eyes.[22] "And that roof of gleaming slate might just as well be a mirror of calm water. I would see that. And as for the shape of those distant hills which haphazardly enclose the landscape, I feel in my hands the power to redesign their soft line according to my own taste. . . . To see is then, as well, to see something else." [23]

How far does Valéry go toward explaining the idea of externality? His interpretation stops far short of completeness. But what induction does not stop short? We do Valéry no injustice in formulating his thought as follows: *Whatever has passed into act is by this very fact in a different order, governed by a different law, than when still virtual;* so that, while the physical world, and especially the human body, is to the eyes possibility, in the eyes as in itself it is act. Therefore it is unknown and of a nature perhaps utterly different from the intimations it gives as possibility, exciting the mind with the notion of concreteness.

> Une Intelligence adultère
> Exerce un corps qu'elle a compris.* ("La Pythie")

Complete induction, or an adequate idea of externality, may never, therefore, be gained unless there are moments in which possibility and act, mind and body, the mechanical and the organic, are apprized as being in a state of undifferentiation. Are there such moments? "O moment, diamant du Temps!" Valéry describes two types of experience in which he finds revealed "that psychical postulate of continuity which resembles in our consciousness the principle of inertia in mechanics" [24] sought already at the time of the Leonardo essay. The first of these is the moment of *meditation,* the second that of *construction.* In meditation, as when the poet looks on the Mediterranean Sea from the graveyard at Sète, time shimmers and thought is a dream. "The soul enjoys its light pure of things. Its silence is the totality of its speech, and its repose composed of the sum of its powers. It knows itself equally far from all names and all forms. No shape has yet altered or constrained it. The least judgment would stain its perfection." [25] Construction,

---

* "An adulterous Intelligence exercises a body *it* has understood."

on the other hand, of which the supreme example is architecture, enables the mind to go the full gamut of its ingenuity, transforming even the human body into an equation, so that the radical undifferentiation of body and mind, act and possibility, the organic and the mechanical, is shown forth. "O sweet metamorphosis! This delicate temple, no one knows it, is the mathematical image of a girl of Corinth, whom I happily loved." [26]

The question remains, finally, how Valéry can represent with the limited symbols of poetry a principle of continuity identical with total consciousness in which, as in complete induction, the vain or tumultuous hydra biting its own tail is transformed into Apollo's perfect diadem. The mind that is "naked, stripped, and reduced to the supreme poverty of potency without aim; victim, masterpiece . . . without instincts, almost without an image" [27] must find a construction to express not the act which it does not possess, but the virtuality of this act. Hence Valéry uses poetic symbols to represent consciousness as an infinitely variable series of virtual acts, "entre le vide et l'événement pur." The poet on the one hand employs the technique of modulation to obtain a "charme continu" expressing the undisturbed continuity of a consciousness that remains attached to no single thing. It knows itself by preference as "ténèbres éveillées," and in this resembles music, the most perfect of the virtual acts of thought, and composed of nothing but recurrence. And on the other hand, Valéry employs the technique of prolepsis or anticipation, representing the mind's unattainable desire for a consonant image on which its power could rest, and showing consciousness as a discontinuous sequence of virtual acts, each with the symmetry and luminosity of the single act of sight most perfect in painting.

Valéry's concern with continuity and induction resumes both the major problem of art and a fundamental problem of post-Cartesian thought. Before Descartes, pure representation, at least in the Christian tradition, had its source in the soul's representation of God, one always virtual, but never complete except in mystical union, and then ineffable. Man being in the fallen state, his soul must go on a pilgrimage, and Medieval poetry and thought seek the analogue of this pilgrimage very frequently in the Song of Songs but, supremely, in Christ. The soul cannot attain God through an inspection of the things of this world, for these are also, or even more bitterly, in the fallen state. If the soul is affected by the things of this world it is impure: the only purity for man lies in the imitation of Christ, as the only hope for his soul lies in the mediation of Christ. Neither man nor his soul, therefore, can be preserved unless his life and his faculties seek the mediation of Christ, and the Church, Christ's temporal incarnation and visible continuance. But Descartes breaks away from the mediated vision, and supports his break by appending the continuity of life, creation, and thought directly to God.[28] After Descartes, the pure vision is of necessity mystical and profane, seeking an unmediated understanding of the world. The modern poet labors under the sign of sacred profanity. Orthodox and unorthodox suffer this in like measure. "The way up and the way down, one and the same" is the ancient epigram with which Eliot prefaces a major work. "There is no such duality," writes Claudel, as a religious and a profane Universe, there is but a single Revelation transcribed in a measureless, continuous and reciprocally translatable language." The life of Christ is no longer the apparent background and principle to every legitimate association of ideas. Can a new principle be found?

Valéry's poem "La Dormeuse" has the strength to resume the essential meditations of post-Cartesian thought: this in itself might serve to prove the continuity of human consciousness both in the instant and in time. The poet looks at a sleeping girl, and in this moment of sleep, when the soul is least present to the observed body, asks an inevitable question: what is it that preserves this body both in itself and to the sense? Or, what makes the act of knowledge possible?

There must be something which sustains thought, and something which sustains the object to thought. The existence of this something would not in itself explain knowledge unless that which sustains in the object to thought is identical to that which sustains thought itself. Only in the light of such a hypothesis can we understand all those dicta that relate to the possibility of intuition, for example Aristotle's statement in the *Metaphysics:* "Actual knowledge is always at one with its object." This being true, we would find in every recorded experience of perfect knowledge a question implicit on the identity of knower with known and on the subject of this identity.

The primary experience of the poet who beholds La Dormeuse is the notion of repose. It seems as if this notion were the objective result of the woman's actual sleep; thus the poem begins with the question of the nature of this sleep so total that it is transferred by a kind of spontaneous induction from the object to the mind. Two distinct ideas enter into the notion: first that something so vital, so breathing, so instinct with movement as this girl can appear as if in absolute repose; then that something in absolute repose can affect an observer.

Neither the soul nor the composite of soul and body is adduced in explanation of the invincible calm and its effect, though both suggest themselves. The hypothesis of soul is rejected, perhaps because *âme* has received a sentimental connotation, perhaps because it is evident that what is subdued by sleep is the soul, perhaps because the poet knew too well Aristotle's distinction between soul and mind, the former being defined as the actuality and principle of movement in its particular body. The hypothesis of the composite is rejected because this calm is "more powerful than a tear," that is to say, is more at rest, and of more power to affect, than some thing which moves the observer only insofar as it is interpreted as evidence of the composite, i.e. of the soul's action on the body.

If neither the separate soul nor the composite of soul with body sufficiently explains the notion of repose given by La Dormeuse to the poet, only one supposition remains, that the body itself has induced such surpassing calm. But only in sleep or under the species of sleep is the human body perceivable as a separate entity. It is always the phenomenon of sleep which gives rise to the idea of the body as such. So out of the sleep of Adam rose the body of Eve. And beholding this girl asleep it appears a miracle, almost as great as that of original creation, that where the wakeful consciousness is absent the body should survive, and with such purity of evidence.

It is this thought of the body surviving despite the soul's absence which leads to a first intuition of the nature of perfect knowledge. For though physical sleep has made possible the perception of the body as a separate entity, it does not explain why the body so perceived should give rise to its description in terms of an unmoved mover. The repose attributed by the poet to the body of La Dormeuse is not a privation, produced by the absence of the moving soul, but a principal and positive quality. It is in fact the *vis inertiae* isolated as a primary law of nature by Descartes, Galileo, and Newton. The law and its fruitful applications are consequent on a full recognition that the body has a subsistence quite apart from the presence of a "soul."

This recognition, however, does not characterize perfect, so much as mathematical, knowledge. The poet in the presence of La Dormeuse does more than mark the conservation of her body, soul being absent or, at most, potential. His amazement is directed to the fact that this pure body is perceptible, and as if by action of its very repose. It is evident that the fact of conservation does not in itself explain the fact of perception. Yet the poet's last verse—"ta forme veille et mes yeux sont ouverts"—clearly suggests that the same force of repose which has conserved the object for perception must be equally present in the perceiving subject for an act of knowledge to take place.

The intuition, then, that an identical power sustains knower and known appears to be a necessary component of any true act of knowledge. Yet perception is not explained. If the faculty of knowing is always at rest, and if what is to be known, namely the body under the species of sleep, is always at rest, then mind and body are distinct and separately preserved substances and perception either an illusion or the result of a curious "action at a distance." Now this, evidently, constitutes the dilemma of Descartes.

Yet the fact of sense perception never becomes a major cause of perplexity to Descartes because it is envisaged as the purely mechanical contact of two or more bodies. Descartes rediscovers and affirms Aristotle's axiom that "nothing is felt except by contact." [29] The return to an account of perception in terms of direct contact would have been of the greatest importance in bridging the gap between sense experience and perfect knowledge if it had not been described as a purely mechanical process. For the Schoolmen had postulated intelligible or intentional species as mediate between knower and known, and this, though not without psychological validity, had only served to strengthen the case against the natural or unfallen powers of the human intellect. Yet Descartes' conviction of the primarily mechanical nature of physical event is so strong that even the sensuous manifold, light, color, sound, is thought(as still in modern science) to be occasioned by a contact of particles: that we interpret a certain kind of contact as light, another as sound, and so forth is considered an effect neither of the body nor of the soul but of their strict union. But concerning the character of this union Descartes is most reticent. He will say merely that our senses inform us not of the nature of things but only in what way they are harmful or beneficial.[30] Such a view, however, can explain only why we think this thing desirable and that repulsive: it does not explain why the senses interpret certain impulses (*attouchments*) as light, others as sound. The problem is not confronted till Berkeley's *New Theory of Vision;* even there the immediate interpretation of marks of sight in terms of touch is called arbitrary and, as in Descartes, referred to Providence. A definite advance has however occurred insofar as it is recognized that the interpretative power of the senses is in no way deducible from a description of sense experience in terms of mechanical contact. Though Berkeley falls back on Providence for the final cause, and on the principle of the association of ideas for the efficient cause, the problem whether the immediate interpretation given by the senses to physical event is more than arbitrary remains untouched.

Thus formal philosophy is, after Descartes, forced to a total consideration of the fact and necessity of perception. Not that the medieval philosopher was indifferent to it. The inevitability of sense experience is perhaps the dominant tragic factor in the confession of St. Augustine. He intimately knows the nisus with which images, often simple and arbitrary, can take hold of the mind. St. Thomas emphasizes that the soul in order to understand must revert to phantasms. But whereas these philosophers evidently view the necessity of sense perception as a sign that an originally divine intellect is now united to a corruptible body, modern philosophy tends to the very opposite conviction. So much so that Berkeley can think of equating the *esse* of things with their *percipi*.

The poet who beholds the sleeper is amazed at the fact of perception. For what has moved the sense, and continues to move it, if both the faculty of knowing and the possible object are in absolute repose? It cannot be the separate soul, it cannot be the composite of soul with body, it cannot be the separate body. The poet gives this mover the name of "form"; it charms his eyes into their unceasing vigil. But this form, whether the origin or the product of perception, does not correspond to the term in Aristotle and the Thomistic philosophers. There the soul is represented as the form and actuality of the body; but here it is the body which appears as the form and actuality of the soul! Yet not the body under the species of sleep. *The subject of the poet's experience is the body known under the species of wakefulness.* Valéry is pursued by the idea that he might come to "see" his own body. He has accepted with rare consistency that all knowledge is of one's body: between person and person there is simply visibility. If one's own body, the locus of perception, should become the subject of perception, the virtual act of consciousness would become the perfect act of knowledge, mind and body knowing each other's function. This constitutes the desire of Narcissus in search of his body—"Ephémère immortelle si claire devant mes yeux!" Such desire, however, is not satisfied by means of the sleeper or any other thing. Narcissus can see himself only in that very clear water of unspecified composition which holds the eternal promise of self-prehension. And is not the elusive fountain for Narcissus exactly what God is for Malebranche, that medium, sought by post-Cartesian thinkers, in which a direct intuition of the living body could be realized?

Aristotle wrote: "Both sleeping and waking presuppose the existence of soul, and of these waking corresponds to actual knowing, sleeping to knowledge possessed but not employed." [31] To understand the body under the species of wakefulness is to know it in the act of knowing. Mathematical knowledge has for its object the sleeping body, which remains uniform and incapable of using or exhibiting the knowledge it possesses. Aesthetic and perfect knowledge have for their object the wakeful body, namely the body in the exercise of a continuous primary act of knowledge, that of perception. In perception knowledge is truly act.

It is the recorded experience of all our poets that there exists an identity between perception and creativity.[32] The immediate interpretation given by the senses to physical event can only be understood by analogy to the act of original creation. Descartes failed to achieve this understanding. "Conservation and creation differ only according to different modes of thought, and not actually." [33] Perception therefore remains an unexplained fact. Yet even Descartes harbored the thought that there is an identity between the act of perception and that of divine creation. But unlike modern philosophers and poets he still retained the notion of *creation by separate species* and hence believed this identity to be revealed only in that act which enabled the mind to formulate clear and distinct ideas. Therefore his statement that conservation and creation do not differ. But they do differ: whereas conservation does not imply perception, creation does. "And God said: 'Let there be light.' And there was light. And God saw the light, that it was good." Valéry's sleeping woman the form of whose body forces the eyes to self-knowledge, Rilke's water-carrier possessed of a secret repose which will suddenly bear fruit, Hopkins' hidden heart which stirs for the equilibrium of the windhover until overtaken by a despairing desire to render through body or word the roll and rise and carol of creation whereby all things imitate their creator even to self-destruction, Wordsworth's repose under the dark sycamore from which there issues a creation accomplished by the blended might of mind and Nature—all is part of a new argument from perceptibility.

Hence the desire for a perception pure of all percepts need not in the modern poet involve a denial of the necessity of sense experience or of the reality of sense objects. It is unmistakably perception desired and experienced as the plenary manifestation of a creative presence. Every withdrawal to the heart of sound and sight, every inversion of the sense, every evocation of ideal blindness, every reduction to a state of spiritual poverty, every imagination of death, every intuition of the bare fact of being alive repeats the same human testimony that we possess now or did possess or do potentially possess an image of the miracle of creation. And though this testimony is, in modern writings, merely human, deprived by will or necessity of sacred example, yet the procession is clear and loud and admissible into evidence. Nor is the record complete. We have at our disposal a body of lost evidence which will gradually appear as vast to us as the lost heritage of classical antiquity to the artists of the Renaissance. Descartes scruples to say that, looking out of a window, he *sees* certain men passing in the street, for what is actually perceived are hats and coats which could be covering artificial machines moving by clockwork: he does not therefore see men but *judges* they are men, having understood by the exclusive power of judgment residing in his soul what he thought to see with his eyes. But William Blake has no doubt concerning his eyes which see at sunrise a host of angels sanctifying God in the words of the prophet Isaiah. "I question not my Corporeal or Vegetative Eye any more than I would Question a Window concerning a Sight. I look thro' it and not with it." Perhaps we have only begun to understand the creative power of the senses, the extent to which they are enabled to give immediate, real interpretions.

Each of the poets here studied has tried to conceive a pure representation distinguished from that of Jewish or medieval Christian thought in that its motive and terminal object is identified not with the God of the Testaments, but with Nature, the body, or human consciousness. Though Valéry is nearest to one for whom the soul has no windows, even Valéry seeks to know by knowing his body. But it were foolish to say, what has so often been said, that the Jewish tradition by its emphasis on the incorporeality of God, and the Christian by its emphasis on the creatureliness of man, did no justice to sense perception as a way to joy or as a way to wisdom. Who can possibly say this who has read and understood "The heavens declare the glory of God"? But how could any poet who read it, and the literature from which it is taken, and made it into a daily and sacred part of his mind, conceive or praise in any other way? It is still strong enough.

The difference between the poet in the Judeo-Christian tradition and the modern poet does not lie in the brain or in the bodily eye, but in the postulate and the efficiency of a sacred text. The pursuit of Wordsworth, Hopkins, Rilke, and Valéry is to the same end as that of a Christian mystic like Meister Eckhart: pure representation, a vision unconditioned by the particularity of experience, a will removed from wilfulness and the search for relation, knowledge dissociated from self-ends, the mind freed from its obsession with utility—*das unerkennende Erkennen*. But whereas the older poet, even when as extreme as Meister Eckhart, knew and acknowledged mediation, the modern either does not acknowledge or does not know a mediator for his orphic journey. He passes through experience by means of the unmediated vision. Nature, the body, and human consciousness—that is the only text.

THE NEW PERSEUS

Ich habe kein Dach über mir, und es regnet mir in die Augen. MALTE LAURIDS BRIGGE

Iᴛ ɪs sᴀɪᴅ that Perseus, when he went to slay the Medusa, was given by Athene a resplendent mirror to escape the monster's direct glance, which would have turned him into stone. Perseus, accordingly, looked in the mirror, cut off the Gorgon's head, and from her blood there sprang the winged horse Pegasus which with one stamp of its foot produced Mount Helicon's sweet fountain, dear to the Muses. But the new Perseus is a different kind of hero. He disdains or has lost Athene's mirror, and goes against the monster with naked eye. Some say that, in consequence, he is petrified; others, that he succeeds but the fountain of Pegasus is a sweet-bitter brew.

As poets, Wordsworth, Hopkins, Rilke, and Valéry are at one in their quest for a pure representation. But as *modern* poets they are related by their effort to gain pure representation through the direct sensuous intuition of reality. Each has a greater or lesser trust in the unmediated vision; or it may simply be that Athene's mirror is irreparably broken. The eye and the senses are made to supply not merely the ornaments but the very plot of truth. The body itself becomes, in its contact with the physical world, the source and often the end of cognition. Not only the four poets here considered, but the majority of poets, beginning with the romantics, refuse any but human and sensory intermediaries to knowledge, seek the hellenic innocence of the senses, and create like Novalis a new communion hymn around an old question:

> Wer hat des irdischen Leibes
> Hohen Sinn erraten? *

* "Who has divined the high meaning of the earthly body?"

Their doubting of the mediated vision, moreover, suggests that though they are, like Novalis, often professed and active believers, these poets no longer understand a concept of divine creation operative in medieval Christian thought and reaching the zenith of its artistic expression in the period between Dante and Milton. The essential contribution of Judeo-Christian to Greek philosophy is considered to be a view of the world as directly created by God.[1] One of the finest passages in the *Confessions* tells how St. Augustine, seeking God by reflecting on the beauty of the earth, finds that all things on earth can give him only one answer: we are not He, yet He made us.

> I asked the earth, and it answered me, "I am not He"; and whatsoever are in it confessed the same. I asked the sea and the deeps, and the living creeping things, and they answered, "We are not thy God, seek above us." . . . And I replied unto all the things which encompass the doors of my flesh; "Ye have told me of my God, that ye are not He; tell me something of Him." And they cried out with a loud voice, "He made us." (Chapter 10)

But the modern poet has suffered a distinct loss in the power to represent the world as a created thing. Milton is perhaps the last who, with the strength of despair, can render the act of divine creation in its full imaginative splendor. Two ideas are basic to the medieval view of divine creation, and both are textually evident in the first chapter of Genesis: that of the world as a sequence of perfect creations, and that of man as the absolute creation. The first, of the world as an instantaneous creation, is given with glorious detail of sound and thought in the seventh book of *Paradise Lost*. When the sixth day comes, God speaks:

> The Earth obey'd, and straight
> Op'ning her fertile Womb teem'd at a Birth
> Innumerous living Creatures, perfet forms,
> Limb'd and full grown: out of the ground up rose
> As from his Lair the wild Beast where he wons
> In Forest wild, in Thicket, Brake, or Den;
> Among the Trees in Pairs they rose, they walked: (VII, 453 ff.)

The delight in pre-existent perfect forms, of nature or art, reached a last height in Milton, is sustained in the principles of the eighteenth century, but falls amid the general decay and indistinction of genres evident in the theory and practice of the romantic artists, a decay almost complete at the present time, when no philosophy—religious, historical or aesthetic—can restore a feeling for the *genre tranché*.

The second concept, of man as the absolute creation, that is, formed in the image of God, crown and master of created things, having nothing in common with these except the fact of createdness, and createdness out of dust, is equally emphasized in Milton, even more clearly than in the biblical accounts, and with prevenient pathos:

> Let us make now Man in our image, Man
> In our similitude, and let them rule
> Over the Fish and Fowl of Sea and Air,
> Beast of the Field, and over all the Earth,
> And every creeping thing that creeps the ground.
> This said, he form'd thee, *Adam,* thee O Man
> Dust of the ground, and in thy nostrils breath'd
> The breath of Life; and his own Image hee
> Created thee . . .   (VII, 519 ff.)

Yet modern poets are haunted by the indifference of man and nature; the dust of the earth from which God formed the rest of creation by act of word, and the breath which he breathed into man by special act, are no longer separate but interpenetrating elements, and acts distinguished not in kind but in continuous time. Thus Wordsworth is strongly influenced by his feeling for continued revelation, and even the orthodox poet envies "the horror and the havoc and the glory" which all creation with the seeming exception of man possesses; [2] while Rilke almost goes so far as to reproach Christ for the resurrection of Lazarus, considering this a disturbance of natural process.[3] It is clear that a view of creation as immanent and continual has replaced the view of created things as instantaneously created, and of man as the absolute creation.[4]

The loss of the first concept, of instantaneous and perfect creation, brings to modern poetry its first major difficulty. The only
thing that will spring up fully-formed to the unmediated vision is
accidence or fortuitousness. Blake said that he could stare at the
knot in a piece of wood until almost mad. We remember the
"smooth spoon" of Hopkins. Nerval never forgets a young English
girl seen biting into a lemon; he must accommodate her in his
myth-haunted consciousness. In Wordsworth the mystic moment is
for the most part brought on by a commonplace event ("It was in
truth an ordinary sight"). Some of the poets even construct theories
on accidence. Rilke is the extreme case. He refuses to ignore any
event, however slight; a dog, a bowl of roses, the stray sound of a
violin—"Das alles war Auftrag." His concept of "thing" is in response to such attempt, for the "thing" is a fragmentary event, without determined contour, and simply that. The "thing" resembles
to a curious degree Hopkins' view of inscape and instress. With
Hopkins the act of attention or caught attention receives value
per se: "All the world is full of inscape and chance left free to act
falls into an order as well as a purpose: looking out of my window
I caught it in the random clods and broken heaps of snow made by
the cast of a broom." [5] Valéry seems at first an exception. He is in
direct reaction to the systematic accidentalism of Hugo and the
mystical accidentalism of Nerval. Writing in 1920, Valéry realized
that the symbolist movement provided only a short interlude of
pure poetry. His successors "have again opened on the accidents of
being the eyes we had closed in order to make ourselves more akin
to its substance." [6] One need only compare the fine use of accident
and accidence in Proust to the gross effects of chance in Balzac to
perceive the advance in consciousness which has occurred, and
which in modern psychology and increasingly in modern criticism
is called (after Taine) the technique of significant detail. One could
go on fairly endlessly, pointing out that the problem of accidence
arises at the same time strongly in painting—the subordination of
the detail to the whole is the main aesthetic preoccupation of
Delacroix's *Journals,* and Baudelaire in an early "Salon" compares
Delacroix and Hugo to the detriment of the latter:

Too materialist, too attentive to the surfaces of nature, M. Victor Hugo has become a painterly poet; Delacroix, always respectful of his ideal, is often without knowing it a poetic painter.[7]

But here we touch on the theories of local color and word-painting, which express the unmediated eye's attempt to grasp a physical reality by purely sensory means, theories which are variously denounced in the course of the century.[8] We should not forget to add that Valéry is only a seeming exception: he would use and reproduce by technical means the continual but rarely grasped parthenogenesis in consciousness of rhythm and word. Valéry is also responsible for a most perfect derationalization of sight: after him, the surrealists will free all the senses, and have their finest poet in Eluard whose main, inexhaustible theme is "la vie immédiate." Are not all these poets, in the words of Eliot, "distracted from distraction by distraction"? Modern poetry would evolve a style dealing with "immediate" rather than with "general" nature.

The loss of the second concept, of man as absolute creation, brings a second major concern. The fear (sometimes the desire) arises that the physical world has a fatal influence on human life—"Et la matière, hélas, devint fatalité." [9] * This concept of a material or environmental fatality has been popularized to such an extent by modern sociological theories that one does not always realize its relatively recent importance. Its authority lies, of course, in social, economic, and scientific developments. The concept presupposes a secret undifferentiation or even identity of organic and inorganic life, as is already set forth in Diderot's *Rêve d'Alembert* (1761) and Schelling's *Von der Weltseele* ("a hypothesis of the higher physics"). In Schelling's preface of 1806 one may find formulated in swift and imaginative manner themes that are obsessive and even tragic in poets like Novalis, Poe, Nerval, Baudelaire, and Hugo, themes that reach Rilke. These poets are all in one way or another haunted by the idea of reification.

But a third, perhaps most important, consequence, implicit in the loss of the Bible account of divine creation, is the modern

* "And matter, alas, became fatality."

poet's concern with the *inherent* arbitrariness of symbols. Though it was Adam who named every living creature, he did so at the behest and under the aegis of God (Genesis 2:19-20). Though words have a merely arbitrary or conventional relation to their referents, they are assured of a sacred origin. As words they are arbitrary, but as symbols divine; and the same holds for any other system of reference including that of the orders of creation, inasmuch as marked by the mark of God. As things they are what they are, but as symbols they are divine. The bread and wine on the tongue is, like the word, only bread and wine, and yet, as Claudel says, "Chair de Dieu sur ma langue, consacre mon cœur et mon principe."

However, those poets who have forsaken the literary and the spiritual authority of a sacred text not only feel the unavoidable inadequacy that dogs conventional ways of expression (a stimulus in all times for artistic creation), but feel this inadequacy as inherent in all the works of man, as his one constant dilemma, his pain from childhood on, his existential anguish. For nothing now declares God of itself, but all is the work of man, including the testaments; and all is profane as it is sacred, and cannot be more than his conceptions which remain conceptions. Symbols are only such by pretense, and the entirety of life is caught up in this pretense. Everything is *in potentia* equally sign and equally symbol.

In the romantic poets the leveling of symbols or the fusion of *genres* still has a distinct social and religious aim. Wordsworth's *Peter Bell* and *The White Doe of Rylstone* were written with the avowed attempt of showing the "humblest departments of daily life" as suitable for both poetic and religious inspiration. The same motive works in *The Prelude,* which sacrifices the high argument of Milton for the personal history of a simple agrarian life. In France we have the somewhat later example of Lamartine's *Jocelyn,* itself in the line of Rousseau, and of course Victor Hugo acting as Christian Democrat in his famous preface to *Cromwell.* Germany has for its *cause célèbre,* besides Shakespeare, Goethe's *Wilhelm Meister,* which Novalis at first praises for its domestication of the marvelous, then condemns as a *Candide* against the poetic spirit. But Friedrich Schlegel already moves away from the

consciousness of the social and religious cause when he describes
the mingling of trivia and magnalia in *Wilhelm Meister* as an instance of romantic irony; [10] for romantic irony, as the expression
of the artist's entire freedom vis-a-vis the materials of experience,
already denotes a sense for the inherent inadequacy of all symbols
as such, and leads to the now conventional stage tricks of Pirandello
as well as to the present, almost universal, acceptance of the element
of playfulness in art.

By the time of Hopkins, the dilemma is acute even in the orthodox
religious artist. Though Hopkins may have been aware in "The
Windhover" of the significance of the falcon as a type of Christ, he
suspends this knowledge, choosing indeed a falcon, but a local one.
His poem testifies to the fact that the *res creatae* are no longer
known as an object of contemplation leading the observer by degrees to God, but as one compelling him to God through the intuition of an inconceivable physical force felt present equally in
every particular thing. Just as Van Gogh's conception of the starry
night renders not so much this night with its indubitable peace
as the despair of the artist in finding a visual form adequate to the
mind's simultaneous perception of an immense calm and an equally
immense power, so "The Windhover" expresses by its asyndetic
style and sprung rhythm not only the instress of the falcon, but also
the artist's creative will to represent the divine as a physical force.

But not till Rilke and Valéry is the essential indifference of subject matter realized in full. No event seems now to have a greater
intrinsic claim on the artist than any other. The subject of a poem,
said Valéry, is as foreign to it and as important as his name is to a
man. Rilke accepts and is able to poetize the most varied subjects,
substantiating what phenomenology calls the original right of all
data.[11] It is clear that there are no more "poetic" objects. If Valéry's
poetry centers on a minimum of symbols, the sea, the air, the sun,
a tree, this is not an aesthete's prejudice but an arbitrary limitation
which confers on them the power of abstract variables which re-
cover individual meaning only if the *entire* system of signs wherein
they participate is understood. The poetry of Mallarmé likewise
forces the reader to the understanding of an entire system, which
acts almost like a separate language, for what is denoted by the

words is not, as Mallarmé has declared, the conventional thing itself, but the *effect* of a thing, and ideally, of its sign, i.e., their immediate impact on the cleared consciousness.

What, therefore, started in romanticism as a religious and a social concern (is continued in realism as the humanitarian and positivist belief that "whatever is worthy to exist is also worthy to be known") [12] reaches Hopkins as a problem in expression, and appears in Rilke and Valéry almost free from its religious, social, positivist, and expressionist foundations as a frank acceptance of the inherently arbitrary character of human symbols. *In the beginning was the fable.*[13]

There are two major paths taken by the poets in their struggle against the arbitrariness of symbols. The first is to accept the arbitrary basis of language and to make it both specific and total as in music. Poetry is to be purified of all effects not proper to it, that is to say, of all effects also found in other sign systems. One such effect is the utilitarian, another the emotional, a third could be the pictorial. What is left? First of all, absolute internal consistency, as in pure mathematics. That is why Valéry and Mallarmé cannot be understood except in their totality, but are then understood totally in every line. Second, effects which, though not as yet totally known, may be related to the imminent (rather than immanent) formations of consciousness.

This also has a bearing on another, often parallel, path chosen by the poets to overcome arbitrariness, one which is an exploration of the inner motion and incipient meanings of human speech as such: the discovery of the *voice* of the spoken word. Only in this way can poetry rival the example of painting and the plastic arts to which it is so strongly attracted. Instead of giving conventional names to things, it would, like the painter, take them away and render instead the immediate "figure" of the senses, which in this case especially is that of speech as pure voice. "Wird euch langsam namenlos im Munde?" [14] The poetry of Rilke and Valéry are living instances of anominization; Hopkins also desires the "inscape" of speech. But what both methods—the essentializing of the word's arbitrariness and the discovery of the spoken word's voice—have in common, is the attempt to find and to represent things *immedi-*

ately significant, *aesthetic* things, signs of the creative nature of perception.

The modern poet has committed himself to the task of understanding experience in its immediacy. He has neglected the armature of the priest—the precautionary wisdom of tradition—and often, the inculcated respect for literary models. But therefore he only, and the more strongly, knows the need of mediation. The quest of the new Perseus becomes a quest for tokens of mediation, or "immediation," panentheistic symbols. The mirror must be restored. But the mirror remains Athene's gift, or that of God, in any case a supernatural gift. Does the modern poet's unarmed vision find its symbols of mediation?

In Wordsworth some are provided by the poet's sensitivity to atmospheric media, mists rolling down valleys on November days, the organic wreaths which nourished him in his youth, mountain mists, glittering light, a trembling lake, or even smoke rising from the woods of the Wye. But there is one special phenomenon, very clear already in the *Descriptive Sketches,* that of dilation. We shall give only its most famous instance, occurring in the first book of *The Prelude* during the young boy's stolen trip in an elfin pinnace:

> lustily
> I dipped my oars into the silent lake,
> And, as I rose upon the stroke, my boat
> Went heaving through the water like a swan;
> When, from behind that craggy steep till then
> The horizon's bound, a huge peak, black and huge,
> As if with voluntary power instinct,
> Upreared its head. I struck and struck again,
> And growing still in stature the grim shape
> Towered up between me and the stars, and still,
> For so it seemed, with purpose of its own
> And measured motion like a living thing,
> Strode after me.   (I, 373 ff.)

Wordsworth is not writing fiction; this is a correctly observed optical phenomenon which the sensitive eye may experience at twilight or near-dark if it keep steady on one point. But for Wordsworth dilation was a primary experience and is interpreted as a sign of Nature's mediating presence.

Not only atmospheric media, but also organic and material media may provide these symbols. Luminosity of any kind, but especially that which seems to have its source in earth or sea attracts the poet. When Wordsworth describes the daffodils "flashing" upon the inward eye, it may be more than a metaphoric expression. He tells us also that he felt in his childhood days "Gleams like the flashing of a shield." Students of eidetic psychology [15] have shown that Wordsworth had an immense power for visual retention; and one must take him literally when he writes of moments such as these:

> oh, then, the calm
> And dead still water lay upon my mind
> Even with a weight of pleasure, and the sky,
> Never before so beautiful, sank down
> Into my heart, and held me like a dream!
>
> (*The Prelude*, II, 170 ff.)

From these come Wordsworth's views on the forming of the imagination through the direct agency of Nature; and it seems likely that the eyes do have the ability to retain and emit certain types of luminosity. The experience of the drowned mind helps to explain how Wordsworth came to his apocalyptic vision of a drowned world, symbol for the immanence of a sustaining spirit.

Similar experiences of dilation and of terrestrial luminosity are encountered in other poets who are in search of a mediator, and especially in a poet we have not treated, Nerval. The myth of the lost sun is central to his work. At one point he writes that one never sees the sun in dreams, although one may have a perception of an even greater clarity coming from self-luminous bodies. He then gives the following description of a dream:

> The lady I followed, moving her lively body forward with a motion that caused the folds of her dress in changing taffeta to glitter, graciously placed her bare arm around a long stem of hollyhock, then started to grow under a clear ray of light in such a manner that the garden slowly took her form, trees

and flowerbeds becoming the roses and ornaments of her garment; while her figure and her arms printed their contours
on the sky's purple clouds. Thus she passed from my sight in
a process of transfiguration, for she seemed to disappear into
her own greatness. "Oh! do not leave me! I cried . . . for
Nature dies with you!" [16]

Both dilation and special luminosity are present; there is even the
measured motion which is characteristic of experiences of dilation,
and Aurelia transformed into the earth would provide the necessary mediation; but here the theme of nature's ambivalence in-
trudes, for Nerval seeks a human mediator, a new Beatrice, and
fears that Aurelia's death and transfiguration, here foreshadowed
and later verified, will leave him once again with the impersonal
God of Lucretius "impuissant et perdu dans son immensité."
Hugo's "Le Satyre" will also present a dilated God; while Rilke in
his *Sonnets to Orpheus* (I, XXVI) will give a version of the "scattered" God. These instances likewise express the very same desire
for a mediating figure of panentheistic character.

The "ether" theory worked strongly on the poetic imaginations of
the romantic period. Both Herder and Schelling have remarkable
panegyrics on the atmosphere. For Herder it is the "Sensorium of
the omnicreative God." [17] Schelling regards it as the medium ensuring the intercommunication of all the forces of Nature, and sees in
this concept of the creative ether his great chance to join Greek philosophy with modern nature philosophy ("Naturphilosophie"). [18]
The very same linking is made, and most beautifully, by his school-
friend Hölderlin—"Vater Aether!" Even Hopkins still professes
an interest; indeed, he once intended to write a treatise concerning
air. The blueness of the air, with its intense color and power of
shielding earth from the sun, becomes for him a principle of mercy
and a sign of Mary:

> Whereas did air not make
> This bath of blue and slake
> His fire, the sun would shake,
> A blear and blinding ball
> With blackness bound and all

> The thick stars round him roll
> Flashing like flecks of coal,
> Quartz-fret, or sparks of salt,
> In grimy vasty vault.
> Through her we may see him
> Made sweeter not made dim.[19]

But Hopkins' final and main torment was that he felt his body literally that of Christ or in Christ, that he could not distinguish his "sweating self" from the physical force in him which he took to be divine and which at moments impelled him to self-destructive action shadowed in the world of nature. The body itself, the "God-made-flesh," [20] becomes an ambivalent symbol of divine mediation.

In Rilke there is also found an impulse to a self-consuming act, represented in images of explosive dilation—"das Aufgehen." This opening up signifies a revelation of Nature that returns to Nature. The fate of the hero in the sixth Duino Elegy is characterized as "Sein Aufgang ist Dasein"—he knows no existence that is not at the same time revelatory self-sacrifice. The poet of the sonnets to Orpheus would become an echoing glass self-shattered. In *Malte Laurids Brigge* the image of explosive dilation is especially obsessive: "Das Lachen quoll aus ihren Munden wie Eiter aus offenen Stellen." * Yet these also are turned into symbols of mediation. The echo of the torn and scattered Orpheus dwells in Nature to mediate Nature:

> O du verlorener Gott! Du unendliche Spur!
> Nur weil dich reissend zuletzt die Feindschaft verteilte,
> Sind wir die Hörenden jetzt und ein Mund der Natur.†

In a letter of 1914 Rilke interprets the smile of the Egyptian statues at Karnak to signify "the denudedness of a secret, so thoroughly secret at each point and place, that there is no need to hide it." This open secret is the fertility principle of Nature: "everything phallic is perhaps only . . . an interpretation of the Human

---

* "Laughter ran from their mouths like pus from open wounds."

† "O lost God! You infinite trace! Only because enmity finally tore and scattered you are we now those who hear and a mouth for nature."

and Secret in the light of Nature's Open Secret. I cannot think
of the Egyptian divinities' smiling without being reminded of the
word 'pollen.' " [21] Is not the open secret of Nature, so secret at
every point that it need not be hidden, identical with the scattered
Orpheus' emanation, his infinite trace? And are not both figures
dependent on Rilke's feeling for gravity (Die Schwere) or directionless direction, by means of which everything is felt to turn or
summon to a common center indistinguishable from the circumference? In Schelling's *Concerning the World-Soul,* the following
is found:

> Inasmuch as . . . the God dwelling in the weight of things
> shows himself everywhere as center, and reveals the infinity of
> his nature, which the false imagination seeks in infinite space,
> entirely in the present and at every point, he by this annuls
> that vacillating and vague character of the imagination which
> attempts in vain to join the unity to the ubiquity, and the
> ubiquity to the unity of Nature.[22]

"Das alles war Auftrag"!—The image of the scattered and now
immanent God, open and secret at every point, all circumference
yet all center, represents the God of Gravitation and his Mediator
Orpheus, who sacrificed himself to sing and order reality without
choice or refusal, since the divine is indistinguishably in every element of life.

Yet the will to experience all things without choice or refusal
and in their immediacy is not fully realized even by Rilke. The
example of Orpheus does not always suffice. The poet is compelled
to find further symbols, and one of them is a mirror, the *impersonal*
mirror. It is this mirror of which Malte has such great need. For
it enables the observer oppressed by experiences he cannot shake
off, all of them in some mysterious way pointing to him, both to
represent these fully and yet to deny them any personal significance.
He will look in this mirror, reproducing all things without sup-
pression but also with complete coldness, and he will say—not
"this refers to me" but—*this is* ("nicht: das bin ich; nein: dies
ist"). [23]

Rilke's finest symbol of mediation for the unrevealed and sense-oppressive world, however, is that of the interior and sleeping girl, found in the *Sonnets to Orpheus* (I,2): "Sie schlief die Welt." The sleeper is a real girl who has found mysterious direct entry into the ear. One suspects that though entering through the eyes she could not have found sleep in the poet's eyes; but they are by-passed, and hardly appearing she is already invisible and beds down in a more interior sense. She does not rage in or torment the poet, but appears to his perception and, perceived, falls asleep in him as if just mature not only in body, but also in the mind. Her sleep, then, signifies both the first maturity of the body, and its simultaneous maturity in the mind. Rilke describes here a direct sense intuition, such as all our poets seek: the girl who first was the object of perception resumes then all objects of perception, and finally becomes perception itself, through which the world is seen so intimately that it ceases to be seen. Rilke, then, has a vision-in-the-sleeper or, as he sometimes describes it, vision-in-the-blind-angel,[24] where the mediate senses and contour of the body are lost, the body becoming itself one subsuming and penetrable sense.

The sleeper, however, is already touched by death, for nothing entirely human can become symbol for the mediating presence. Her death, moreover, coincides with the first moments of physical maturity. These sonnets were written for Wera Ouckana Knoop who at the passing of childhood was attacked by a mysterious glandular disease and died before the age of twenty. Rilke cannot distinguish spiritual from physical fulfillment, and physical fulfillment from death. Yet this is the persistent crisis of all those poets for whom Christ and the Testaments no longer suffice as mediation. The physical world must have part in the new mediation, but in the physical world the evidence in favor of life is indistinguishable from the evidence in favor of death.

Several strange figures of mediation, human and inhuman at the same time, therefore appear in modern poetry. They are all more or less reified. The first of these is Wordsworth's Blind Beggar.[25] He stands propped against the wall like a puppet. He reminds us of the blind Hermit in *The Borderers* and of the Leech Gatherer. Wordsworth gazes on him as if admonished from another world; his mind turns with the might of waters.

The second of these strange figures is Rilke's Patient. He appears most hauntingly in *Malte Laurids Brigge*. Malte sits in the hospital, to the left of him a girl with bulging eyes and rotting gums, and to the right

> whatever it was at the right of me, I could recognize it only after some time had passed. It was a huge, immovable mass, which had a face and a large, heavy, motionless hand. The side of the face that I saw was empty: quite without marks of character and without thoughts, and it was eery how the suit resembled that of a corpse clothed for the coffin. . . . Its hand had been placed on the trousers, there where it lay, and even the hair was as though combed by those who wash the corpses, and like the hair of stuffed animals, set in rigid lines. I observed everything with interest, and the thought came that this then was the spot reserved for me; I was sure I had now finally reached that place in my life where I would remain.[26]

This thing without senses, almost without face, arouses no horror; the tone of naration is almost that of one who suffers from paramnesia, and is a means of self-protection, for Malte recognizes the patient as an index of his own fate. But of course Rilke also has his blind man (and woman). The poem "Pont du Carrousel" presents a remarkable resemblance between his figure and Wordsworth's, the blind man being described as "the dark entrance into the underworld among a race with superficial senses." [27]

A third example is found in Nerval. The loss of a mediator is his consuming theme. Having lost Aurelia, and being once again in the asylum, he sees a young ex-soldier who had refused to eat for six weeks. The soldier is fed by a long rubber tube inserted into the nose.

> The scene made a great impression on me . . . I was face to face with an indefinable being, taciturn and patient, sitting before the supreme gates of existence like a sphinx. . . . He seemed to me placed between life and death, like a sublime interpreter, like a confessor predestined to hear those secrets of the soul which words would not dare to or could not transmit. He was the ear of God without the intermingling of a

stranger's thoughts. I spent whole hours in self-examination, my head close to his and holding his hands.[28]

In Hopkins no such figure is found, but the embers are there, bleak, inert, yet bursting and gashing flame as if of their own will. If Valéry has escaped, it is because he accepts incommunicability. But even in Valéry there is that almost inhuman luminosity of the eyes, the magic and mysterious mirror by means of which Narcissus hopes to know his own body.

When, therefore, the new Perseus looks directly at the Medusa two things are found to happen: he turns into stone, or draws the mediating mirror out of his own eyes. The first event is expressed as the experience of reification, which includes a curious tone of much modern literature, both extremely apathetic and extremely sense-observant, to be found in Rilke's *Malte Laurids Brigge,* Camus' *L'Etranger* and Faulkner's *The Sound and the Fury*.[29] One could, no doubt, interpret it as resulting from a fear of existential reality, but though it is this, it is also a fear inherent in the attempt to gain an unmediated, direct sense intuition. The second event is expressed by an "irrealization" of the eyes. It is in the very nature of symbols, and peculiar to the modern poet only insofar as he would counteract the eyes by an appeal to the body as the common root of all sensing, and this may serve to explain modern (romantic and post-romantic) emphasis on synaesthesia. Sometimes, of course, as in Valéry, such irrealization is accomplished not by recourse to synaesthesia, but to sheer visibility, which denies to perception both innate or acquired ideas as well as the material impress of matter, leaving consciousness in uninterrupted play or in repose between sight and idea. Both the experience of reification and that of the irrealization of the eyes are by chance found together in a prose fragment of Eluard's. It is given here without further comment:

> First I was overcome by a great yearning for solemnity and pomp. I felt cold. All my being, living and corrupt, aspired to the rigidity and majesty of the dead. Then I was tempted by a mystery in which forms play no part. Inquisitive about a

washed out sky from which the birds and the clouds are ban-
ished. I became the slave of the pure faculty of sight, the slave
of my unreal and virgin eyes, ignoring both the world and
themselves. A tranquil power. I suppressed the visible and the
invisible, I lost myself in a mirror without silvering. Indestructible, I was not blind.[30]

But a further conclusion imposes itself, which, though unsought,
must stand at the end of these essays, like the moral at the end of
a fable written for its own sake. The four artists here considered,
chosen from among the greater modern poets, have in varying degree and even when most Christian, lost the full understanding of
revealed religion, accepted the individual quest for truth and
forced by this same quest to seek mediation, sought it neither in
Christ nor in tradition but in the very things that caused them to
seek: personal experience and sense experience. The escape from
the circle of despair is then made by various forms of panentheism,
or pantheism in the redefinition of Novalis: "the idea that everything may become an organ or mediator of God if I raise it to
this." [31] But who confers this raising power, and on whom? Even
if the answer to the first part of the question is God, the answer to
the second part is always the artist. It is the artist who, acknowledged or not, pretends to the role of mediator.

Wordsworth is a turning point. Though steeped in the volume
which displays the written promise, the mystery, the life which cannot die, he refused this comforter and shield against human suffering, noting all signs of human decay, every natural or incidental
wastage of life, the beggars, Margaret, idiocy; pitying even a poor
man's horse shelterless in the beating rain, or a broken pane of glass
glittering senselessly in the moor's dreary moonlight. Yet with
thoughts and images of grief assailing him, Wordsworth still finds
mental repose, but never, except in his revised work, by reference
to revelation, and to the Sufferer, Christ. His moments of mysticism
and consolation are not, like those of previous Christians, described
as an *excessus menti*, they are instead an *accessus menti* giving to
the human mind not annihilation but full consciousness of the
subsistence and indestructibility of a life in which it shares:

> Sensation, soul and form
> All melted into him. They swallowed up
> His animal being; in them did he live
> And by them did he live. They were his life.
> In such access of mind, in such high hour
> Of visitation from the living God,
> He did not feel the God; he felt his works;
>
> .   .   .
>
> Ah! *then* how beautiful, how bright appeared
> The written promise; he had early learned
> To reverence the volume which displays
> The mystery, the life which cannot die;
> But in the mountains did he *feel* his faith
> There did he see the writing—All things there
> Looked immortality, revolving life,
> And greatness still revolving, infinite.[32]

Thus revelation recedes as the proof-text for the rightness or wrongness of actions human or divine. Personal experience becomes the sole authority and source of conviction, and the poet a new intermediary. Nor is the new role of the artist comparable to the ancient conceptions of him as *poeta vates*. The slogan will indeed be used, but only in the way slogans are used. The modern poet is the Experimenter and, not rarely, the Self-Tormentor. His real mediation is to accept and live the lack of mediation. "The divine on earth must accept human status. It must propose its own enigma to itself." [33] And not acknowledging a sacred text, the poet is also coming to refuse the concept of literary authority so firmly accepted by continental classicism and with continuing influence even to the present day. The poet in our day who wishes to use traditional themes and marks of style is forced to write in what is becoming an entirely new genre, that of parody.

Yet the unmediated vision is far from absolute. The experiment has only started which, clearing the mind for the shock of life, would in time overcome every arbitrary god of the intellect, thus to achieve a perfect induction and a faultless faith.

BIBLIOGRAPHY
AND NOTES

De Sélincourt, Ernest, ed. *The Prelude.* Oxford, The Clarendon Press, 1926.

De Sélincourt, Ernest, ed. *The Letters of William and Dorothy Wordsworth; the Middle Years.* Oxford, The Clarendon Press, 1937.

De Sélincourt, Ernest, and Helen Darbishire, eds. *The Poetical Works of William Wordsworth.* Oxford, The Clarendon Press, 1940–49. 5 vols.

De Sélincourt, Ernest, ed. *Journals of Dorothy Wordsworth.* New York, The Macmillan Co., 1941. 2 vols.

Grosart, Alexander B., ed. *The Prose Works of William Wordsworth.* London, Edward Moxon, Son, and Co., 1876. 3 vols.

Peacock, Markham L., ed. *The Critical Opinions of William Wordsworth.* Baltimore, Johns Hopkins Press, 1950.

1. For "statement" of emotion see Josephine Miles, *Wordsworth and the Vocabulary of Emotion,* Univ. of Calif. Pub. in English, Vol. 12 (Berkeley and Los Angeles, 1942), *passim.*
2. "Regeneration," *Silex Scintillans.*
3. Grosart, 2, 55.
4. See remarks of F. A. Pottle on "Emergent Idiom" in *The Idiom of Poetry* (Ithaca, 1946).
5. See *Prelude,* Bk. II, ll. 302–22, especially ll. 315–20 (all refs. are to 1850 version):

> the soul,
> Remembering how she felt, but what she felt
> Remembering not, retains an obscure sense
> Of possible sublimity, whereto
> With growing faculties she doth aspire,
> With faculties still growing . . .

6. The use of blank verse in "Tintern Abbey," *The Prelude,* and *The Excursion* was not so inevitable as it now seems. "Tintern Abbey" was composed in July, 1798, the same year that the poet conceived *The Recluse;* and in a notebook stemming from the same year and containing fragments of his new epic, Wordsworth had already noted Dr. Johnson's warnings on the danger of this measure (See *The Prelude,* p. xxx, n. 2):

> Dr. Johnson observed, that in blank verse, the language suffered more distortion to keep it out of prose than any inconvenience to be apprehended from the shackles and circumspection of rhyme. This kind of distortion is the worst fault that poetry can have; for if once the natural order and connection of the words is broken, and the idiom of the language

violated, the lines appear manufactured, and lose all that character of enthusiasm and inspiration, without which they become cold and insipid, how sublime soever the ideas and the images may be which they express.

It would therefore be a mistake to think Wordsworth chose blank verse for its theoretical adequacy to "language really used by men." The reverse might seem more likely: blank verse in the eighteenth century is considered as that poetic measure farthest removed from the natural order and easy flow of words. Many factors combined to establish this opinion, chief of which is the example of Milton, whose "lapidary" style is countenanced with uneasiness: Johnson finds in it "neither the easiness of prose, nor the melody of numbers." And even Shakespeare, whose verse has in our day been taken as Milton's natural antithesis insofar as he is supposed to have produced a verse most sensitive to common speech, is not always allowed this virtue in the eighteenth century; Sir Joshua Reynolds, arguing that art requires a necessary deviation from the natural, refers in 1786 to his language as "the language of blank verse, so different from common English." Although there is a tradition of colloquial blank verse in the eighteenth century, Words-worth acknowledges only the *Seasons* of Thomson, and this not for its style, termed vicious and tainted by false ornaments, but for taking its inspiration from external Nature. Adding to this the obvious fact that most of the *Lyrical Ballads,* as the title suggests, are not in blank verse but in a rhythm, rhyme, and language of ballad style suggested by the *Reliques* of Percy, we may consider it as certain that Wordsworth did not choose the measure for his major productions simply because he thought it naturally or conven-tionally suited to "language really used by men."

Why, then, did he choose it? For the very reason, probably, that had caused the 18th century to mistrust it: it was the measure used, and used as if determined, by Milton. Goldsmith's remark, "Nothing but the greatest sublimity of subject can render such a measure pleasing," is a common belief of that century and helps to clarify Wordsworth's intention. He wished to use a measure reserved for the highest kind of subject in order to treat of "the life in common things," but especially because he would thus imitate and rival Milton. One would not be wrong in regarding *The Recluse* as a powerful criticism of Milton's work—by no means an attack or attempted refutation, but a criticism that accepts Milton's thought even to the measure in which he writes, although trying to correct his subject from the sublime to the familiar, from the enthusiastic to the human. Milton is for Words-worth a lasting experience, in relation to which he is continually forced to define himself, and without which his poetry would never have achieved that philosophic stature at which he aims from the very outset, when both he and Coleridge speak of his epic venture as a "philosophic" poem.

7. A fine description of these two moments is given by Wordsworth in defense of

his sonnet, "With ships the sea . . ." in a letter to Lady Beaumont, 1807 (Peacock, pp. 408–9):

> I am represented in the Sonnet as casting my eyes over the sea, sprinkled with a multitude of Ships, like the heavens with stars . . . in a kind of dreamy indifference with respect either to this or that one. . . . All at once, while I am in this state, comes forth an object, an individual, and my mind, sleepy and unfixed, is awakened and fastened in a moment. "Hesperus, that *led* The starry host" is a poetical object, because the glory of his own Nature gives him the pre-eminence the moment he appears; he calls forth the poetic faculty, receiving its exertions as a tribute; but this Ship in the Sonnet may, in a manner still more appropriate, be said to come upon a mission of the poetic Spirit, because in its own appearance and attributes it is barely sufficiently distinguished to rouse the creative faculty of the human mind. . . . The mind being once fixed and roused, all the rest comes from itself. . . . My mind wantons with grateful joy in the exercise of its own powers, and, loving its own creation. . . .

The difference between Wordsworth's and Milton's poetic inspiration is also clear from this letter. The subjects Milton deals with are considered in themselves worthy and beautiful. Those that Wordsworth considers need the concurrence of the creative mind. As the poet grows older he will put more and more emphasis on the conferring powers of the imagination ("the soul of Man, communicating its creative energies to the images of the external world." Peacock, p. 422).

8. These are references to various parts of *The Prelude* that tell of Wordsworth's poetic ambitions left behind for the celebration of humbler matter. See *Prelude*, Bk. I, 169 ff., 586.

9. See above, n. 7.

10. *Journals, 1*, 11 (The Alfoxden Journal, 1 March, 1798).

11. *Prelude*, Bk. IV, 295 ff.

12. *Prelude*, Bk. V, 438 ff.

13. *Ibid.*, 453 ff.

14. *Prelude*, Bk. I, 33 ff.

15. *Prelude*, Bk. VI, 592 ff.

16. *Prelude*, Bk. V, 364 ff.

17. Cf. Wordsworth's own comment on the passage as it first appeared under "Poems of the Imagination." Quoted by N. P. Stallknecht, *Strange Seas of Thought* (Durham, 1945), p. 55:

> Guided by one of my primary consciousnesses, I have represented a commutation and transfer of internal feelings, co-operating with external accidents to plant, for immortality, images of sound and sight, in the

celestial soil of the Imagination. The Boy, there introduced, is listening, with something of a feverish and restless anxiety, for the recurrence of the riotous sounds which he had previously excited; and, at the moment when the intenseness of the mind is beginning to remit, he is surprized into a perception of the solemn and tranquilizing images which the Poem describes.

Cf. De Quincey's commentary on Wordsworth in *Literary Reminiscences* (Boston, 1874), also given by Stallknecht, p. 60. While Stallknecht's remarks are observant, Arthur Beatty is constrained by his very narrow view of the active principle in Wordsworth to state that this experience is "An experience that was not Wordsworth's own," evidently in contradiction to the poet's express assertion "Guided by one of my own primary consciousnesses." See Arthur Beatty, *William Wordsworth, His Doctrine and Art in Their Historical Relations* (1st ed., Madison, 1922), ch. 8 and p. 220. The Boy of Winander episode was one of the earliest of *The Prelude* to be composed; it seems expressly conceived to illustrate the generous influence of Nature on the imagination, being found as part of "The Ruined Cottage" (De Sélincourt, *Poetical Works*, 5, 346), the germ of what was to become *The Excursion,* and there prefaced as follows:

> My playmates! brothers! nurs'd by the same years,
> And fellow-children of the self-same hills,
> Though we are moulded now by various fates
> To various characters, I do not think
> That there is one of us who cannot tell
> How manifold the expedients, how intense
> The unwearied passion with which nature toils
> To win us to herself, and to impress
> Our careless hearts with beauty and with love.
> There was a Boy (etc. as *Prelude,* 1805) . . .

Cf. also Wordsworth's comments on the Samphire gatherer "hanging" on the cliff, in preface to 1815 ed. of *Lyrical Ballads.*
18. *Prelude,* Bk. I, 330 ff.
19. *Prelude,* Bk. XII, 272 ff.:

> Oh! mystery of man, from what a depth
> Proceed thy honours. I am lost, but see
> In simple childhood something of the base
> On which thy greatness stands

20. *Prelude,* Bk. I, 94 ff.
21. *Prelude,* Bk. IV, 150–8.
22. To avoid misunderstanding, it should once more be stressed that Words-

worth did not have a theory of divine inspiration. See, e.g., his letter-preface to *Peter Bell* (De Sélincourt, *Poetical Works*, 2, 331):

> The Poem of Peter Bell, as the Prologue will show, was composed under a belief that the Imagination not only does not require for its exercise the intervention of supernatural agency, but that, though such agency be excluded, the faculty may be called forth as imperiously, and for kindred results of pleasure, by incidents within the compass of poetic probability, in the humblest departments of daily life.

It is precisely in this that our poet differs from Milton. But the fact remains that he cannot initiate the creative process by an act of will, unless he wishes to produce a poetry of the fancy. It is to the initiating, to the calling forth that the principle of generosity refers; he may not test the soul out of his will. We note also that the creative activity is more easily started by the "untuned," than by the "splendid" scene. Wordsworth's liking for sterner nature has been interpreted by G. Wilson Knight ("The Wordsworthian Profundity," in *The Starlit Dome*, 1941) as stemming from a lack of the sexual drive. Similar comments are to be found in the works of Empson and Trilling. The theme of denudation is too universal and deep-rooted to be profaned by such partial analysis. The sternness of Nature is taken by the poet as a test of both his faith and his creative strength. See De Sélincourt, *Poetical Works*, 5, 319, "The Recluse" (Appendix A), ll. 163 ff.:

> Stern was the face of Nature; we rejoiced
> In that stern countenance, for our Souls thence drew
> A feeling of their strength.

23. *Prelude*, Bk. I, 430 ff.
24. *Journals*, *1*, 6 (Alfoxden Journal, 1 Feb. 1798).
Ibid., p. 125 (Grasmere Journal, 17 March 1802).
25. *Prelude*, Bk. IV, 90 ff.
26. *Journals*, *1*, 82 (Grasmere Journal, 24 Nov. 1801).
27. There are remarkable similarities between Wordsworth's and Schelling's philosophy of Nature. For both, the essential harmony and adaptedness of man and Nature is revealed through an aesthetic intuition, an imaginative act, a transcendental synthesis. We immediately think of Wordsworth's "blended might" of man and Nature when we read the following question which Schelling poses in "Über das Verhältniss der bildenden Künste zu der Natur," a speech that had visible repercussions on Coleridge's *Poesy or Art*:

> Wie können wir jene scheinbar harte Form [i.e. of Nature] geistig gleichsam schmelzen, dass die lautre Kraft der Dinge mit der Kraft unseres Geistes zusammenfliesst, und aus beiden nur ein Guss wird?

But the difference is also and immediately apparent. For Schelling, Nature presents at first glance hardness of form and reserve. For Wordsworth Nature is always of generous aspect—the pastoral farms are green to the very door. For Schelling it is a question of "thawing out" Nature by an epistemological event (not act; see n. 34) producing what Wordsworth specifically calls a "creation."

28. *Prelude,* Bk. VII, 44 ff.
29. De Sélincourt, *Poetical Works, 5,* 5, ll. 63–71.
30. See Geoffrey Keynes' edition of *Complete Prose and Poetry* (New York, Random House, 1927), pp. 1026–7.
31. Grosart, *2,* 138 ff.
32. *L'Imagination,* though not published till 1806, was written between 1785 and 1794. In the preface one finds this on the interaction of the imagination and its objects:

> Quand j'ai voulu exprimer comment les objets modifient l'imagination, comment ils sont eux-mêmes modifiés par elle, il m'a suffi de peindre l'action réciproque des eaux sur le rivage, et du rivage sur les eaux:
>
>> Du mobile océan tels les flots onduleux
>> Vont façonner leurs bords, ou sont moulés par eux.

These are bad verses but sufficient to express what must have been a late eighteenth-century and commonplace attempt to combine the tradition of Locke with that of Descartes.

33. *Prelude,* Bk. VIII, 437.
34. A. N. Whitehead in his well-known chapter on "The Romantic Reaction" (*Science and the Modern World,* 1926) has recruited Wordsworth for his camp, pointing out that

> What the theory [i.e. his and Wordsworth's] does is to edge cognitive mentality away from being the necessary substratum of the unity of experience. That unity is now placed in the unity of an event. Accompanying this unity there may or there may not be cognition.

Wordsworth does indeed edge cognitive mentality away from being the necessary substratum of the unity of experience. But not, perhaps, because he is a precursor of Whitehead's theory of organism. The transcendent unity of event as event is in Wordsworth dependent on an inherent and metaphysical principle of generosity. To say, as Whitehead does, that accompanying this unity of event there may or there may not be cognition is a statement true of, for example, Faulkner's idiot in *The Sound and the Fury* but inapplicable to the experience of Wordsworth, where as long as the principle of generosity is active the meeting of mind and Nature inevitably results in cognition, in an epistemological event. Though Wordsworth may also insist on the activity of the mind and the necessity for the mind to impose its spiritualizing power on the scene before it, he never thinks this activity could be initiated or willed by the unaided mind. The poem for

Wordsworth, the aesthetic intuition, is not the result of an epistemological act but of an epistemological event: a mutual and transcendent principle of generosity has gone into action. What is edged away as the necessary substratum of the unity of experience is the will toward relational knowledge.

35. For the origin and development of powers, presences, and "plastic" nature see Joseph W. Beach, *The Concept of Nature in Nineteenth-Century Poetry* (New York, 1936).

36. Dr. Johnson's definition of the sublime in his "Life of Cowley."

37. *Prelude,* Bk. III, 133–4.

38. De Sélincourt, *Poetical Works,* 5, 335, "The Recluse" (Appendix A), I. 642.

39. *Paradise Lost,* Bk. XII, 641.

40. *Excursion,* Bk. II, 327 ff.

41. *Paradise Lost,* Bk. XII, 303–4. I do not think this has ever been pointed out.

42. De Sélincourt, *Poetical Works,* 5, 4 (Preface to ed. of 1814), ll. 47–55.

43. *Journals, 1,* 8–9 (Alfoxden Journal, 8 Feb. 1798).

44. *Prelude,* Bk. I, 473 ff.

45. *Journals, 1,* 6 (Alfoxden Journal, 1 Feb. 1798).

46. De Sélincourt, *Poetical Works,* 5, 347, Appendix B.

47. See *Prelude,* Bk. V, The Boy of Winander episode, ll. 384–8.

48. *Prelude,* Bk. IV, 323 ff.

49. See also G. Wilson Knight (*The Starlit Dome,* 1941) on the "marriage metaphor." The water imagery has been keenly studied quite recently, though its central significance is not entirely understood, by Florence Marsh in *Wordsworth's Imagery* (New Haven, 1952), esp. chap. 5, "Sounds, Waters, Man-made Structures."

50. De Sélincourt, *Poetical Works,* 5, 317, "The Recluse" (Appendix A), l. 126.

51. *Excursion,* Bk. IV, 755.

52. *Journals, 1,* 139 (Grasmere Journal, 29 April 1802).

53. *Excursion,* Bk. IV, 1132–47. Cf. Wordsworth's account of whence he drank the visionary power, *Prelude,* II, 306 ff.: "listening to the notes that are/ The ghostly language of the ancient earth."

54. *Prelude,* Bk. V, 127 ff.

55. *Prelude,* Bk. V, 10 ff. Cf. W. H. Auden, *The Enchaféd Flood* (New York, 1950).

56. *Excursion,* Bk. III, 368 ff.

57. In the "Supplementary Preface" of 1815. See Grosart, 2, 138.

58. The hermit and the hermitage were of course popular accouterments of Italian and English gardens in the latter half of the eighteenth century. See C. B. Tinker, *Painter and Poet* (Cambridge, 1938). This does not affect the fact that Wordsworth used the figure for his own purpose.

59. We consider this type of vision in the concluding chapters. One could compare *Prelude,* Bk. II, 302 ff.:

for I would walk alone
Under the quiet stars, and at that time
Have felt whate'er there is of power in sound
To breathe an elevated mood, by form
Or image unprofaned . . .

See also the fragment given below, entitled "Redundance."

60. Wordsworth may, for example, be interpreted along eidetic lines, as German scholars have shown—at times convincingly. See Gerhard Hensel, *Das
Optische bei Wordsworth* (Marburg, 1930), and the less interesting E. Schu-
macher, *Einheit und Totalität bei Wordsworth* (Marburg, 1930). Both are
under the influence of E. R. Jaensch, a pioneer of eidetic psychology and
professor at that time at Marburg.

61. See Basil Willey, *Nineteenth Century Studies* (London, 1949), pp. 9, 10.

62. *Excursion*, Bk. IV, 1207–24.

63. E.g., "Über Anmut und Würde." The concept of "Die schöne Seele" is based
on (what we have called) the constraint of love.

64. *Journals, 1*, 136 (Grasmere Journal, 22 April 1802).

65. It refers of course indirectly to the dilemma of the Ode, the passing of the
visionary gleam.

66. Cf. Coleridge's "The Aeolian Harp": "A light in sound, a sound-like
power in light."

67. "Ode on the Power of Sound," composed 1828.

68. Wordsworth uses "stationary" elsewhere to mean "in martial order."
See the "Thanksgiving Ode": "Firm as a rock in stationary fight," De Sélincourt, *Poetical Works, 3*, 157.

69. Cf. the last stanza of the "Ode on the Power of Sound":

A Voice shall finish doubt and dim foreseeing,
And sweep away life's visionary stir;
The trumpet . . .

70. (1) ll. 70–5. (2) ll. 126 ff.

71. We are ready to support this rather far-reaching contention with a detailed
study of the theme "The Waters of Judgement" in the earlier work of Wordsworth, especially in *The Borderers*.

72. See n. 64 above.

73. De Quincey in his essay "On Wordsworth's Poetry" draws attention to this
image, though with respect to another poem where the waterfall is actually
described as "frozen by distance."

The Fragment "Redundance"

The following fragment is given by De Sélincourt in Appendix B to his edition
of *The Excursion*, in *Poetical Works, 5*, 346. It dates from the time of "Tin-

tern Abbey" and the early passages of *The Prelude,* being found in one of the manuscripts containing "The Ruined Cottage." We quote it to suggest once again how vital the image of the earth as an ebbed ocean is to the poet. The "subduing of the eye" seems to us one of the major themes in Wordsworth. The eye is to be made as effective as the ear, light to be made as visionary in its qualities as sound, though, in the final analysis, even sound tends to give way to a nondescript sense entirely without image. The term "I stood" is not unimportant. It is always used in connection with mystical moments, suggesting perhaps that the simple, physical act of standing is perceived as the effect of a sustaining force. But why is the fragment called "Redundance"?

>   Not the more
> Failed I to lengthen out my watch. I stood
> Within the area of the frozen vale,
> Mine eye subdued and quiet as the ear
> Of one that listens, for even yet the scene,
> Its fluctuating hues and surfaces,
> And the decaying vestiges of forms,
> Did to the dispossessing power of night
> Impart a feeble visionary sense
> Of movement and creation doubly felt[.]

HOPKINS

Abbott, Claude C., ed. *The Letters of Gerard Manley Hopkins to Robert Bridges.* London, Oxford University Press, 1935. (Cited as *Letters.*)

Bridges, Robert, and W. H. Gardner, eds. *Poems of Gerard Manley Hopkins.* New York and London, Oxford University Press, 1948. (Cited as *Poems.*)

House, Humphry, ed. *The Note-Books and Papers of Gerard Manley Hopkins.* London and New York, Oxford University Press, 1937. (Cited as *Note-Books.*)

1. Hopkins' interest in the realia which give rise to the metaphors and cognates of various languages is exemplified in his disquisition on "Horn" which would do credit to a Meyer-Lübke. *Note-Books,* p. 5 f. (24 Sept. 1863).
2. *Note-Books,* p. 53 (22 Jan. 1866).
3. "The Starlight Night," *Poems,* p. 70.
4. Letter to Bridges (Nov. 1882) in *Poems,* p. 240. F. R. Leavis, *New Bearings in English Poetry* (New York, 1950), p. 172, seems to be the only one of the commentators to have clearly understood the physical basis of Hopkins' poetry: "His words and phrases are actions as well as sounds, ideas and images, and must . . . be read with the body as well as with the eye."
5. "I wake and feel the fell of dark, not day"; *Poems,* pp. 68 ff.
6. *Poems,* pp. 101–2.
7. "The Caged Skylark," *Poems,* p. 75.
8. The suggestion of R. V. Schoder, "What Does the Windhover Mean?" in

Immortal Diamond: Studies in Gerard Manley Hopkins, ed. Norman Wey-
and (New York, 1949), chap. 9. Father Schoder's article appears to be the
most sensible of those published up to date on "The Windhover." There is
no reason, however, to suppose that "rung" refers only to the falcon's spiral
ascent. We point out with respect to "buckle" (see p. 62) that Hopkins uses
words to indicate physical actions or their effect rather than a particular
thing or relation. "Rung" is used here to suggest (1) the stress exerted on a
bell and its consequent ringing out; (2) the stress on the rein of a horse in
order to control and direct it, creating perhaps a whiplike snaking in the rein
parallel to that in the "wimpling wing"; (3) the spiral motion of flight.
Hopkins might have said that all three actions have the same "inscape" or
"instress."

9. See "The Blessed Virgin Compared to the Air We Breathe," *Poems,* p. 100:

> I say that we are wound
> With mercy round and round
> As if with air: the same
> Is Mary, more by name.

The blue-bleak embers are (as will become evident) a symbol for the man-
and God-deserted Christ, and of a sudden flaring up in glory and resurrection.

10. "Spelt from Sibyl's Leaves," *Poems,* p. 105.

11. "The Wreck of the Deutschland," *Poems,* p. 26.

12. Father Schoder, on the other hand, thinks "shine" refers to the plough.
This may be so, but such a view neglects the kinaesthetic basis of Hopkins'
imagery. With "down" elsewhere the poet refers clearly to, or mimics, a
strong, almost muscular, movement:

> I walk, I lift up, I lift up heart, eyes,
> Down all that glory in the heavens to glean our Savior,
> ("Hurrahing in Harvest")

13. *Note-Books,* p. 130 (12 March 1870).

14. See Austin Warren, "Instress of Inscape," in *Gerard Manley Hopkins,* by
the Kenyon Critics (Norfolk, New Directions, 1945). See also W. A. M. Peters,
Gerard Manley Hopkins (London and New York, 1948). Both are fine treat-
ments. It may be added that the terms "instress" and "inscape" occur for the
first time in a fragmentary exposition on Parmenides, *Note-Books,* pp. 98–
102. See also Preface to *Note-Books,* p. xxv. This fragment anticipates the
important "That Nature is a Heraclitean Fire and of the comfort of the
Resurrection (see discussion above, pp. 57, 59). A careful study of the two
terms as used in the fragment will show that Hopkins' epistemology is contained here almost *in toto* and much before his acquaintance with Duns
Scotus (August 1872).

15. Cf. *Note-Books,* p. 140: "What you look hard at seems to look hard at you."

16. Cf. Letter to Bridges, in *Letters,* pp. 290–2 (25 Sept. 1888). In his 1868 notes on Parmenides he mentions that philosopher's two principles of fire and earth: " 'ethery flame of fire, comforting the heart . . . marvellously subtle, throughout one with itself, *not* one with the other' " and " 'unmeaning . . . night, thick and wedgèd body.' " *Note-Books,* p. 102.

17. (And do they so?) *Silex Scintillans.*

18. Bridges informs us that two texts of this poem quote "Nam expectatio, . . ." (*Poems,* p. 240.) The "but dost that long" could be interpreted as "art eternal, resilient."

19. From the comments on the *Spiritual Exercises* of St. Ignatius. *Note-Books,* p. 309 (20 Aug. 1880).

20. From "That Nature is a Heraclitean Fire."

21. Peters (*Gerard Manley Hopkins,* p. 19) makes some excellent suggestions in noting that Hopkins habitually associates the sound of bells and the flame of fire, and especially that we should read, or rather hear

> AND the fire that breaks from thee then, a billion
> Times tolled lovelier, more dangerous, O my chevalier!

Peters says, "The words 'fire' and 'tolled' show how the instresses of the bird in action, of fire and of tolling bells, are joined in one poetic experience."

22. Cf. remarks of W. H. Gardner which point to the same thing but fall short of entire understanding: "God the Son assumes *all* Nature; hence the individual, intrinsic degree of Christ sums up the degrees of all men. The whole sonnet is a poetic statement of the Scotist concept that individual substances, according to the metaphysical richness of their being, make up one vast hierarchy with God as their summit." Cited in *Poems,* p. 239, from the author's *Gerard Manley Hopkins: A Study of Poetic Idiosyncrasy in Relation to Poetic Tradition* (New Haven, Yale University Press, 1948), *1.*

23. "The Wreck of the Deutschland," *Poems,* p. 65.

24. In a discussion on what the word is generically speaking, Hopkins comes to the conclusion that it is properly neither the thing referred to nor the emotional response it may call up in the reader, but "the expression, *uttering* of the idea in the mind. That idea itself has its two terms, the image (of sight or sound or *scapes* of the other senses), which is in fact physical and a refined energy accenting the nerves, a word to oneself, an inchoate word, and secondly the conception." *Note-Books,* pp. 95–6 (9 Feb. 1868). This precept dispenses with all exclusive hypotheses concerning the word "buckle." For there is, in Hopkins, the audacious attempt to conceive words generically, as beings in their own right and not only as carriers of an idea. In some of his later poems everything tends to become subordinate to a method of rhythmic stuttering, as it were, that would make the word a point, the strongest and non-referential intention of speech, inseparable from the nervous effort which precedes it:

> I cast for comfort I can no more get
> By groping round my comfortless, than blind
> Eyes in their dark can day or thirst can find
> Thirst's all-in-all in all a world of wet. (*Poems*, p. 111.)

The final tendency of Hopkins is toward pure speech, what he might call the inscape of speech. And "buckle," therefore, is in the nature of a pure speech movement, an "explosive," that cares little about grammatical precision. See the discussion above, p. 62.

25. *Note-Books*, p. 144 (22 April 1871).

26. *Note-Books*, pp. 149–150 (8 July 1871).

27. "God's Grandeur," *Poems*, p. 70.

28. My own term. It means to suggest that the senses develop a figure of their own as organically as the body itself.

29. With the exception of Novalis in one poem, the "Hymn" of *Geistliche Lieder*.

30. *Letters*, p. 304 (29 April 1889).

31. *Appreciations*, "Coleridge," 1865, 1880. Pater was a tutor at Oxford while Hopkins was there, and Hopkins seems to have attended his lectures on Greek philosophy.

32. Especially chap. 6, "Word-Painting."

33. *Letters*, p. 267 (6 Nov. 1887).

34. We would not for a moment suggest that Hopkins is unorthodox. He is against tradition. Cf. his eulogy on Christ's body in one of the sermons, *Note-Books*, p. 265 (23 Nov. 1879). Hopkins may simply be said to interpret strictly and literally the doctrine of the physical resurrection.

35. "We may think of words as heavy bodies, as indoor or out of door objects of nature or man's art." *Note-Books*, p. 223 (lecture notes).

36. The following passage is added not for the sake of proof but for interest, for if the principle be accepted that the lower can only be understood through the higher, and never the higher through the lower, then the understanding of poetry may never come from a perusal of the author's prose work, though this may catch light from a previous understanding of his poetry: ". . . grace is any action, activity, on God's part by which, in creating or after creating, he carries the creature to or towards the end of its being, which is its self-sacrifice to God and its salvation. It is, I say, any such activity on God's part; so that so far as this action or activity is God's it is divine stress, holy spirit, and, as all is done through Christ, Christ's spirit. . . . It is as if a man said: That is Christ playing at me and me playing at Christ, only that it is no play but truth; That is Christ *being me* and me being Christ." This is also in the spirit of the *Spiritual Exercises* and comes from Hopkins' comments on St. Ignatius in 1880. *Note-Books*, p. 332 (30 Dec. 1881).

RILKE

Ausgewählte Werke. Leipzig, Insel-Verlag, 1942. 2 vols.
Das Buch der Bilder. Leipzig, Insel-Verlag, 1913.
Duino Elegies, tr. J. B. Leishman and Stephen Spender. London, Hogarth Press, New York, W. W. Norton, 1939.
Erste Gedichte. Leipzig, Insel-Verlag, 1913.
Gesammelte Briefe. Leipzig, Insel-Verlag, 1936–40. 6 vols. (Cited as *GB, 1, 2,* etc.)
Gesammelte Werke. Leipzig, Insel-Verlag, 1930. 6 vols. (Cited as *GW, 1, 2,* etc.)
Neue Gedichte. Leipzig, Insel-Verlag, 1911–13. 2 vols.
Die Sonette an Orpheus. Leipzig, Insel-Verlag, 1923.
Tagebücher aus der Frühzeit. Leipzig, Insel-Verlag, 1942.

1. "Childhood," in *Silex Scintillans.*
2. E.g., "Vigilien," No. 4, in *Erste Gedichte,* p. 43.
3. "Orpheus. Eurydike. Hermes," *Neue Gedichte, 1,* 92.
4. P. 358.
5. "Gesang der Frauen an den Dichter," *Neue Gedichte, 1,* 22.
6. Religion "ist keine Pflicht und kein Verzicht, es ist keine Einschränkung: sondern in der vollkommenen Weite des Weltalls ist es: eine Richtung des Herzens." To Ilse Blumenthal-Weiss, 28 December 1921, *GB, 5,* 76. Also Malte's remark concerning Abelone: "Konnte ihr wahrhaftiges Herz sich darüber täuschen, dass Gott mehr eine Richtung der Liebe ist, kein Liebesgegenstand?" *GW, 5,* 242.
7. Rilke is conscious of the root *Zug* in *Bezug.* Cf. Fourth Elegy, "Wir sind nicht einig. Sind nicht wie die Zugvögel verständigt." *Bezug* denotes an instinctive and transcendent orientation.
8. It would be rash to try to describe here what modern or ancient philosophy intends by *phusis.* But since we mean a parallel conception whenever we use the term "physical order," it may be useful to append a definition of Heidegger's (in *Holzwege*): "Wir nennen es [i.e. *phusis*] die Erde. Von dem was das Wort hier sagt, ist sowohl die Vorstellung einer abgelagerten Stoffmasse als auch die nur astronomische eines Planeten fernzuhalten. Die Erde ist das, wohin das Aufgehen alles Aufgehende und zwar als ein solches zurückbirgt."
9. Rodin is said to have recognized in Baudelaire "einen, der sich nicht von den Gesichtern hatte beirren lassen und der nach den Leibern suchte, in denen das Leben grösser war, grausamer und ruheloser." *GW, 4,* 313–14. And about "hands": "Es gibt eine Geschichte der Hände, sie haben tatsächlich ihre eigene Kultur, ihre besondere Schönheit; man gesteht ihnen das Recht zu, eine eigene Entwickelung zu haben, eigene Wünsche, Gefühle, Launen und Liebhabereien." *GW, 4,* 327–8.

10. E.g., Bordieu: "s' il n'y a qu'une conscience dans l'animal, il y a une infinité de volontés; chaque organe a la sienne. . . . Les abeilles perdent leurs consciences et retiennent leurs appétits ou volontés."

11. "Er schuf Körper, die sich überall berührten und zusammenhielten wie ineinander verbissene Tiere, die als ein Ding in die Tiefe fallen; Leiber, die horchten wie Gesichter und ausholten wie Arme; Ketten von Leibern, Gewinde und Ranken, und schwere Trauben von Gestalten." *GW, 4,* 336.

12. "Ähnlich wie die Sprache nichts mehr mit den Dingen gemein hat, welche sie nennt, so haben die Gebärden der meisten Menschen, die in den Städten leben, ihre Beziehung zur Erde verloren;" in Rilke's early essay on Painting, "Worpswede," *Ausgewählte Werke* (Leipzig, 1938), *2,* 230–1.

13.   Du, der mit dem Aufschlag,
                  wie nur Früchte ihn kennen, unreif
                  täglich hundert Mal abfällt vom Baum der gemeinsam
                  erbauten Bewegung, (der, rascher als Wasser, in wenig
                  Minuten Lenz, Sommer und Herbst hat)—
                  abfällt und anprallt ans Grab:

14. *Sonnette an Orpheus,* Zweiter Teil, p. 47.

15. "Der Ölbaumgarten," *Neue Gedichte, 1, 20.*

16. "Herbsttag," *Buch der Bilder,* p. 45.

17. ". . . entschlossen und schicksalslos wie eine Ewige, steht sie neben ihm, der sich verwandelt. Immer übertrifft die Liebende den Geliebten, weil das Leben grösser ist als das Schicksal." *Ausgewählte Werke, 2,* 171–2.

18. "Orpheus. Eurydike. Hermes," *Neue Gedichte, 1,* 92.

19. "Starker Stern."

20. "Gegen-Strophen," *Letzte Gedichte,* in *GW, 3,* 457.

21. "Die Frucht," *Ausgewählte Werke, 1,* 365.

22. "Verkündigung," *Buch der Bilder,* in *GW, 2,* 72–3.

23. "Es winkt zu Fühlung," *Letzte Gedichte,* in *GW, 3,* 452.

24.   Feigenbaum, seit wie lange schon ists mir bedeutend,
                  wie du die Blüte beinah ganz überschlägst
                  und hinein in die zeitig entschlossene Frucht,
                  ungerühmt, drängst dein reines Geheimnis.
                  Wie der Fontäne Rohr treibt dein gebognes Gezweig
                  abwärts den Saft und hinan: und er springt aus dem Schlaf,
                  fast nicht erwachend, ins Glück seiner süssesten Leistung.
                  Sieh: wie der Gott in den Schwan.
                          . . . . Wir aber verweilen,
                  ach, uns rühmt es zu blühn, und ins verspätete Innre
                  unserer endlichen Frucht gehn wir verraten hinein.

25. Rilke came to know Meister Eckhart in 1905 (see his letter to Gräfin Luise Schwerin, 5 June 1905, *GB, 2,* 73 f.). Eckhart is the first to use *gelassen* in a mystical sense according to Grimm, *Deutsches Wörterbuch* (Leipzig, 1897), *4, 1,* 2865.

26. "Starker Stern."

27. "Der Berg," in *Neue Gedichte*, 2, 116.

28. "Die bewegte, lebendige Welt, einfach und ohne Deutung gesehen als Anlass zu Dingen." *GB, 1, 382.*

29. "Der Goldschmied," in *Ausgewählte Werke, 1, 158.*

30. Ninth Duino Elegy.

31. "Vom Tode Maria," in *Das Marienleben*, in *GW, 2.*

32. Ninth Duino Elegy.

33. *Sonnette an Orpheus*, Zweiter Teil, pp. 47, 48.

34. *Die Weise von Liebe und Tod des Cornets Christoph Rilke, GW, 4, 27.*

35. *Sonnette an Orpheus*, Zweiter Teil, p. 47.

36. "Der Turm," in *Neue Gedichte, 1, 75.*

37. See Rilke's description of a Rodin *Karyatide*. We give this passage in full to suggest not only the importance of *tragen* to Rilke but also his conception of will and destiny in terms of physical weight: "Und dann die *Karyatide*. Nicht mehr die aufrechte Figur, die leicht oder schwer das Tragen eines Steines erträgt, unter den sie sich doch nur gestellt hat, als er schon hielt; ein weiblicher Akt, knieend, gebeugt, in sich hineingedrückt und ganz geformt von der Hand der Last, deren Schwere wie ein fortwährender Fall in alle Glieder sinkt. Auf jedem kleinsten Teile dieses Leibes liegt der ganze Stein wie ein Wille, der grösser war, älter und mächtiger, und doch hat seines Tragens Schicksal nicht aufgehört. Er trägt, wie man im Traum das Unmögliche trägt, und findet keinen Ausweg. Und sein Zusammengesunkensein und Versagen ist immer noch Tragen geblieben, und wenn die nächste Müdigkeit kommt und den Körper ganz niederzwingt ins Liegen, so wird auch das Liegen noch Tragen sein, Tragen ohne Ende. So ist die *Karyatide*." *GW, 4, 340–1.*

38. "Und sogar die Steine älterer Kulturen waren nicht ruhig. In die hieratisch verhaltene Gebärde uralter Kulte war die Unruhe lebendiger Flächen eingeschlossen, wie Wasser in die Wände des Gefässes. Es waren Strömungen in den verschlossenen Göttern, welche sassen, und in den stehenden war eine Gebärde, die wie eine Fontäne aus dem Steine stieg und wieder in denselben zurückfiel, ihn mit vielen Wellen erfüllend." *GW, 4, 320.*

39. *Sonnette an Orpheus*, Zweiter Teil, p. 51.

40. We deal here with a very fundamental perception. Cf. *Briefe an einen jungen Dichter*, Rome, 29 October 1903, where Rilke recounts some of his first impressions:

"Unendlich lebensvolle Wasser gehen über die alten Aquädukte in die grosse Stadt und tanzen auf den vielen Plätzen und breiten sich aus in weiten geräumigen Becken und rauschen bei Tag und erheben ihr Rauschen zur Nacht, die hier gross und gestirnt ist und weich von Winden. Und Gärten sind hier, unvergessliche Alleen und Treppen, die nach dem Vorbild abwärts gleitender Wasser erbaut sind,—breit im Gefäll Stufe

aus Stufe gebärend wie Welle aus Welle." Also: "Auf einmal weiss ich
viel von den Fontänen, den unbegreiflichen Bäumen aus Glas." See
Tagebücher aus der Frühzeit.

41. *Sonnette an Orpheus,* Zweiter Teil, p. 52.
42. See *Sonnette an Orpheus,* Zweiter Teil, p. 49: "O Brunnen-Mund . . ." and
the poem enclosed in a letter to Frau L. Tronier-Fundier, 1919.
43. ". . . die Eigenschaften werden Gott, dem nicht mehr Sagbaren abgenom-
men, fallen zurück an die Schöpfung, an Liebe und Tod." To Ilse Jahr, 22
February 1923, *GB 5,* 196.
44. Ninth Duino Elegy.

VALÉRY

Eupalinos; ou l'architecte: précédé de l'âme et la danse. Paris, La Nouvelle
Revue française, 1924.
Lettres à quelques-uns. Paris, La Nouvelle Revue française, 1952.
Mélange. Paris, La Nouvelle Revue française, 1941.
Poésies. Paris, La Nouvelle Revue française, 1930.
Selected Writings. New York, New Directions, 1950.
Variété. Paris, La Nouvelle Revue française, 1948. 5 vols. (Cited as *Variété
I, II,* etc.)

1. For Valéry's interest in the "charme continu" of a poem, a sustained equality
and continuity of effect, see especially two essays: "Fragments des mémoires
d'un poème," *Variété V;* and "Situation de Baudelaire," *Variété II.*
2. See "Poésie et pensée abstraite," *Variété V.*
3. ". . . les alexandrins sentent trop la prose trèsfacile, sont trop énervez et
flasques." *Préface de la Franciade,* 1587.
4. The following remark from "Le Prince et la Jeune Parque," (*Variété V,*
120–1) is well known: "Mon dessein était de composer une sorte de discours
dont la suite des vers fût développée ou déduite de telle sorte que l'ensemble
de la pièce produisît une impression analogue à celle des *récitatifs* d'autrefois.
Ceux qui se trouvent dans Gluck, et particulièrement dans *l'Alceste,*
m'avaient beaucoup donné à songer. J'enviais cette ligne."
5. See Epigram of the poem. The sexual figure is, of course, not absent, but
it is no longer principal, only a variant.
6. ". . . la putain retentissante qui appelle éternellement les hommes." *Eupalinos,* p. 195.
7. Cf. Rilke's description of the angels in his second Duino Elegy:

> Spiegel, die die entströmte eigene Schönheit
> wiederschöpfen zurück in das eigene Antlitz.

8. The basic series may be diagrammatically shown as

$$am \begin{cases} aime, \ m\hat{e}me, \ extr\hat{e}me \ \ldots \\ amer, \ mer, \ air, \ or \ \ldots \end{cases}$$

9. ". . . sa puissance en pleurs perd tous ses diamants."

10. *Eupalinos*, p. 217.

11. *L'Ame et la danse* (in same vol. with *Eupalinos*), p. 62: "Cette femme qui était là est dévorée de figures innombrables."

12. *Ibid.,* pp. 66–71.

13. *Eupalinos,* pp. 132–3.

14. "Au sujet d'Eurêka," *Variété I,* 125: "Nous n'avons point chez nouns de poètes de la connaissance. Peut-être avons-nous un sentiment si marqué de la distinction des genres, c'est-à-dire de l'indépendance des divers mouvements de l'esprit, que nous ne souffrons point les ourages qui les combinent."

15. *Mélange,* p. 17: "Une écume s'allume, *de temps à autre,* sur le champ de la mer, et ces *temps* sont créés par le hasard."

16. *Ibid.* p. 41: "Ici, la mer ramasse, reprend ses innombrables dés et les rejette."

17. *Ibid.,* p. 156: "L'inexplicable ici, peut-être aurait-il pour image la *distance?* L'action à distance, l'induction, etc.??"

18. *Variété I,* 269. "Introduction à la méthode de Léonard de Vinci."

19. *Ibid.,* p. 257.

20. *Ibid.,* p. 233: "La conscience des pensées que l'on a, en tant que ce sont des pensées, est de reconnaître cette sorte d'égalité ou d'homogénéité."

21. *Ibid.,* p. 211: "Couleur et douleur; souvenirs, attente et surprises; cet arbre, et le flottement de son feuillage, et son variation annuelle, et son ombre comme sa substance, ses accidents de figure et de position, les pensées très éloignées qu'il rappelle à ma distraction—*tout cela est égal.* . . . Toutes choses se substituent—ne serait-ce pas la définition des *choses?*"

22. The essay contains many other echoes of H. Poincaré, one of the finest French mathematicians. The concept of reasoning by recurrence ("mathematical induction") appeared for the first time in the article where Valéry saw it, "Sur la nature du raisonnement mathématique," *Revue de Métaphysique et de morale,* 2 (1894), 371–84.

23. *Variété I,* 235: "l'imitation consciente de mon acte est un nouvel acte qui enveloppe toutes les adaptions possibles du premier."

24. *Leonardo da Vinci's Notebooks,* tr. Edward McCurdy (New York, 1923), p. 239.

25. ". . . tout ce qui passe de l'état lourd à l'état subtil, passe par le moment du feu et de lumière." *L'Âme et la danse,* p. 60.

26. *Variété I,* 262.

27. *Ibid.,* p. 242.

28. *Essai d'explication du Cimetière marin* (Paris, La Nouvelle Revue française, 1933).

29. *Mélange,* p. 96.

PURE REPRESENTATION

1. *Republic* Bk. VI, l. 508b.
2. *Lettres à quelques-uns* (Paris, La Nouvelle Revue française, 1952), "à P. Louys," 15 May 1916, p. 114: "que faut-il penser de cette pratique: Crever les yeux à l'oiseau pour qu'il chante mieux. Expliquer et développer (3 pages)."
3. *Prelude* II, l. 305 f.
4. Claude C. Abbott, ed., *Further Letters of Gerard Manley Hopkins* (New York, Oxford University Press, 1938), pp. 79–80.
5. No. 122 in the third edition of the *Poems,* ed. R. Bridges and W. H. Gardner.
6. *The Notebooks and Papers of Gerard Manley Hopkins,* ed. Humphry House (1937); p. 262 f. From a sermon delivered in 1879.
7. *Ibid.,* p. 249.
8. *Ibid.,* p. 190.
9. *Gesammelte Briefe,* 2, 432.
10. *Ibid.,* p. 434.
11. *Novalis Schriften,* ed. Paul Kluckhohn, *3,* 230:

> "Bedeutender Zug in vielen Märchen . . . dass wenn der Mensch sich selbst überwindet, er auch die Natur zugleich überwindet—und ein Wunder vorgeht . . . z. B. die Verwandlung des Bären in einen Prinzen, in dem Augenblicke als der Bär geliebt wurde . . . Vielleicht geschähe eine ähnliche Verwandlung, wenn der Mensch das Übel in der Welt lieb gewönne—in dem Augenblicke, als ein Mensch die Krankheit oder den Schmerz zu lieben anfinge, läge die reizendste Wollust in seinen Armen— höchste positive Lust durchdrängte ihn. Könnte Krankheit nicht ein Mittel höherer Synthesis sein?"

12. *Gesammelte Werke, 4,* 56:

> Irgendwo habe ich einen Mann gesehen, der einen Gemüsewagen vor sich herschob. Er schrie: Chou-fleur, Chou-fleur, das fleur mit eigentümlich trübem eu. Neben ihm ging eine eckige, hässliche Frau, die ihn von Zeit zu Zeit anstiess. Und wenn sie ihn anstiess, so schrie er. Manchmal schrie er auch von selbst, aber dann war es umsonst gewesen, und er musste darauf wieder schreien, weil man vor einem Hause war, welches kaufte. Habe ich schon gesagt, dass er blind war? Nein? Also er war blind. Er war blind und schrie. Ich fälsche, wenn ich das sage, ich unterschlage den Wagen, den er schob, ich tue, als hätte ich nicht bemerkt, dass er Blumenkohl ausrief. Aber ist das wesentlich? Und wenn es auch wesentlich wäre, kommt es nicht darauf an, was die ganze Sache für mich gewesen ist? Ich habe einen alten Mann gesehen, der blind war und schrie. Das habe ich gesehen. Gesehen.

13. *Ibid.*, p. 8.

14. "Abschrift aus dem Taschenbuch an Lou Andreas-Salomé," *Gesammelte Briefe, 5,* 350. We give the translation on p. 126 of J. B. Leishman's and Stephen Spender's edition of the *Duino Elegies* (New York, 1939).

15. *Ibid.*, p. 76: "Es war da wie ein grosses totes Tier, das einmal, als es noch lebte, meine Hand gewesen war oder mein Arm. Und mein Blut ging durch mich und durch es, wie durch einen und denselben Körper."

16. *Lettres à quelques-uns,* p. 163.

17. *Selected Writings* (New Directions, 1950), p. 238.

18. *Variété I,* 241.

19. *Ibid.*, p. 210.

20. *"Rendre purement possible ce qui existe; reduire ce qui se voit au purement visible,* telle est l'oeuvre profonde." *Mélange,* p. 96.

21. *Selected Writings,* p. 253.

22. Cf. Berkeley's *An Essay towards a New Theory of Vision* (1709).

23. See n. 19.

24. ". . . ce postulat psychique de continuité qui ressemble dans notre connaissance au principe de l'inertie dans la mécanique." *Variété I,* 258.

25. "L'âme jouit de sa lumière sans objets. Son silence est le total de sa parole, et la somme de ses pouvoirs compose ce repos. Elle se sent également éloignée de tous les noms et de toutes les formes. Nulle figure encore ne l'altère ni la contraint. Le moindre jugement entachera sa perfection." ("Méditation avant Pensée"), *Mélange,* p. 95.

26. From *Eupalinos* in *Selected Writings,* p. 174.

27. *Variété I,* 208.

28. By means of a theory of "creation continuée"; see *Discours de la Méthode,* ed. Étienne Gilson (Paris 1930), p. 36; and Gilson's notes pp. 340 ff. It is to be noted that Berkeley's argument in his *New Theory of Vision,* that the arbitrary yet inevitable connection of visible with tangible ideas is the work of God, must also depend ultimately on the concept of continued creation. For what is necessary yet also arbitrary cannot be considered a law of nature.

29. See the *Réponses aux quatrièmes objections.* Descartes bases his position on Aristotle's *De Anima,* Bk. III, chap. 13.

30. *Les Principes de la philosophie,* Deuxième Partie, 2, 3; Quatrième Partie, 198.

31. *De Anima.*

32. Of the multitude of recognitions, explicit and implicit, which could here be adduced, we choose only the following well-known statement that has influenced philosophers and poets to the present day. It expresses in concise form the concept of a *creative imagination* which haunts the reflective powers of romantic and later artists: "The primary Imagination I hold to be the living power and prime agent of all human perception, and as a repetition in the finite mind of the eternal act of creation in the infinite I AM." Coleridge, *Biographia Literaria,* chap. 13.

33. "C'est une chose que la lumière naturelle nous fait voir clairement, que la conservation et la création ne diffèrent, qu'au regard de notre façon de penser, et non point en effet." *Méditation troisième.*

THE NEW PERSEUS

1. See Étienne Gilson, *L'Esprit de la philosophie médiévale* (Paris, 1932), esp. chap. 4, "Les Êtres et leur contingence."

2. Hopkins. See above, p. 133.

3. See Walther Rehm, "Der Dichter und die Toten," *Orpheus* (Düsseldorf, 1950), p. 563. This book has proved very informative on modern ideas of the poet as mediator, although its erudition at times obscures a great argument.

4. Charles Kingsley welcomed the *Origin of Species* with ". . . now they have got rid of an interfering God—a master-magician as I call it—they have to choose between the absolute empire of accident and a living, immanent, ever-working God." I take this quotation from Charles E. Raven, the Gifford lecturer, who in his *Natural Religion and Christian Theology* (Cambridge, 1953) tries to discount St. Augustine's view of the natural world as a *massa perditionis,* insisting that original Christianity recognized the "continuity of nature and supernature." The finding of sufficient proof-texts to support this view is a major task for the modern theologian, and already quite apparent as early as Schelling and Coleridge.

5. See *Selections from the Notebooks of G.M. Hopkins,* ed. T. Weiss (New Directions).

6. *Variété I,* 113.

7. "Salon de 1846," article on Eugène Delacroix, in *Curiosités esthétiques,* ed. Jacques Crepet (Paris, 1923) pp. 106–7: "Trop matériel, trop attentif aux superficies de la nature, M. Victor Hugo est devenu un peintre en poésie; Delacroix, toujours respectueux de son idéal, est souvent à son insu un poète en peinture." Baudelaire will change his mind about Hugo in "Réflexions sur mes Contemporains," *L'Art romantique.*

8. See especially the key article of Désiré Nisard, "M. Hugo en 1856," *Mélanges,* 2, 55 ff. The issue of the possibility of a material representation in literature was taken up with perspicuity by Irving Babbitt in his *New Laocoon.* Babbitt perceives that the originality of romantic and postromantic literature is in its word painting, its use of "local impressions," but condemns this. The only academic critic to render it some justice before the present generation is Gustave Lanson in his *L'Art de la prose* (Paris, 1911), though this deals mainly with prose. "Après Bernadin de Saint-Pierre, le mot, instrument de pensée ou de sentiment, est appliqué à la stricte notation de la perception des sens" (p. 207).

9. Hugo, "Le Satyre."

10. See his *Gespräch über die Poesie* (1800).

11. Edmund Husserl, *Ideas*, tr. W. R. Boyce Gibson (New York, 1952), paragraph 26. The original edition of the *Ideen* was published in 1913.

12. A dictum from Bacon's *Novum Organum*.

13. "Au sujet d'Eurêka," *Variété I*, 145.

14. *Sonnette an Orpheus*, Erster Teil, XIII. The immediate reference is to the taste of fruit.

15. See the works of E. R. Jaensch and his school, e.g., Gerhard Hensel, *Das Optische bei Wordsworth* (Marburg, 1930).

16. *Aurélia*, chap. 6, Première Partie:

> La Dame que je suivais, développant sa taille élancée dans un mouvement qui faisait miroiter les plis de sa robe en taffetas changeant, entoura gracieusement de son bras nu une longue tige de rose trémière, puis elle se mit à grandir sous un clair rayon de lumière, de telle sorte que peu à peu le jardin prenait sa forme, et les parterres et les arbres devenaient les rosaces et les festons de ses vêtements; tandis que sa figure et ses bras imprimaient leurs contours aux nuages pourpres du ciel. Je la perdais ainsi de vue à mesure qu'elle se transfigurait, car elle semblait s'évanouir dans sa propre grandeur, "Oh! ne fuis pas! m'écriai-je . . . car la nature meurt avec toi!"

17. *Ideen zur Geschichte der Menschheit* (1784), *3*, Erster Theil, Fünftes Buch.

18. *Von der Weltseele* (1798). See especially the last chapter.

19. "The Blessed Virgin Compared to the Air We Breathe."

20. "The Soldier."

21. *Gesammelte Briefe* (Leipzig, 1939), *3*, 368: to Lou Andreas-Salomé, 20 Feb. 1914.

22. F. W. J. von Schelling's *Sämmtliche Werke* (Stuttgart, 1857), 2 Pt. 1, 366:

> Indem . . . der Gott in der Schwere sich überall als Mittelpunkt zeigt, und die Unendlichkeit seiner Natur, welche die falsche Imagination in endloser Ferne sucht, ganz in der Gegenwart und in jedem Punkte gibt, hebt er eben damit jenes Schweben der Imagination auf, wodurch sie vergebens die Einheit der Natur mit der Allheit und die Allheit mit der Einheit zu vereinigen sucht.

23. *Requiem* (für eine Freundin).

24. E.g., in his experience at Toledo, described in a letter to Ellen Delp, 27 Oct. 1915, *Gesammelte Briefe, 4,* 80:

> Erscheinung und Vision kamen gleichsam überall im Gegenstand zusammen . . . als ob ein Engel, der den Raum umfasst, blind wäre und in sich schaute. Diese, nicht mehr von Menschen aus, sondern im Engel geschaute Welt, ist vielleicht meine wirkliche Aufgabe.

25. *Prelude* VII, ll. 637 ff.

26. *Gesammelte Werke,* 5, 73–4:

> was rechts von mir war, konnte ich erst nach einer Weile erkennen. Es war
> eine ungeheure, unbewegliche Masse, die ein Gesicht hatte und eine grosse,
> schwere, reglose Hand. Die Seite des Gesichts, die ich sah, war leer, ganz
> ohne Züge und ohne Erinnerungen, und es war unheimlich, dass der Anzug
> wie der einer Leiche war, die man für den Sarg angekleidet hatte . . . Die
> Hand hatte man auf diese Hose gelegt, dorthin wo sie lag, und sogar das
> Haar war wie von Leichenwäscherinnen gekämmt und war, wie das Haar
> ausgestopfter Tiere, steif geordnet. Ich betrachtete das alles mit Auf-
> merksamkeit, und es fiel mir ein, dass dies also der Platz sei, der für mich
> bestimmt gewesen war, denn ich glaubte nun endlich an diejenige Stelle
> meines Lebens gekommen zu sein, an der ich bleiben würde.

27. *Buch der Bilder.* The poem is relevant enough to be quoted in its entirety:

> Der blinde Mann, der auf der Brücke steht,
> grau wie ein Markstein namenloser Reiche,
> er ist vielleicht das Ding, das immer gleiche,
> um das von fern die Sternenstunde geht,
> und der Gestirne stiller Mittelpunkt.
> Denn alles um ihn irrt und rinnt und prunkt.
>
> Er ist der unbewegliche Gerechte,
> in viele wirre Wege hingestellt;
> der dunkle Eingang in die Unterwelt
> bei einem oberflächlichen Geschlechte.

28. *Aurélia,* chap. 6, Seconde Partie:

> Ce spectacle m'impressionna vivement . . . je rencontrais un être indé-
> finissable, tâciturne et patient, assis comme un sphynx aux portes suprêmes
> de l'existence. . . . Il me semblait placé ainsi entre la mort et la vie, comme
> un interprète sublime, comme un confesseur prédestiné à entendre ces
> secrets de l'âme que la parole n'oserait transmettre ou ne réussirait pas à
> rendre. C'était l'oreille de Dieu sans le mélange de la pensée d'un autre.
> Je passais des heures entières à m'examiner mentalement, la tête penchée
> sur la sienne et lui tenant les mains.

29. Cf. J. P. Sartre's "A propos de 'Le Bruit et la fureur': La Temporalité chez
Faulkner," *Situations* I. Sartre's entire work could be considered as a critique
of reification: "La Chose" is his principal enemy.

30. *La Pyramide humaine* (1926):

> D'abord un grand désir m'était venu de solennité et d'apparat. J'avais
> froid. Tout mon être vivant et corrompu aspirait à la rigidité et à la
> majesté des morts. Je fus tenté ensuite par un mystère où les formes ne

jouent aucun rôle. Curieux d'un ciel décoloré d'où les oiseaux et les nuages sont bannis. Je devins esclave de la faculté pure de voir, esclave de mes yeux irréels et vierges, ignorants du monde et d'eux-mêmes. Puissance tranquille. Je supprimai le visible et l'invisible, je me perdis dans un miroir sans tain. Indestructible, je n'étais pas aveugle.

31. "Blütenstaub," fragment no. 74. *Novalis Schriften,* ed. P. Kluckhohn, 2, 28.

32. De Sélincourt, *Poetical Works,* 5, 382–3, "The Ruined Cottage," ll. 130–36, and 145–152; also *ibid.,* p. 15, ll. 205–229.

33. Victor Hugo in *William Shakespeare:* "Sur la terre, il faut que le divin soit humain. Il faut qu'il se propose à lui-même sa propre énigme."

INDEX

MAJOR CONCEPTS

Attributes of the poetic faculty, 45

Complete interpretation, x, xiii, 35ff., 45

Continuity: as major problem of art, 147ff.; representation by Valéry, 147–8; unconditioned continuity of mind and the role of symbols, 127, 128

Experience and symbols of 'immediation': ambivalent figures of mediation, 169; artist as mediator, 172–3; dilation, 164f.; 'ether,' 166; Hopkins, 166–7; imperative of total experience, 168; impersonal mirror, 168; interior sleeper, 169; luminosity, 165f.; Nerval, 165–6; Novalis' definition of pantheism, 172; Rilke, 167–9; self-consuming act, 167; Valéry, 171; Wordsworth, 164–5

Imageless vision or pure representation: defined, 128–9; two modes in Hopkins, 134; two modes in Rilke, 140f.; two modes in Wordsworth, 132; two principles of perfect knowledge in Valéry, 145; ultimate meaning for the modern poet, 153–5

Induction and retroduction, 124, 145, 146, 147ff.

Perception and knowledge: argument from perceptibility, 152–3; bridging of the gap, 148–53; identity between perception and creativity, 153–4; as subject of poet's experience, 152

Symbol: assuring continuity of consciousness, 127f.; character of ideal system of symbols, 128–9; difference between symbols of poetry and those of other arts, 128; expression of identity, 44–5, 93, *passim;* relation of sign and symbol, 127

Tyranny of the eye: in Hopkins, 132–4; in Rilke, 134–41; in Valéry, 141–6; in Wordsworth, 128–32; function of symbols in relation to experience of sight, 127–9; 'irrealization of the eyes,' 171; recurrent figure of the blind man, 129, 131, 136, 170; 'reification,' 171; synaesthesia, 89ff., 128, 134, 171

Unmediated vision: attempt to represent immediate sensa, 163f.; concept of environmental fatality, 160; concern with inherent arbitrariness of symbols, 161–4; Descartes' break with mediated understanding, 148; direct sensuous intuition of reality, 156f.; disesteem of sacred text and literary authority, 173; loss of traditional concept of divine creation, 157f.; mark of modern poet, 154–5; parody a new genre, 173; poet as experimenter, 173; rendering of circumstance and fortuitousness, 159–60; revelation receding as proof-text, 154–73; sacred profanity, 148; Wordsworth as turning point, 172–3

WORDSWORTH

Absence of divine machinery, 3, 161

Absence of will toward relational knowledge, 5f., 8, 38f., 45, 182–3 n.34

HOPKINS

RILKE

VALÉRY